OCCASION[AL PAPER]

IMF-Supported Programs in Capital Account Crises

Atish Ghosh, Timothy Lane, Marianne Schulze-Ghattas,
Aleš Bulíř, Javier Hamann, and Alex Mourmouras

INTERNATIONAL MONETARY FUND
Washington DC
2002

Production: IMF Graphics Section
Figures: Sanaa Elaroussi
Typesetting: Alicia Etchebarne-Bourdin

Cataloging-in-Publication Data

IMF-supported programs in capital account crises/Timothy Lane . . . [et al.].—Washington, D.C.: International Monetary Fund, 2002.

p. cm.—(Occasional paper, ISSN 0251-6365; no. 210)

Includes bibliographical references.
ISBN 1-58906-082-2

1. International Monetary Fund—Developing countries. 2. Capital movements—Developing countries. 3. Financial crises—Developing countries. 4. Balance of payments—Developing countries. 5. Crisis management—Developing countries. I. Lane, Timothy D. (Timothy David), 1955–. II. International Monetary Fund. III. Occasional papers (International Monetary Fund); no. 210.

HG3891.I43 2002

Price: US$20.00
(US$17.50 to full-time faculty members and students at universities and colleges)

Please send orders to:
International Monetary Fund, Publication Services
700 19th Street, N.W., Washington, D.C. 20431, U.S.A.
Tel.: (202) 623-7430 Telefax: (202) 623-7201
E-mail: publications@imf.org
Internet: http://www.imf.org

recycled paper

Contents

Text Tables

Appendix Tables

Text Figures

Appendix Figures

The following symbols have been used throughout this paper:

. . . to indicate that data are not available;

— to indicate that the figure is zero or less than half the final digit shown, or that the item does not exist;

– between years or months (e.g., 2000–01 or January–June) to indicate the years or months covered, including the beginning and ending years or months;

/ between years (e.g., 2000/01) to indicate a fiscal (financial) year.

"Billion" means a thousand million.

Minor discrepancies between constituent figures and totals are due to rounding.

The term "country," as used in this paper, does not in all cases refer to a territorial entity that is a state as understood by international law and practice; the term also covers some territorial entities that are not states, but for which statistical data are maintained and provided internationally on a separate and independent basis.

Preface

During the 1990s, a number of emerging market countries faced capital account crises, in which sudden reversals of capital inflows forced large and abrupt current account adjustments, often with pervasive macroeconomic consequences. The nature and scope of these crises presented challenges that differed considerably from those of more traditional adjustment programs. Given the dominant role of private capital flows, estimates of sustainable current account positions—and the appropriate balance between financing and adjustment—were subject to much greater uncertainty, the impact of macroeconomic policies on market confidence became critical, and structural policies had to address a variety of vulnerabilities that lay at the root of the crises.

This paper reviews the design of and experience with IMF-supported programs formulated in response to capital account crises in the 1990s, focusing on the experiences of eight countries: Turkey (1994), Mexico (1995), Argentina (1995), Thailand (1997), Indonesia (1997), Korea (1997), the Philippines (1997), and Brazil (1998). The review was prepared by a staff team under the general guidance of Jack Boorman, Director of the Policy Review Department. The staff team comprised Timothy Lane (Chief, Policy Review Division), Aleš Bulíř, Atish Ghosh, Javier Hamann, Alex Mourmouras, and Marianne Schulze-Ghattas.

The authors are grateful to numerous colleagues at the IMF for detailed comments on the paper: to Sibabrata Das, Tricia Gillett, and Ivetta Hakobyan for research assistance; and to Olivia Carolin, Brian Gallo, Fernanda Gusmao, and Sylvia Palazzo for secretarial assistance. Jacqueline Irving of the External Relations Department edited the manuscript and coordinated production of the publication.

The opinions expressed in the paper are those of the authors and do not necessarily reflect the views of the IMF or of its Executive Directors.

I Introduction

Increasing globalization of capital markets poses new challenges for the design and implementation of IMF-supported programs. These challenges have been thrown into sharpest relief in recent capital account crises, during which rapid reversals of capital inflows brought about large and abrupt current account adjustments with pervasive macroeconomic consequences.

The reversal of capital inflows in these recent crises occurred very suddenly, reflecting a sharp shift in market sentiment. This contrasts with the situation that more traditional programs were designed to tackle, where ongoing macroeconomic imbalances generally result in a relatively gradual deterioration on the external side. Although concerns over the sustainability of current account deficits and exchange rate pegs played a role, they do not explain the suddenness and magnitude of the shifts in the capital account. Various other vulnerabilities, such as adverse public debt dynamics (Brazil and Turkey), a risky public debt management strategy (Mexico), and pervasive financial sector weaknesses (e.g., Indonesia, the Republic of Korea, and Thailand) appear to have been critical in changing investor confidence.

Given the differences in their origins, IMF-supported programs in capital account crisis were confronted with challenges that differed considerably from those of more traditional IMF programs.[1] Given the dominant role of private capital flows, estimates of sustainable current account positions and financing needs were subject to much greater uncertainty, the impact of the programs on market confidence became critical, and policies had to address a variety of vulnerabilities that were at the root of the crises.

There are three main reasons for focusing on a comparison of the programs formulated in response to these crises. First, the crisis cases raise issues of whether the policy response in the context of IMF-supported programs took adequate account of what was distinctive about these crises; this is particularly important in formulating an appropriate response to other capital account crises that will inevitably occur in the future. Second, they raise the more general question of whether, or to what extent, macroeconomic policies can influence the adjustment process once a crisis has erupted. Third, some of the problems confronted in these crisis cases, and the issues of crisis prevention they raise, are, writ large, those faced by other countries in the context of financial globalization.

This paper examines the experience with IMF-supported programs in the context of eight capital account crises in the 1990s. In some cases, new IMF-supported programs were formulated in response to a crisis, while in two of the countries (Argentina and the Philippines), IMF-supported arrangements that were in place at the beginning of the crisis were extended and augmented, and policies were modified. The sample includes Turkey (1994), Mexico (1995), Argentina (1995), Thailand (1997), Indonesia (1997), Korea (1997), the Philippines (1997), and Brazil (1999).[2] The paper focuses on the broad macroeconomic strategy of these programs in addressing the crises: the financing and external adjustment envisaged and the role of macroeconomic and structural policies. The chronology of events in the individual countries is presented in Appendix V.

[1]Capital outflows, of course, are a general characteristic of balance of payments crises, such as those in the heavily indebted countries of the 1980s. However, the magnitudes involved in the capital account crisis countries, stemming from stock imbalance and vulnerabilities, made their nature qualitatively different. It would also be fair to say that, within the economics profession, there has often been very little consensus on the nature of the crises, or the appropriate policies for dealing with them. Krugman (2001) discusses the evolution of thinking about such crises.

[2]Dates refer to the year of original program approval, except in the cases of Argentina and the Philippines. Argentina (1995) refers to the Ninth Review and Extension of the extended arrangement approved in March 1992; Philippines (1997) refers to the Fourth Review and Extension of the extended arrangement approved in June 1994.

II Pre-Crisis Conditions and Emergence of the Crisis: Implications for Program Design

Unlike in the cases of most IMF-supported programs, pre-crisis vulnerabilities in capital account crisis countries reflected various stock disequilibria and structural weaknesses more than purely macroeconomic imbalances. The crises were manifested in sharp exchange rate movements and massive capital outflows, far in excess of initial imbalances. The focus of program design, and of macroeconomic and structural policies, therefore, was on restoring confidence, to stem and reverse capital outflows.

Pre-Crisis Conditions and Emergence of the Crisis

Pre-program conditions in capital account crisis countries differed in important respects from those prevailing in most other countries that adopted IMF-supported standby and Extended Fund Facility (EFF) arrangements in the past decade. For one thing, with the exception of Turkey (1994), which suffered from erratic growth and high inflation, most traditional macroeconomic indicators were, *on average*, more favorable: fiscal imbalances were smaller, inflation was lower, and growth was stronger (see Table 2.1).

Current account deficits prior to the crises *were* substantial but they were the counterpart of large private capital inflows that in most cases had been sustained for years. Although current account deficits were, to varying degrees, an ingredient of the crisis in all countries, these deficits in and of themselves do not explain the abruptness and magnitude of the reversals of capital flows. In some countries, notably Mexico and Thailand, current account deficits were very large, but overall external debt was manageable and solvency was not a concern.[3] Although the capital inflows registered in the pre-crisis years could not necessarily be expected to persist, the magnitude of these flows gave little warning that the adjustment in the capital account would be as sudden and severe as that which eventually took place. Nor did the appreciation of the real effective exchange rate, experienced in varying degrees in most countries in the years prior to the crises, foreshadow the sudden sharp depreciations, with significant overshooting, that occurred (Figure 2.1). In fact, in the majority of the countries considered, the crisis intensified *after* the initial exchange rate adjustment. In the absence of other vulnerabilities, current account adjustment and a correction of the real exchange rate could have been achieved in a more orderly fashion, although perhaps not without some temporary turbulence.[4]

The large capital outflows were thus less the underlying cause of the crises than their manifestation. The underlying vulnerabilities primarily reflected stock imbalances—high levels of public debt, maturity or currency mismatches in the structure of private sector liabilities, or highly leveraged positions[5]—and the correction of these imbalances would likely have entailed at least some macroeconomic disruption, even in the absence of the very large capital outflows that eventually transpired. The precise propagation mechanism between these stock imbalances and the currency crises varied across countries. As many "second-generation" crisis models would suggest, however, the market's perception that the authorities

[3]For a general discussion of solvency and current account sustainability, see Milesi-Ferretti, Maria, and Razin (1996); for an application to pre-crisis conditions in Mexico, see Calvo (1996).

[4]Although some observers have pointed to the role of unsustainable current account deficits and associated real exchange rate misalignment in the lead-up to the Mexican crisis (see Dornbusch and Werner (1994)), there is a growing consensus that traditional flow disequilibria cannot explain the virulence of recent capital account crises and that other types of vulnerabilities triggering self-fulfilling expectations on the part of investors were a key factor in these crises. Views differ as to the link between these vulnerabilities and shifts in expectations, and the element of randomness in the latter. See Calvo and Mendoza (1996) and Sachs, Tornell, and Velasco (1996) for analyses of the crisis in Mexico; and Corsetti, Pesenti, and Roubini (1998), Lane and others (1999), Boorman and others (2000), Radelet and Sachs (1998), and Krugman (1998), for discussions of the Asian crisis.

[5]Calvo and Mendoza (1996) emphasize the distinction between vulnerabilities related to traditional flow disequilibria and increasingly important vulnerabilities arising from stock disequilibria.

Table 2.1. Selected Macroeconomic Indicators for Capital Account Crisis Countries

	t–3	*t*–2	*t*–1	*t*	*t*+1
Capital account crisis countries[1]					
Real GDP (growth, in percent per year)	6.0	5.4	3.8	–5.5	5.1
Consumer price index (growth, in percent per year)[2]	12.5	8.2	5.3	8.9	6.8
Fiscal balance (as percent of GDP)	–1.2	–1.8	–3.5	–4.6	–3.5
Current account (as percent of GDP)	–3.7	–4.2	–3.7	3.5	2.6
Official reserves (in months of imports)	3.2	3.3	2.4	3.6	4.0
External debt (as percent of GDP)	37.4	38.5	43.7	66.6	53.4
Other program countries[1]					
Real GDP (growth, in percent per year)	–2.2	0.0	–1.6	2.1	3.1
Consumer price index (growth, in percent per year)[2]	38.6	32.0	21.7	32.9	21.0
Fiscal balance (as percent of GDP)	–7.0	–5.5	–5.1	–3.6	–3.3
Current account (as percent of GDP)	–2.5	–3.5	–4.2	–3.2	–3.7
Official reserves (in months of imports)	1.4	1.7	1.7	2.3	2.4
External debt (as percent of GDP)	63.2	61.3	63.0	65.9	59.8

Source: IMF, *World Economic Outlook*.
[1]See Appendix I for sample definitions.
[2]Sample median.

might be reluctant to raise interest rates—in some cases because of vulnerabilities in the corporate and financial sectors, in others because of the adverse impact on public debt dynamics—may have been an important factor that helped trigger self-fulfilling runs on the currency.

The fact that the vulnerabilities were mainly related to stock imbalances, rather than traditional flow disequilibria, complicated the macroeconomic policy response and created an environment in which it became rational for investors to run for the exit in response to relatively small changes in information about the fundamentals.[6] The sources of these vulnerabilities differed across crises: in the Latin American countries and Turkey, they were primarily rooted in the public sector; in Asia, in the private sector.

The Mexican crisis of 1994–95 demonstrated that such vulnerabilities do not necessarily reflect long-standing imbalances but can build up relatively quickly, particularly when the policy response fails to come to grips with emerging difficulties. Prior to the crisis, in 1992–93, public finances were on a sound footing, with a surplus of the nonfinancial public sector, declining public and external debt ratios, and short-term external debt more than covered by official reserves. In 1994, however, as a combination of domestic political shocks (uncertainty about the election outcome and internal armed conflict), rising international interest rates, and a hesitation to tighten monetary policy had resulted in substantial reserve losses, the government swapped large amounts of peso-denominated treasury bills for U.S.-dollar indexed bills both to reduce its funding costs and to underscore its commitment to the exchange rate peg. Although the move reduced interest payments in the short run, it also increased the government's exposure to exchange rate risk significantly. By early 1995, Mexico was facing an external funding crisis in the wake of the floating of the peso as doubts about the government's ability to service its maturing obligations led to massive outflows.

In contrast, the crises in Turkey (1994) and Brazil (1998) primarily reflected considerations that were medium-term in nature, related to adverse public sector debt dynamics.[7] Although public sector debt ratios were comparable to those in other countries,

[6]This argument suggests that certain types of weak fundamentals not only make it possible that the economy moves to a bad equilibrium, they make it likely. For a similar view, see Corsetti, Pesenti, and Roubini (1998). Calvo (1996) develops a similar argument in the context of a formal model, which accommodates multiple equilibria but, through additional equations, produces a unique equilibrium that is highly sensitive to parameter changes.

[7]In Turkey and Mexico, there were also weaknesses in the financial sector, particularly related to inadequate prudential regulation and supervision.

Figure 2.1. Exchange Rate Movements in Capital Account Crisis Countries

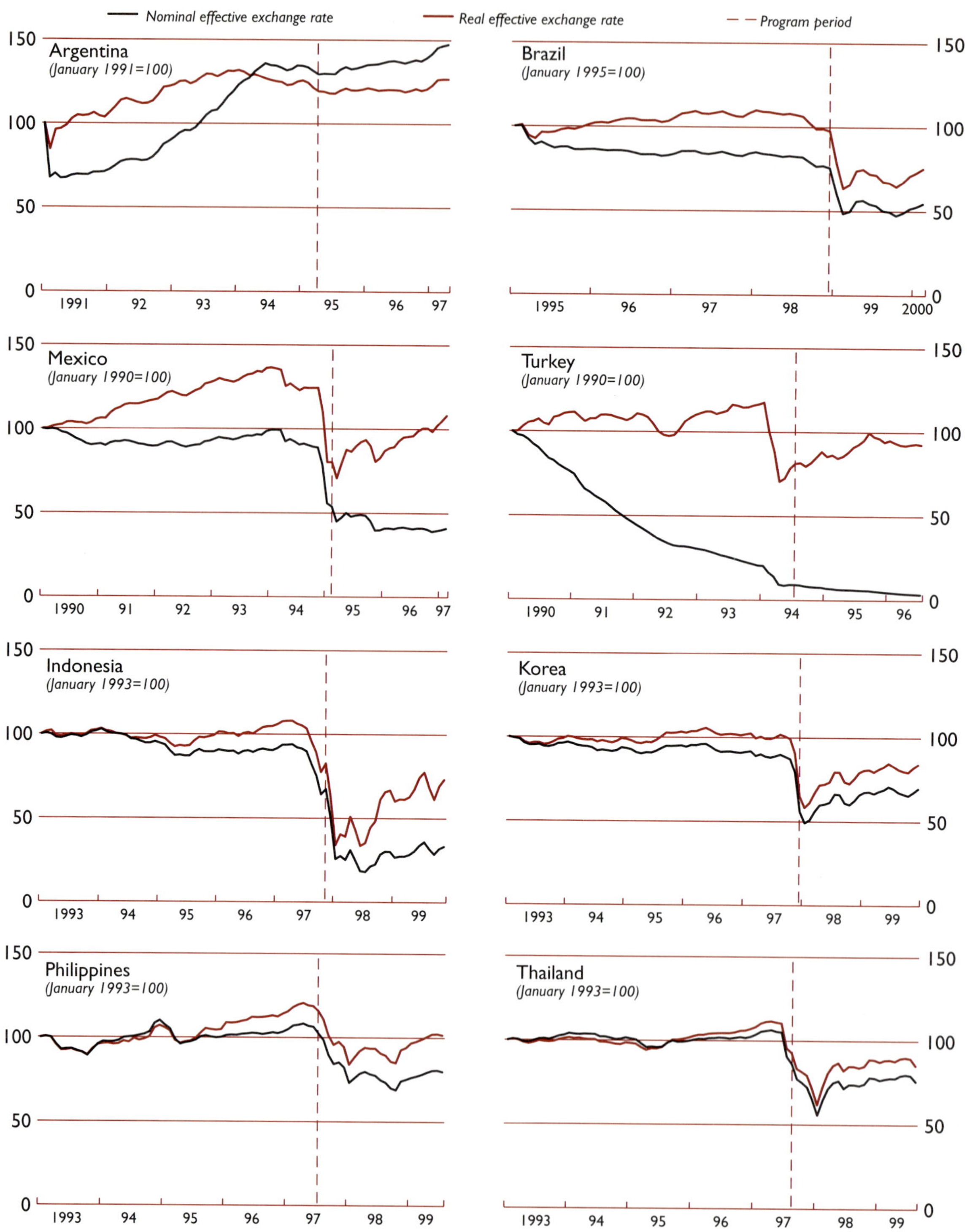

Sources: IMF, *Information Notice System*; and IMF staff estimates.

the legacy of high inflation—ongoing in Turkey and only recently conquered in Brazil—and low policy credibility was reflected in high real interest rates and a correspondingly large burden of this debt on the fiscal accounts; each country ran large and increasing deficits in the run-up to its financial crisis. Moreover, this situation gave rise to an inherent policy dilemma: any monetary accommodation for exchange rate depreciation threatened to accelerate or reignite inflation, but raising interest rates in response to a shift in the capital account could also fuel inflation through "unpleasant monetarist arithmetic,"[8]—that is, by aggravating the already heavy debt servicing burden of the public sector.

This dilemma was at the core of Brazil's vulnerability to contagion in the aftermath of the Asian and Russian financial crises, undermining market confidence in the exchange rate peg despite a comfortable cushion of official reserves (in relation to imports or short-term debt). Temporary interest rate hikes failed to stem capital outflows amid doubts about the government's ability to achieve a sustained fiscal consolidation. The dilemma continued as the IMF-supported program sought to maintain the exchange rate peg, and was only resolved once structural fiscal reforms gained credence and the peg was replaced by a more credible monetary policy framework.

Argentina, like Brazil, had a history of high inflation, which had been stabilized a few years before the Mexican crisis of 1994–95. In contrast to Brazil, however, its policy credibility was buttressed by a currency board-type arrangement and, with the fiscal position close to balance in 1992–93, public sector debt dynamics were not a concern. Moreover, with external debt accounting for over 70 percent of total public sector debt, the fiscal position was partially insulated from changes in domestic financing conditions. But two weaknesses of these arrangements nevertheless made Argentina especially vulnerable to the effects of the Mexican crisis: reliance on external financing, which made the government dependent on sentiments in international capital markets, and the severely limited ability to absorb bank balance sheet weaknesses that the currency board arrangement imposed on the central bank. These concerns triggered an external funding crisis as the government temporarily lost access to international capital markets amid massive withdrawals of bank deposits and large capital outflows.

Pre-crisis conditions in the Asian program countries differed significantly from those in Latin America and Turkey. These countries had a strong track record of low inflation and fiscal positions that had, on average, been close to balance (Indonesia, Korea, and Philippines) or in surplus (Thailand) and public sector debt ratios that were either very low (Korea and Thailand) or declining steadily (Indonesia and Philippines). The vulnerabilities that exposed these countries to a shift in market sentiment were rooted in the private sector, reflecting both weak financial systems and fragilities in heavily indebted corporate sectors. As in other countries, these vulnerabilities created a serious dilemma for monetary and exchange rate policy.

The weaknesses in the financial systems in Asia are by now well known: financial institutions ill equipped to handle risk; inadequate regulation and supervision; highly leveraged corporate sectors; and substantial unhedged and short-term foreign borrowing—encouraged, in part, by remaining controls on long-term flows (Korea) or special facilities (Thailand) and by the implicit guarantee of a pegged exchange rate.

The proximate trigger of the Asian crisis was a decline in export growth, against the background of weakening demand in partner countries, some real exchange rate appreciation especially as the U.S. dollar (to which these countries' currencies were explicitly or implicitly pegged) strengthened against the yen, and a sharp decline in prices for key exports, notably semiconductors, which in varying degrees affected many countries in the region. In Thailand, the resulting drop in exports prompted a reassessment of the sustainability of the country's large current account deficit and of inflated domestic asset prices. Asset prices began to decline, and the downturn of the economy increasingly exposed the vulnerabilities in the financial sector and led to capital outflows and increasing pressures on the exchange rate.

Contagion from the crisis in Thailand quickly spread throughout the region, affecting, among others, the Philippines, Indonesia, and, eventually, Korea. Like Thailand, these countries hesitated to raise interest rates and initially tried to support the exchange rate through intervention. (Indonesia, however, did attempt an initial hike in interest rates that was later reversed.) As in other countries, this policy failed to solve the flow disequilibrium in the foreign exchange market, while creating (in Indonesia and the Philippines) or severely aggravating (in Korea) imbalances between the stocks of short-term debt and usable reserves. These imbalances provided additional incentives for investors to run for the exit, particularly in Korea. Faced with significant reserve losses,[9] these countries were eventually forced to abandon their implicit or explicit pegs.

[8]See Sargent and Wallace (1985).

[9]In Korea, direct reserve losses were limited, but the central bank effectively lost usable reserves by shifting a large part of its foreign exchange holdings to foreign branches and subsidiaries of Korean banks, which faced difficulties rolling over their short-term liabilities.

Despite differences in the underlying causes of the crises, the broad pattern of balance of payments developments before and during the onset of the crises is strikingly similar in the capital account crisis countries (Figure 2.2). Prior to the crises, private capital inflows averaged 4–6 percent of GDP, matched by current account deficits of similar orders of magnitude (official capital and reserve flows being relatively small). In each of these countries, the initial response to the shift in private capital inflows was to try to maintain the implicit or explicit currency pegs through large-scale intervention and reserve losses. With the exception of Argentina, the pegs were abandoned and the counterpart to private capital outflows was official financing together with current account adjustment. One notable difference between Latin America and Turkey, on the one hand, and the Asian crisis countries, on the other, was the duration of the capital outflows when the crises broke. In Latin America and Turkey, capital outflows tended to be sharper—substantial, but of (relatively) short duration. In East Asia, by contrast, capital outflows lasted for several quarters (and, in some cases, inflows have yet to resume on a sustained basis). Eventually, though usually only after a wrenching macroeconomic adjustment, private capital outflows subsided or were even reversed, allowing for a buildup of reserves. In turn, this pattern of capital flows had profound implications for program design, the need for financing, and the appropriate role of macroeconomic policies.

Implications for Program Design

When the countries turned to the IMF for support,[10] they had already encountered one or several waves of capital outflows. Faced with the dilemma that both sharp increases in interest rates and a depreciation of the exchange rate would likely have serious negative effects, most of these countries had tried to counter the outflows through some form of exchange market intervention, which was largely sterilized. In the process, they had incurred significant reserve losses, which in some cases (Korea, Mexico, and Thailand) had led to a virtual depletion of net reserves, significantly increasing the risk of a full-fledged funding crisis. With the exception of Turkey, all of the countries had some form of exchange rate peg prior to the crisis,[11] but by the time the programs were negotiated only Argentina and Brazil were still maintaining their pegs. (The initial program in Brazil explicitly sought to maintain the peg; however, the rate had to be floated soon after the program was approved.) The other countries had already experienced substantial depreciations of their exchange rates, which generally exceeded pre-crisis estimates of possible overvaluations. These capital outflows, if extrapolated, would require massive shifts in current account balances well beyond what seemed consistent with medium-term sustainability and what would have been considered adequate prior to the crisis.

These circumstances held three key implications for program design. First, in the immediate run, restoring confidence required convincing financing strategies that alleviated concerns about the countries' ability to meet their maturing obligations. Second, the fundamental thrust of macroeconomic policy had to be directed more at stemming capital outflows than at fostering greater external adjustment (as in traditional programs). Third, restoring confidence required addressing the various vulnerabilities that had prompted the shift in market sentiment in the first place.

As discussed below, none of these desired criteria for program design would be easy to achieve. If programs were successful in restoring confidence, the large official financing would be superfluous. But given uncertainty about market reactions, programs ran the risk that the projections of market turnaround on which they were predicated would turn out to have been overly optimistic. At the same time, assuming the worst case scenario—or heavy-handed attempts at private sector involvement—could undermine confidence further and exacerbate outflows.

On macroeconomic policies, monetary policy faced a dilemma: should policies be tightened to stem outflows, or eased to forestall an excessive weakening of economic activity (or a worsening of the public debt dynamics)? Fiscal policy could play a key part where there were underlying weaknesses in public sector finances. Beyond this, however, fiscal policy's role was difficult to define because the contribution it could make to external adjustment depended critically on the response of the private sector to the crisis, which was difficult to predict.

Finally, addressing structural vulnerabilities was relatively more straightforward in the countries where these vulnerabilities were primarily rooted in the public sector and where the required policy adjustments fell primarily in the domain of the IMF's traditional expertise. In contrast, in the countries where the structural vulnerabilities were rooted in the private sector and required extensive structural reforms in the financial system and the corporate sector, the vulnerabilities presented a new set of challenges.

[10]As noted above, two of the countries had arrangements in place at the time of the crisis that had either lapsed (Argentina) or were about to expire (Philippines).

[11]Korea did not have a formal peg but had pursued a policy of keeping the real effective exchange rate relatively stable.

Figure 2.2. Balance of Payment Developments
(In percent of quarterly GDP)

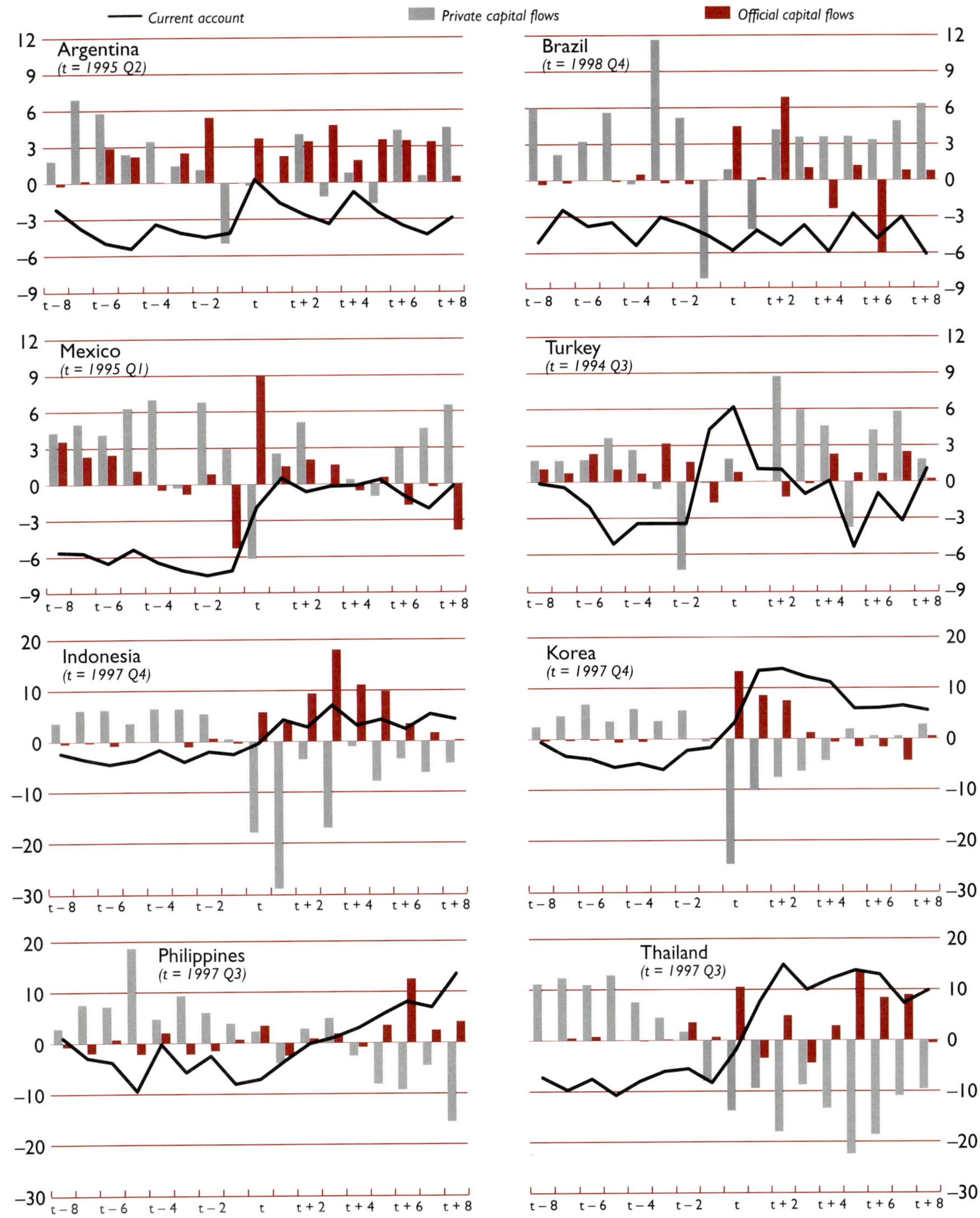

Source: IMF, *International Financial Statistics.*

III Program Financing

The magnitude and suddenness of the reversals of capital inflows that characterized capital account crises gave financing a particularly prominent role in IMF-supported programs designed in response to these crises. Despite exceptionally large official financing, some concerted private sector involvement, and the announcement of confidence-building measures, the catalytic effect of programs in reversing outflows failed to materialize, at least in the short run—necessitating unprogrammed and extraordinarily severe macroeconomic adjustment.

Introduction

The major challenge in designing official financing packages in capital account crises stemmed from the dominant role of private capital flows in determining macroeconomic outcomes, and the potential for these flows to change dramatically in response to shifting market sentiment. In a prototypical "confidence crisis," the link between official financing and current account adjustment may be different from the traditional trade-off in IMF-supported programs. Instead of a smooth trade-off between adjustment and financing, there could be a strong catalytic effect of official financing such that, if the combination of official financing and policies is strong enough to restore market confidence, the official financing package would, ex post, likely be superfluous. Indeed, most of the capital account crisis programs were predicated on just such a catalytic effect of official financing.[12] But at least in the cases reviewed here, confidence was *not* restored sufficiently rapidly to achieve this favorable outcome. Instead, programs were left with a substantial financing gap—often reaching several percent of GDP—which, arithmetically, had to be filled with a combination of official financing, private sector involvement (broadly construed), and unprogrammed, ex-post current account adjustment.[13]

The sheer magnitude of these flows and the speed with which they were reversed meant that capital account crises posed problems that were both quantitatively larger and qualitatively different from those addressed in typical IMF-supported programs. As such, existing modalities for dealing with these crises had to be adapted or new instruments introduced. For instance, the Supplemental Reserve Facility (SRF) was introduced at the time of the Korea program to provide IMF resources that were exceptionally large and front-loaded. Similarly, in the latter programs, there was increasing recourse to coordinated private sector involvement rather than relying solely on the strength of the program to catalyze a decentralized private sector response. Nevertheless, as discussed below, the experience of the capital account crisis countries raises important questions of whether the scale of official financing and efforts at private sector involvement were adequate.[14]

Private Capital Flows: Projections and Outcomes

The initial financial projections in the programs were based on the assumption that both their policy content and the official financing package would trigger a broadly favorable market response. Although this strategy inherently entailed certain risks—and indeed, in several cases, market reactions were significantly less favorable than projected—it meant that the programmed current account adjust-

[12]One hypothesis is that there exists a threshold level of official financing below which confidence is not restored, and that official financing (in the cases reviewed here) never reached that threshold. Such a judgment would have to relate the size of the financing packages to the size of the stock imbalances underlying the crises. In any event, the absence of a strong catalytic effect in any of the programs reviewed here makes it difficult either to prove or disprove this hypothesis.

[13]Of course, different combinations of these would have very different ramifications for the evolution of the crisis and the real economy.

[14]The adequacy of official financing and private sector involvement must, of course, also be gauged in the context of the overall program, including the design and implementation of macroeconomic and structural policies; these are presaged in the following section, and taken up more fully in Chapter V.

Table 3.1. Medium-Term External Debt Stability
(As percent of GDP)

	External Debt End-*t*–1	Current Account Balance						
		Actual	Required balance[1]		Program		Outcome	
		Year *t*–1	Year *t*	Adjustment[2]	Year *t*	Adjustment[2]	Year *t*	Adjustment[2]
Argentina (1995)	33.3	–4.3	–2.5	1.8	–2.0	2.3	–1.9	2.3
Brazil (1999)[3]	30.7	–4.3	–0.5	3.8	–3.6	0.7	–4.7	–0.4
Mexico (1995)[3]	33.8	–7.0	–1.1	6.0	–4.3	2.7	–0.6	6.5
Turkey (1994)	36.9	–3.5	–1.6	2.0	–0.8	2.7	2.8	6.4
Indonesia (1998)[3]	63.3	–1.7	–3.7	–1.9	–2.2	–0.5	4.2	5.9
Korea (1998)[3]	28.1	–1.7	–1.5	0.1	–0.6	1.1	12.7	14.4
Philippines (1998)[3]	61.6	–5.3	–4.9	0.4	–3.4	1.9	2.4	7.6
Thailand (1997)	59.6	–7.9	–4.8	3.0	–5.0	2.9	–2.1	5.7
Thailand (1998)[3]	72.3	–2.1	–2.7	–0.6	–3.0	–0.9	12.8	14.9

Sources: IMF, *World Economic Outlook* database; IMF, MONA database; and IMF staff estimates.

[1]Minimum current account balance required to stabilize ratio of external debt-to-GDP, assuming no real exchange rate appreciation; estimate as of year *t*–1 for year *t*.

[2]Implied adjustment, equal to year *t* minus year *t*–1.

[3]Date refers to year *t*, which differs from the program approval year.

ment could, in principle, be anchored in economic fundamentals such as medium-term external sustainability. A simple yardstick of such sustainability is the current account balance required to stabilize the external debt-to-GDP ratio over the medium-term (Table 3.1). This yardstick is not without its shortcomings: in particular, the larger the initial stock of debt, the greater the implied "sustainable" deficit. Moreover, when the initial stock of debt is above moderately high levels, it may be desirable to reduce the debt-to-GDP ratio. Stabilizing the debt ratio has the virtue of simplicity (although a number of other benchmarks could also be considered).[15]

From Table 3.1 it is evident that, with the exceptions of Indonesia and Korea (and Thailand, in 1998), stabilizing the ratio of external debt to GDP required at least some current account adjustment. Turning to the programmed current account adjustments, it is evident that in most cases the targeted current account balances were sufficient to achieve medium-term stability of the ratio of external debt-to-GDP.[16] Indeed, in Korea and Indonesia, the programmed current account balances exceeded those required for medium-term debt stability by at least 1 percent of GDP.

The large projected swings in these countries' current accounts were less a reflection of the ambitiousness of the programs than a recognition that private capital outflows would likely force substantial corrections. Even these programmed swings, however, pale in comparison to the outcomes (Table 3.1). In almost every instance, the current account swing was larger than planned—often by a substantial margin.[17] Thus, in Turkey, instead of a deficit of about 1 percent of GDP, the outturn was a surplus of more than 2½ percent of GDP; in Indonesia, the outturn was a surplus of 4.2 percent of GDP instead of a deficit of 2.2 percent of GDP; and in Thailand and Korea, the current account swing was some 13–15 percentage points of GDP larger than expected. In large part, these current account swings corresponded to larger-than-anticipated capital outflows (Table 3.2).[18]

[15]Thus, another methodology for assessing current account deficits uses a comparison with the current account-to-GDP ratio that would stabilize the ratio of net foreign liabilities at some specified level, such as 40 percent (see IMF, 2000b). Examining the implications of such indicators is left for future work.

[16]In Brazil and Mexico, although the programmed current account balances fell short of the "required balances," these countries expected foreign direct investment (FDI) inflows of about 2 percent of GDP.

[17]As discussed in Chapter IV below, the forced current account corrections, in turn, implied wrenching macroeconomic adjustment and sharp declines in economic activity.

[18]The main exception is Brazil, where capital outflows were larger than projected, but were financed by a rundown of reserves rather than by current account adjustment. It should also be noted that capital outflows from Korea in 1998 amounted to about 4½ percent of GDP, so that much of the current account surplus partly reflected the authorities' deliberate policy of resisting a reappreciation of the nominal exchange rate and accumulating foreign exchange reserves during 1998 as well as a sharp contraction in domestic demand.

Table 3.2. Program and Actual Balance of Payment Developments
(As percent of GDP)

	Capital Account[2]			Current Account		
	Program[3]	Outcome	Error[4]	Program[3]	Outcome	Error[4]
Argentina (1995)	1.4	1.2	–0.3	–2.3	–1.9	0.4
Brazil (1999)[1]	5.9	2.5	–3.5	–4.7	–4.7	–0.1
Indonesia (1998)[1]	1.8	–7.9	–9.7	–5.0	4.2	9.1
Korea (1998)[1]	4.8	–4.4	–9.1	–0.7	12.6	13.4
Mexico (1995)	5.0	–0.3	–5.2	–5.0	–0.6	4.4
Philippines (1998)[1]	4.8	–0.4	–5.2	–3.3	2.4	5.7
Thailand (1998)[1]	5.5	–12.1	–17.5	–4.7	12.7	17.5
Turkey (1994)	–0.9	–1.9	–0.9	–0.6	2.0	2.6

Sources: IMF, *International Financial Statistics* and IMF staff estimates.
[1]Date refers to year *t*, not program approval year.
[2]Differs from standard presentation of capital and financial account by the exclusion of the use of IMF resources and the change in reserve assets, and the inclusion of errors and omissions.
[3]In percent of actual (not program) GDP; differs from Table 3.1 and Table 4.1 for this reason.
[4]Error = Outcome – program projection.

From Table 3.2, it is striking that capital account projections in these crises have displayed a systematic tendency toward overoptimism, with projection errors ranging from about ½ percent of GDP (Argentina) to 3½–5 percent of GDP (Brazil, Mexico, and the Philippines) and 10–17 percent of GDP in Indonesia, Korea, and Thailand.[19]

Were these projections simply unrealistic? Capital flows are difficult enough to project in traditional IMF-supported programs; in capital account crises the stock vulnerabilities make it all the more challenging.[20] Table 3.3 lists some of the potential stock vulnerabilities, some of which were the driving forces behind the eventual crisis.

In any assessment of the stock vulnerabilities, two caveats must be borne in mind. First, it is not always clear which "stocks" are at risk: is it the external credit lines of the financial sector, or does it extend to the debt of the corporate sector as well? Moreover, as the crisis evolves, different stocks can become increasingly vulnerable. Thus, a crisis that originates in the public sector finances could, via exchange rate depreciations and real interest rate increases, spread to the financial and corporate sectors. Second, even if the appropriate stock can be identified, it is usually far from clear how much is at risk and subject to outflows.[21]

The precise nature of the capital outflows differed across countries. Where they reflected weakness in the public finances and rollover risk of government debt, they are somewhat easier to project since at least the amounts falling due are known. Where they reflected weaknesses in the corporate and financial sectors (mainly Asia), projections would have required detailed balance sheet analyses, which were not available at the time. Moreover, certain structures of the country's external liabilities—short-term versus long-term, private versus public—may make it particularly difficult to forecast the behavior of capital flows. Although there are too few observations to undertake any formal analysis, the evidence does suggest that the largest projection errors occurred in the Asian countries, which were also the most vulnerable in terms of short-term indebtedness. Not surprisingly, moreover, errors in projecting capital flows also tended to be larger when creditors were private rather than official, and when borrowers were dispersed (proxied by private versus official debtors).

In practice, given the lack of strong theoretical underpinnings, projections of the reflow of private cap-

[19]To focus on projection errors of the flows, the program current and capital accounts are expressed in terms of actual GDP (not program GDP).

[20]Most theoretical frameworks model capital flows responding to current and (via exchange rate expectations) prospective interest differentials and an overall "risk premium."

[21]For instance, although short-term debt is usually considered most "at risk," it is often assumed that trade credit lines, which are collateralized by goods, may be relatively immune. In the case of Korea, however, a large component of the capital outflow in early 1998 was the drying-up of trade credits. A further complication arises from large stocks of derivative instruments (e.g., forwards and swaps in Thailand).

Table 3.3. Selected Stock Vulnerability Indicators[1]
(As percent of GDP)

	Domestic Public Debt[2]	Total External Debt	Private External Debt: Commercial banks' debt, debtor based	Private External Debt: Other private debt, debtor based	Short-Term External Debt (Residual maturity)	Memo Item: Gross Foreign Reserves
Argentina (1994)[3]	15.0	33.3	4.2	5.3	5.9	5.7
Brazil (1998)	36.0	30.7	13.2	4.1	10.5	5.4
Mexico (1994)	27.2	33.8	6.0	6.6	8.3	1.5
Turkey (1993)[3]	9.4	36.9	12.1	10.2	13.5	3.5
Indonesia (1997)	3.0[4]	63.3	35.8	2.8	42.7	7.7
Korea (1997)	7.0	28.1	17.1	7.7	12.4[5]	1.9[6]
Philippines (1997)	29.7	61.6	13.6	17.9	18.0	9.1
Thailand (1997)	4.8	72.3	26.0	30.4	31.3	5.5[7]

Sources: IMF, *World Economic Outlook*; BIS-OECD-IMF Joint Debt Statistics; and IMF staff estimates.
[1]End-of-period stocks.
[2]Excludes quasi-fiscal losses.
[3]Dates refer to year *t*, not to program approval year.
[4]Inclusion of quasi-fiscal losses for Indonesia would raise (imputed) domestic public debt to over 40 percent of GDP at end of fiscal year 1997–98.
[5]Original maturity.
[6]Usable reserves.
[7]Net of forwards and swaps.

ital flows must be determined in an iterative process, in light of likely official financing and reasonable estimates of current account adjustment. A particular difficulty in making projections lies in the largely binary nature of capital reflows: either confidence is restored and capital returns relatively rapidly, or confidence is not restored and there are substantial outflows. Although different investors will have different incentives and risk tolerances, a middle ground, in which "some" confidence is restored and "some" capital returns, is unlikely. Macroeconomic projections must be based on an "average" outcome, however; that is, projected capital flows are the probability-weighted average of the "good case" scenario in which confidence is restored rapidly, and the "bad case" scenario in which confidence is not restored and there are protracted outflows.

The hypothetical alternative of basing programs only on the worst case scenario would have the benefit of protecting the program in the event that a favorable market response does not materialize. But by indicating to markets that the IMF considered further large capital outflows likely, such an approach could—unless official financing or private sector involvement were clearly sufficient to cover it from the outset—contribute to the weakening of market confidence. More importantly, it is not always clear what "worst case scenario" for capital outflows means: should it be limited to short-term external debt, or to include medium- and long-term debt falling due, or to a much wider class of domestic liabilities (such as monetary aggregate M2) that is potentially subject to flight if residents lose confidence in the currency?

Program scenarios are not intended to be unconditional forecasts, being predicated, among other things, on the agreed policies being implemented and the expected official financing being disbursed. Nonetheless, it is striking that, in *every* instance in our sample, the outcome was worse than projected.[22] Even in cases where the magnitude of the error was small, such as Argentina (1995), the program does not appear to have had a strong catalytic effect, at least in the very short run, on private capital flows. In Argentina, shortfalls of flows to the private sector to the tune of almost \$3 billion were offset by the government's regaining access to international capital markets in the latter part of the year. In Brazil in 1999, there was a shortfall of almost \$20 billion (despite significantly higher FDI inflows, partly reflecting privatizations), which had to be financed by a run-down of reserves. Likewise, in Mexico, a shortfall of inflows amounting to some \$15 billion had to be offset by greater official financing. In the Asian

[22]If these projections were unbiased and unconditional forecasts, outturns might be expected to be better than projected in about one-half of the cases.

countries, shortfalls in inflows were offset—and in the case of Korea, more than offset—by much greater adjustment of the current account.[23]

A number of factors explain the less favorable than anticipated market reactions to the initial programs and the failure of some programs to restore market confidence and voluntary access to capital markets. First of all, the credibility of the entire financing package is a key factor influencing the markets. One aspect of this financing is that private investors' behavior was based, to some extent, on their own expectations of aggregate private financing, sometimes generating self-fulfilling liquidity attacks: once a rush for the exits started, there were powerful incentives for more investors to join the queue. Another key factor in some cases is that the size of the official financing packages and uncertainties regarding their availability in certain cases had an important influence on market perceptions. The IMF's own financing was phased and conditional on program implementation, implying that markets could not count on the availability of this financing. In some cases—including, at times, the Mexico, Korea, and the Philippines programs—the accompanying bilateral financing, which constituted a sizable part of the packages, was not assured, and there was scope for markets to test these packages.[24] Perhaps more importantly, the size of the official financing packages was not so large in relation to the stock imbalances of the countries, and uncertainty about how such financing could address these balance sheet weaknesses—particularly as they pertained to the corporate and financial sectors—may have undermined their effectiveness.

A second major element concerns the record of program implementation. In virtually all of the cases, failures in implementation of announced economic policies at some times undermined the credibility of the programs in the eyes of the markets. Such delays were important both to the extent that the policy changes were needed to address the underlying problems and to the extent that, as mentioned, future official financing was conditional on these reforms. For example, the agreement between Brazil and the IMF, reached in early December 1998, initially calmed the markets and eased pressures on reserves. Following this, however, interest rates were reduced excessively and prematurely, while the fiscal package stalled in Congress and the provinces, heightening markets' concerns about the authorities' will to implement the program. Similarly, in Indonesia, the authorities initially raised interest rates but then rolled back the increase a week later; the Korean authorities likewise were reluctant to raise interest rates at the outset. As mentioned earlier, this reflects a more general issue: the credibility of monetary policies in most of these crises was impaired by weaknesses in the financial sector or the public finances that were thought to limit the authorities' scope to raise interest rates.

In addition to these initial shortcomings in program implementation, political developments cast doubt on future implementation. In some instances, the lack of disclosure of adequate and timely information to the markets (and the IMF)—and the revelation of adverse information at the height of the crisis—contributed to adverse market reactions. These have included information on the true financial condition of the countries (Mexico and East Asian countries), the size of the fiscal deficit (of the development banks in Mexico and quasi-fiscal losses of the Thai financial institutions), and the availability of usable foreign exchange reserves (Mexico, Thailand, and Korea). These adverse developments included uncertain election outcomes (Korea), new and untested administrations (Mexico), instability of the political regime (Indonesia), disagreements between central and provincial governments (Brazil), and fragility of the coalition negotiating the program (Thailand).[25]

But while it is always possible to find reasons why confidence was undermined in specific instances, there is a more fundamental issue. There is no country that has not at some time experienced hesitations and lapses in policy implementation, mixed political signals, untimely release of bad news, and uncertainties in particular elements of financing. Such eventualities are a fact of life for IMF-supported programs around the world. The difference is, in a capital account crisis, the country's entire macroeconomic prospects may be hostage to such events—and the markets unforgiving of any lapses. Given this reality, there are important questions concerning the appropriate provision of official financing and efforts at private sector involvement.

Official Financing and Private Sector Involvement

Regardless of the reasons—flaws in program design, slippages in implementation, or simple bad

[23]In addition, as discussed in Box 3.2, there were attempts at private sector involvement after the initial program failed to stem capital outflows.

[24]In some cases, such as Brazil, the original IMF-supported programs sought to maintain formal or informal exchange rate pegs that the markets perceived as lacking credibility.

[25]One exception is Argentina, where the reelection of President Menem in May 1995 gave a boost to confidence as his campaign had been based on the need to maintain the currency board arrangement.

luck—the turnaround in capital outflows took significantly longer than expected. In terms of the traditional mix between "financing" and "adjustment," the outcome was far from optimal: countries clearly underwent excessive external adjustment.

To the extent that there were not voluntary reflows of capital, it is arithmetically true that such adjustment could only be avoided by greater official financing, some form of private sector involvement, or a combination of the two. Beyond the arithmetic of financing gaps, however, two points bear emphasizing. First, in the context of stock imbalances and capital outflows, the size of the financing gap itself may have been endogenous to the form of financing—whether official or private sector involvement (and, within the latter, the precise nature of the private sector involvement). Second, given the balance sheet weaknesses, some macroeconomic disruption and adjustment may well have been unavoidable.

Nonetheless, a collapsing exchange rate and massive capital outflows almost surely exacerbated existing balance sheet weaknesses—and indeed, especially in Asia, contributed to widespread corporate and financial sector bankruptcies. Moreover, granted that the balance sheet corrections meant that some output contraction was largely unavoidable, the capital outflows and corresponding current account adjustments implied that an even greater contraction of domestic absorption was required. Accordingly, there was an argument for avoiding such excessive current adjustment to the extent that a combination of official financing and private sector involvement would permit. (Of course, delivering significantly larger financing, either private or official, is by no means a straightforward matter.)

Official Financing

Compared to previous IMF-supported programs, official financing in capital account crisis programs was exceptionally large (Box 3.1). Practically all of these programs were supported by exceptional access to IMF resources, supplemented by funds from other multilateral institutions and governments (with the IMF's share in the overall financing packages ranging from 16 percent in Turkey, to 44 percent in Brazil, and to almost 70 percent in the Philippines). The need for a coordinated official sector response was necessitated by the large amounts of official funds required to deal with these crises. But reliance on bilateral support was not without its risks. In Indonesia and Korea, funds pledged by bilateral creditors formed a second line of defense but were not subject to well-defined terms and conditions and were never disbursed, contributing to market anxieties that may have influenced the decisions of private creditors to continue to exit.[26] Even in the Mexican program, total financing envisaged under the program was $56.8 billion, of which $40 billion was supposed to take the form of loan guarantees provided by the United States government and $7.8 billion was to come from the IMF. In the event, the U.S. Congress rejected the Administration's request for the loan guarantees, and a smaller contribution from the Exchange Stabilization Fund was arranged instead, with additional IMF resources making up part of the shortfall. Although the program also needed strengthened adjustment (which was undertaken in the context of the program review), uncertainty regarding the financing undoubtedly had an adverse effect on market confidence.

A key aspect of the official financing packages was their phasing. The IMF's support is generally phased and conditional: resources are not immediately available in their entirety at the outset, but are typically spread out evenly over the life of the program and conditional on the adherence to the policy understandings under the program.[27]

A related issue concerns the use of floors on net international reserves (NIR) as performance criteria. Taken to their extreme, and adhered to rigidly, such floors could vitiate the confidence effects of official support, as the country would, in effect, be unable to use the resources provided. In practice, program floors on NIR reflected a number of different considerations. In Brazil, where the initial program sought to maintain the formal exchange rate peg, the NIR floor allowed for substantial intervention.[28] In Asia, NIR floors were generally tighter, reflecting both the very low initial levels of reserves—and hence the need to build up reserves rapidly—and the need to limit sterilized intervention (with the intention that support for the exchange rate should come mainly from increases in interest rates).[29] Nevertheless, the targeted increases in NIR in the initial stages of the programs were more than accounted for by expected dis-

[26]For a fuller discussion of the Asian experience with the so-called second lines of defense, see Lane and others (1999).

[27]See, for example, Guitián (1981).

[28]In Argentina, the other case in which the program sought to maintain the exchange rate peg (in the form of a currency board), the floor on net international reserves was made an indicative target. There was also a performance criterion on "free" international reserves—gross international reserves minus currency issued and legal reserve deposits at the central bank—which allowed the central bank to use its reserves pursuant to its commitments under the currency board.

[29]In some cases, such as Thailand, there were also explicit limits on the amount of sterilized intervention that could be undertaken under the program.

Box 3.1. Official Financing in Capital Account Crisis Programs

Practically all of these programs entailed exceptionally large access to IMF resources,[1] supplemented by funds from other multilateral institutions and governments (with the IMF's share in the overall financing packages ranging from 16 percent in Turkey, to 44 percent in Brazil, and almost 70 percent in the Philippines).

Dealing with a demand for an exceptionally large scale of IMF resources led to a gradual change in practices and the introduction of additional facilities. In the case of the five programs with cumulative access above 300 percent of quota, Mexico, Indonesia, and Thailand were handled as exceptional cases within the framework of existing arrangements. The Supplement in excess of the statutory limit of 100 percent, ranging from 118 percent of quota in Argentina to 1,757 percent of quota in Korea. In contrast, for IMF programs in general, average annual access in stand-by and extended arrangements ranged between 32 and 56 percent between 1990 and 1994, and fluctuated within a 22–100 percent band during those years.

Financing Packages in Capital Account Crisis Programs

		Financing Package (In millions of U.S. dollars)					Financing Package (As percent of)				
Country	Date of Arrangement	IMF	IMF as percent of total	World Bank and other multilaterals	Other	Total	GDP[1]	M2[2]	Capital account[3]	Potential outflows[4]	Short-term debt[5]
Argentina	April-95	2,861	33.0	2,600	3,200	8,661	3.4	16.2	77.2	82.3	95.5
Brazil	December-98	18,262	43.7	9,000	14,538	41,800	5.2	18.3	192.1	66.6	113.9
Indonesia	November-97	10,083	27.9	8,000	18,000	36,083	15.9	31.0	296.6	268.7	50.1
Korea	December-97	20,990	36.0	14,200	23,100	58,290	11.2	27.6	233.0	94.8	62.7
Mexico	February-95	17,843	34.4	—	33,957	51,800	12.3	47.3	169.1	108.0	164.3
Philippines	July-97	1,039	69.8	—	450	1,489	1.8	3.3	18.0	12.9	17.6
Thailand	August-97	3,926	22.9	2,700	10,500	17,126	9.4	11.8	101.6	37.4	37.5
Turkey	July-94	742	16.3	3,800	—	4,542	2.5	13.1	67.4	436.5	24.5

[1]As a percent of U.S. dollar value of GDP for year prior to arrangement.

[2]U.S. dollar value of M2 at the end of the year prior to the arrangement, except for Mexico (1993) and the Philippines (1996).

[3]Capital account, including errors and omissions, of the year prior to the crisis, except for Mexico (1993) and the Philippines (1996).

[4]Potential outflow defined as the cumulative sum over the previous three years of all private capital flows excluding foreign direct investment and errors and omissions.

[5]Short-term debt at the end of the year prior to the arrangement, except for Indonesia, where 1997 was used.

[1]Access to IMF resources exceeded the statutory limit of 300 percent of quota in Korea, Mexico, Brazil, Thailand, and Indonesia, where the exceptional circumstances clause was invoked. In addition, since most of these programs were heavily front-loaded, all of them except the 1994 Turkish program entailed gross purchases over the first 12 months of the arrangement in excess of the statutory limit of 100 percent, ranging from 118 percent of quota in Argentina to 1,757 percent of quota in Korea. In contrast, for IMF programs in general, average annual access in stand-by and extended arrangements ranged between 32 and 56 percent between 1990 and 1994, and fluctuated within a 22–100 percent band during those years.

bursements of external financing, and typically included explicit adjustors for shortfalls in official support.[30] There is little direct evidence of whether, in the cases reviewed here, the existence of an NIR floor may itself have eroded the confidence effects of official financing packages—although more generally it appears that market participants are becoming increasingly aware of various factors that may influence the usability of reserves. The possibility that NIR floors could have such an undermining effect would need to be weighed carefully against the usefulness of NIR floors as a signal that, if breached, there may be a need to reassess policies.

[30]A case in point is Korea, where the original program envisaged a buildup of net international reserves from about $6 billion at the outset of the program in early December 1997, to $11 billion by end-December, with an automatic adjustor for shortfalls in balance of payments support. In the event, not all of the expected amount was disbursed and the NIR floor was automatically adjusted to –$3 billion, which was met.

tal Reserve Facility (SRF), which is not subject to access limits of its own, provided the framework for dealing with the Brazilian program of December 1998. The Korean program preceded the creation of the SRF by two weeks and, while the text of the original arrangement did not mention the SRF, the letter of intent did include a provision to the effect that Korea would request to use the new facility as soon as it became available to members, which occurred on December 19, 1997.

Another notable aspect of the official financing packages was their phasing, with most of these programs having entailed an unusually front-loaded schedule of purchases, particularly after the introduction of the SRF. Although the Argentine and Philippine programs were relatively short-lived, they allowed for the release of about 60 percent or more of total access of IMF resources upon approval. Even where the program's life was three years (Brazil, Indonesia, Korea, and Thailand), some 30 percent of total access was, as a minimum, available at the time of approval, and at least three-quarters of total access was available within the first year of the program.

Access to IMF Resources in Capital Account Crisis Programs

		Access				Phasing of Purchases (As a percent of total access)		
Country	Date of Arrangement	Type[1]	Millions of SDRs	Millions of U.S. dollars[2]	Percent of quota	Upon approval	First six months	First twelve months
Argentina	April-95	EFF (12)	1,815	2,861	118[3]	57.7	71.8	100.0
Brazil	December-98	SBA (36)	13,025	18,262	600[4]	29.2	68.3	86.7[5]
Indonesia	November-97	SBA (36)	7,338	10,083	490	30.0	60.0	75.8
Korea	December-97	SBA (36)	15,500	20,990	1,938[4]	43.2	81.3	90.6
Mexico	February-95	SBA (18)	12,070	17,843	688	43.6	63.4	81.7
Philippines	July-97	EFF (6)	754.7	1,039	119	67.4	100.0	100.0
Thailand	August-97	SBA (34)	2,900	3,926	505	41.4	69.0	75.9
Turkey	July-94	SBA (14)	509	742	79	31.5	46.2	75.7

[1]Length of original arrangement (in months) in parentheses.

[2]Calculated using the average U.S. dollar/SDR rate for the month of approval of the arrangements.

[3]Since a waiver for end-December 1994 was approved at the same time, an additional 18 percent of quota, corresponding to undrawn purchases under the third year of the 1992 EFF, were made available immediately (in addition to the 50 percent shown in the table).

[4]At least part of the funds were made available through the SRF. In the case of Korea, the original arrangement preceded the creation of the SRF by two weeks; however, following the adoption of the SRF, the text of the SBA was amended to specify that the part of the financing during the period December 18, 1997–December 18, 1998 would be available through the SRF.

[5]Under the arrangement, the Brazilian authorities could request, under certain circumstances and subject to completion of Board reviews, that purchases under the SRF be brought forward.

Both the phasing of official financing and the use of NIR floors limit the amount of resources that are immediately available and usable by the country. Part of the logic of providing official financing, however, is to assure foreign creditors that the country has available sufficient resources to meet maturing obligations—and hence that there is no need to rush for the exit. This poses an inherent dilemma, particularly when the program requires structural reforms that can only be instituted over time. Based largely on these considerations, the IMF's financing in capital account crises has generally been more front-loaded than the more typical equal phasing, but the IMF has stopped well short of the extreme of making its entire financing available up front.

Granted that the official financing packages assembled in these cases were both unusually large and unusually front-loaded, inevitably there is a concern about possible "moral hazard" effects in future crises, whereby investors lend imprudently in the expectation of being "bailed out" by public funds. At a theoretical level, such effects are certainly possible; the empirical evidence is, however, much more mixed.[31]

A related issue—concerning moral hazard on the part of policymakers—is whether countries that delayed addressing underlying weaknesses, and in approaching the IMF, were, in effect, "rewarded" with larger packages. This issue is taken up in Appendix II, which uses two different proxies of policy delays—an exchange market pressure index and the loss of reserves relative to short-term debt—and examines their relationship to the size of the official financing package. No empirical evidence is found in favor of the hypothesis that countries that may have engaged in a systematic postponement of adjustment were rewarded with larger official packages in the context of IMF programs.

Private Sector Involvement

In contrast to the provision of official financing, attempts at coordinated private sector involvement, broadly construed, were quite limited, particularly in the earlier crises (Mexico 1994, Turkey 1994, and Argentina 1995). In Brazil and Thailand, there was an attempt at the onset of the crisis to involve the private sector, at least on an informal basis, while in Korea, the exception among the cases reviewed here, direct pressure was applied to international banks to lengthen their credit lines after the failure of the initial program to stem bank withdrawals (Box 3.2).

The initial agreement with Korea's creditor banks was reached in early 1998 and, although capital outflows continued thereafter, these mostly reflected the drying up of trade credit lines, which were not subject to the agreement. Indeed, reaching the agreement with the creditor banks—as well as the strengthening of the policy package (as discussed in Chapter V)—appears to have been a pivotal point in the turning of the Korean crisis.

This raises the question of whether some form of coordinated private sector involvement should have been attempted in more of these cases.[32] Such a strategy could eliminate the risk of relying on voluntary capital reflows, and likely would reduce both the required current account adjustment and the need for official financing.[33] But it is important to recognize that there are limitations to this strategy: private sector involvement cannot always be pulled out, deus ex machina, to fill the unanticipatedly large financing gaps. In some instances, the very mechanics of coordinated private sector involvement would have been challenging; in the case of Mexico, for instance, short of a stay or outright default, which might have been extremely disruptive, the widespread holdings of Tesobonos would have made negotiations with creditors logistically difficult. And while more heavy-handed attempts at private sector involvement might solve the immediate financing gap, it may do so at greater cost in terms of delays in regaining future market access and resumption of voluntary capital inflows. Thus far, the use of capital controls in the face of large capital outflows (not attempted in the cases reviewed here) has met with rather mixed results (Box 3.3).[34]

Beyond the impact on the individual countries, it is also important to bear in mind the implications of private sector involvement as a policy regime. In particular, routinely imposing private sector involvement—especially in a form that would impose losses on investors—could make short-term investors even more skittish, impelling them to exit even more hastily while they have the chance, and exacerbate contagion in the midst of a crisis.[35] Introducing such steps as a standard feature of IMF-supported programs could in some instances offset, or even more than offset, any favorable confidence effects of the IMF's financing.

Given that, even in the most successful cases, there are limits to coordinated private sector involvement—and certainly its less disruptive forms do not by any means enable the authorities to control the capital account[36]—the question arises of whether there should have been greater official

[31]See, for instance, Lane and Phillips (2000).

[32]This could, in principle, have been done in several ways—either separately or in combination. These include moral suasion to induce creditor banks to negotiate a restructuring of credit lines or provide new money, negotiated restructuring of bond debt, payment standstills enforced by exchange controls, or default.

[33]Moreover, to the extent that private sector involvement imposes losses on creditors—which was not the case in either Korea or Brazil—its use could also help alleviate moral hazard.

[34]Theoretical arguments for exchange controls typically appeal to inefficiencies in the operation of capital markets due to, among other things, asymmetric information combined with inappropriate deposit insurance; mismatches between financial intermediaries' long-term assets and short-term liabilities that leave them vulnerable to runs; principal-agent problems that result in herd behavior; the dependence of asset values on expectations, which generates bubbles and peso problems; and problems associated with incompleteness of contingent markets and bounded rationality (Rodrik, 1999).

[35]Any form of negotiated private sector involvement requires both coordinating different creditors and confronting them with a credible threat of default; to be credible, such a threat has to be acted on in some instances. Moreover, any reforms that would make it easy for debtors to restructure bonds or other forms of debt would run counter to the economic rationale for the existence of such debt, which is based on asymmetric information.

[36]Thus, in Brazil, generally considered the most successful case of large-scale private sector involvement among the countries reviewed here, the projection error on the capital account still amounted to some 3½ percent of GDP.

Box 3.2. Private Sector Involvement

The programs considered in this paper offer a variety of experiences regarding the scale and outcome of private sector involvement. In some early programs—Argentina (1995), Mexico (1994), Turkey (1994), and the Philippines (1997)—private sector involvement was not needed or was not attempted. In the case of Argentina, no private sector involvement was needed: the program was successful in restoring spontaneous capital flows and the country's 1995 financing needs were met through voluntary market financing. In the case of Mexico, on the other hand, private sector involvement was not attempted in the face of continuing outflows in early 1995. Rather, the program was revised to feature more adjustment and a modified and more credible official financing package.

Several factors rendered private sector involvement difficult in the case of Mexico. One was that the capital fleeing the country was in the form of assets—the notorious tesobonos—that had diverse ownership and lacked well defined legal and operational rules for restructuring—a problem of all attempts at private sector involvement to date. In fact, only limited progress has been made to date in lifting institutional constraints to restructuring sovereign bonds. Second, although it would be possible to attempt to bail in private banks whose lines needed to be rolled over and which comprised a significant liability, it would be politically difficult to treat so differently bondholders and holders of bank liabilities. In fact, problems posed by the need to maintain inter-creditor equity is another difficult area where only limited progress has been made. Finally, the IMF and bilateral supporters may have been dissuaded from embarking on a risky, unknown process of involving the private sector in January 1995 because of the daunting task of attempting to contact so many bond holders in the midst of a crisis.

In those crises where private sector involvement was attempted, its detailed *form* varied, depending on the circumstances of individual countries. Different mechanisms were employed to achieve the voluntary and cooperative participation of the private sector in providing relief to unsustainable debt positions.[1]

Direct pressure was applied to international banks to lengthen their credit lines (Korea, 1998). Emergency negotiations between the foreign commercial banks with credits to Korea and the new government of Kim Dae Jung took place in the final week of 1998, "under the stewardship and with the moral suasion of G-7 central banks."[2] U.S., Japanese, and European banks agreed to roll over their loans through March, allowing the government time to negotiate a more comprehensive restructuring package. On January 28, Korea and the banks reached agreement on the rescheduling of $24 billion of debt and on a plan to replace the bank loans with sovereign-guaranteed bonds. Twenty-two billion dollars of interbank claims were converted into bonds with a maturity of one to three years and a spread of 225 to 275 basis points over LIBOR.[3] Korea's short-term debt was reduced from $61 billion at end-March 1998 to $41 billion at end-April. The deposits and loans were converted into new loans that carried an explicit government guarantee and were transferable. Korea's experience with private sector involvement is sometimes compared (not very favorably) with the subsequent experience of Brazil because, in the latter case, less pressure was applied by the official community. But the terms of the debt restructuring were such that Korea's bank creditors came out whole.

Informal pressure was exerted on international banks to maintain their credit lines (Thailand, August 1997; Brazil, March 1999). In Thailand, Japanese bank creditors gave informal indications or assurances that they would maintain their credit lines to Thai banks. As part of a reformulated program, Brazil reached a voluntary agreement with creditor banks that they would maintain exposure to the country. This comes closest to an example of voluntary catalysis in our sample of programs. The agreement with commercial bank creditors that they would maintain their credit lines with Brazilian banks at their end-February level was reached following negotiations between the banks, the Brazilian finance minister, and the country's newly appointed central bank governor, without moral suasion or pressure from the creditor countries' central banks. The Brazilian authorities were very concerned about the possibility that by approaching the banks, they could trigger the very run they were trying to avoid. To avoid this, they went to great lengths to make it very clear that they were not attempting to trap banks in a pattern of involuntary lending. Although this approach limited the use of IMF resources to pay off bank creditors, the banks once again did not take a hit—unlike other classes of investors who suffered losses in Brazilian markets.[4]

[1]Other programs have required that the national authorities renegotiate their bond contracts as a precondition for extending IMF assistance (Ukraine, 1998; Romania, 1998; Pakistan, 1999). In some cases, involuntary and unilateral debt restructurings were used, accompanied by capital controls after failure of voluntary debt restructuring offers by the national authorities (Russia, July 1998; Ukraine, autumn 1998). In other instances, precautionary lines of credit with private banks or international development banks were used, which were drawn during times of crisis (Mexico, 1998; Argentina, 1998). For a detailed discussion of private sector involvement issues, see *Involving the Private Sector in Forestalling and Resolving Financial Crises*, ibid.

[2]See Eichengreen (1999).

[3]In January 1998, agreement was reached between the Korean authorities and a group of 13 foreign banks and 33 Korean banks (including overseas branches) to restructure the short-term debt. Bonds and other securitized debt (commercial paper and overnight deposits), derivatives and other off-balance sheet items, and foreign exchange contracts were excluded from the agreement.

[4]Eichengreen (1999).

Box 3.3. Capital Controls

Another tool available to address capital outflows is the imposition of capital controls. Although none of the countries reviewed here adopted such controls,[1] two other countries facing capital account crises—Malaysia and Russia—did adopt explicit capital controls.

Malaysia

The Malaysian capital controls were instituted in September 1998 and required (1) repatriation, by October 1, of all ringgit held abroad; (2) an end to all offshore trading in ringgit and domestic credit facilities for overseas banks and stockbrokers; (3) retention of the proceeds of the sale of Malaysian securities in the country for a year; (4) payment in foreign currency for imports and exports; and (5) central bank approval for the conversion of ringgit into foreign currency.

Comparing Malaysia's performance with these controls to the other Asian countries, some commentators have argued that they were effective, both in terms of stemming capital outflows and in terms of broader macroeconomic benefits.[2] Unfortunately, the Malaysian experience does not provide much of a controlled experiment for examining the efficacy of capital controls.

Specifically, the approach adopted by the Malay authorities at the onset of the 1997 crisis, although not in the context of an IMF-supported program, did not differ greatly from that adopted by Thailand and Korea. Malaysia faced much the same loss of confidence, with capital outflows beginning in mid-1997—like other countries in the region. In response to the crisis, overnight interest rates were raised from 6 percent to 35 percent in July 1997 (although lowered soon thereafter as the authorities adopted more direct means of controlling monetary conditions), and the budget was tightened at the end of 1997. Similar to the other Asian countries, real GDP growth fell from 7.3 percent in 1997 to –7.4 percent in 1998, the real exchange rate depreciated by 20 percent, the stock market declined by some 60 percent, and the current account swung into a surplus of more than 13 percent of GDP.[3] Malaysia's performance must also be viewed in the context of its much more favorable initial conditions than those of its neighbors (for instance, Malaysia's external debt was only 17 percent of GDP).[4]

By the time capital controls were introduced in September 1998, Malaysia had already suffered heavy capital outflows (around $10 billion) so that the base of portfolio investment that could be affected by controls, was already considerably reduced. Moreover, conditions in regional currency and stock markets had already broadly stabilized, export growth had begun to recover, and capital outflows in the region had abated (by the second and third quarters of 1998, for example, growth was turning positive in Korea and Thailand, and capital inflows were resuming in Korea, although not in Thailand). Thus, while Malaysia's growth did bounce back to 5.8 percent in 1999 (compared to 11 percent in Korea and 4 percent in Thailand), it is difficult to know how much of this should be attributed to the imposition of capital controls. The effectiveness in narrower terms of abating capital outflows is also debatable, with net outflows reaching 8 percent of GDP in 1999. Finally, the impact of capital controls cannot be judged solely on the basis of short-run economic considerations. Capital controls appear to have had an impact on foreign direct investment, which had been instrumental in generating rapid economic growth prior to the crisis. Foreign direct investment declined by 26 percent during 1999, possibly reflecting enhanced Malaysia-specific risk. In light of these considerations, Malaysia's case is unlikely to have been the best test of the usefulness of capital controls as a response to a crisis.

Russia

During the first half of 1998, following the Asian crisis and amid growing domestic political uncertainties, Russia suffered from a deterioration in market sentiment and a sharp reversal of capital inflows. From around mid-May 1998, political turmoil resulted in intensifying financial market pressures, with average yields on domestic bonds (GKO) rising from under 30 percent at the start of the month to over 100 percent by the end. The Central Bank of Russia (CBR) responded by raising interest rates from 30 percent to 150 percent, and increasing its sale of foreign exchange to the market. But by mid-July, after sales corresponding to about

[1]With the exception of Thailand, which briefly imposed capital controls in May 1997. These controls were unsuccessful in stemming capital outflows, and the baht was floated two months later.

[2]Using a time-shifted difference-in-differences methodology, Kaplan and Rodrik (2001) argue that the Malaysian controls succeeded immediately in reducing interest rates, stabilizing the currency, and stemming financial panic, thus facilitating a smaller drop in employment and real wages, and allowing a faster recovery in real activity. Their methodology compares Malaysia's performance following September 1998 to the earlier experiences of Korea and Thailand under their IMF-supported programs, while attempting to control for differences in the external environment. As argued below, this is problematic. Others draw somewhat different conclusions. Using a large panel data set and the General Evaluation Estimation technique, Hutchinson (2001) identifies the impact of the crisis on real GDP separately from that arising from participation in an IMF-supported program. He concludes that Malaysia's lack of participation in an IMF-supported program did not help its real performance which was similar to others in the region. Moreover, participation in an IMF-supported program following a crisis does not appear to mitigate or exacerbate output losses.

[3]Appendix V, Table A5.1 provides some selected macroeconomic indicators.

[4]In addition, the initial fiscal position was strong and the regulatory framework for the financial sector was relatively well developed.

one quarter of base money, the strategy proved increasingly untenable as investors continued withdrawing from the treasury bill market.

The announcement in mid-July of a modified economic adjustment program supported by the IMF, with additional resources of SDR8.5 billion, helped ease market pressures temporarily. But confidence was again eroded when the Duma (Russia's lower house of parliament) refused to accept the fiscal measures envisaged in the government's program. GKO yields rose to 300 percent and the Ministry of Finance canceled new auctions. The CBR was forced to provide large credits to the government to meet obligations on maturing GKOs, as well as extending support to commercial banks, essentially sterilizing reserve outflows.

Against this backdrop, the government announced a series of measures on August 17, 1998, which included (1) a widening of the exchange rate band from Rub5.3–7.1 per dollar to Rub6.0–9.5 and elimination of the daily narrow band; (2) suspension of payments on treasury bills maturing before end-1999 and their conversion to longer-term paper; and (3) a 90-day standstill on servicing private external debt (including payments by Russian banks to nonresidents to settle forward foreign exchange contracts that investors had written to hedge their GKO/OFZ holdings).

Market reaction to these measures was extremely unfavorable, in part due to uncertainty about details of the debt conversion scheme. The ruble continued to depreciate despite continued central bank intervention and, in early September, the exchange rate band was completely abolished and the ruble was allowed to float; by year-end, the ruble had depreciated by some 45 percent compared to its pre-crisis level. The devaluation and the de facto default on treasury bills caused the collapse of a large number of banks, the domestic payment system was temporarily impaired, and access to international capital markets was severely disrupted.

The Russian default-cum-devaluation came close to triggering severe disruption in the world financial system, particularly for other emerging market countries, and triggering large stock market corrections in the fall of 1998. The adverse spillovers from the Russian and Brazilian crises provided fresh negative impulses, which contributed to a global slowdown in 1999. Cuts in interest rates by the U.S. Federal Reserve and other central banks and IMF financial assistance to Brazil quickly helped to restore confidence, however.

The crisis had a significant negative impact on Russia's domestic economy and on a number of neighboring countries, although the impact on the real economy was less than initially feared. Although Russian output first contracted sharply in the months following the August 17 devaluation, it stabilized by late 1998, and then recovered sharply. Real GDP growth fell from about 1 percent in 1997 to –5 percent in 1998, before recovering to 3 percent in 1999 and more than 8 percent in 2000. The main factors behind the sharp recovery were significant real exchange rate depreciation, which spurred import substitution, and higher oil prices, which boosted exports and government revenues. In addition, macroeconomic and financial policies were also broadly appropriate. Inflation, which had fallen to 15 percent in 1997, almost doubled to 28 percent in 1998, and then more than trebled to more than 85 percent in 1999. The improvement in the current account, which reached a surplus of 12½ percent of GDP in 1999 and 18 percent of GDP in 2000, was largely due to high energy prices and a sharply lower level of imports, and it was largely offset by large capital outflows.

On the financial side, the crisis took a toll on the banking and payment systems and resulted in a protracted banking crisis. The government debt conversion entailed prolonged and difficult negotiations with nonresident holders of these securities, freezing the government securities market and cutting the government from a major source of financing. The Russian government also lost access to global capital markets and fell behind in its external debt servicing obligations. The national authorities followed a strategy of servicing only the part of foreign debt incurred by the Russian Federation itself and incurred arrears on the inherited debt of the former Soviet Union. Successive rounds of negotiations with Russia's international creditors—including Paris and London Club creditors—are continuing, aiming at debt restructuring agreements. Recently, the national authorities decided to resume full payments on Soviet-era debt to the Paris Club in 2001.[5]

The favorable external conditions lowered the cost to the national authorities of default and of imposing capital controls and helped the government partially repair the damage to domestic debt markets caused by the crisis and default. The government was unable to access domestic or international capital markets in 1998–99 and was forced to resort to central bank financing. Public finances improved rapidly in 1999–2000, however, aided by the forced debt restructuring that shifted the burden of debt payments to 2003.[6] The government used its strong fiscal position to reduce its domestic debt in relation to GDP and to lengthen its term structure. The market in domestic government debt was recreated and the damage that the default inflicted on the government's relationship with investors has been partially repaired. New issues of GKOs were placed with nonresidents in December 1999 and with domestic investors in February 2000. The government is also

[5]At the conclusion of the last Article IV Consultation with Russia in November 2000, the IMF's Executive Board considered that, given Russia's healthy external position, emphasis needed to be placed on normalizing relations with creditors, improving market confidence, and attracting foreign investment.

[6]The federal primary balance moved from a deficit of about 1¼ percent of GDP in 1998 to surpluses of about 2 percent of GDP in 1999 and 6 percent of GDP in 2000.

Box 3.3 *(concluded)*

trying to resurrect other segments of the market in domestic government debt.[7] Progress has been slower in attracting private flows, which have remained below historical levels, although they have been reoriented away from portfolio flows into more stable forms like FDI.[8]

Assessment

Taken as a whole, neither Malaysia's nor Russia's experience with capital controls can provide a definitive test of their usefulness as a crisis fighting measure. A favorable external environment and restrained policies enabled Malaysia and Russia to avoid the worst consequences of exchange controls. In Russia, the government was able to recreate a voluntary market for domestic government paper in the aftermath of the partial default. External private flows may have been affected in both countries, however. Especially in Russia, private capital inflows have remained lower than their already depressed historical levels and structural reforms have lagged behind. Russia could still be vulnerable to a renewed bout of weakness in emerging markets as continued satisfactory macroeconomic performance is highly dependent on oil prices. That said, temporary capital controls appear to be a feasible, albeit second-best, response to crisis. These controls provide some breathing space to countries in crisis. But the longer they are kept in place, the larger are their longer-term costs from circumvention, distortions of saving and investment, the damage to country creditworthiness, and higher financing costs.

[7]For details, see *Oxford Analytica Brief*, November 9, 2001 (Part 1).

[8]Foreign direct investment inflows to Russia, which were extremely low before the crisis, have declined further in the aftermath of the crisis. Gross FDI inflows dropped from $4.8 billion in 1997 to about $2.5 billion annually in 1998–99, although they are projected to rise steadily over the medium term to about $8 billion by 2005.

financing.[37] Conceptually, greater official financing may be appropriate even if it does not have a catalytic effect on private flows, since it may be used to offset the "excessive" current account adjustment.[38] This argument, however, must be put in perspective. Consider the case of Thailand, where in 1998, capital outflows amounted to some 12 percent of GDP, while the financing package—provided by creditors including the IMF, other multilaterals, and bilaterals—amounted to about 9 percent of GDP. Thus, even if the full amount were to be disbursed within one year—and were all used to offset capital outflows during 1998 (rather than to build foreign exchange reserves)—official financing would have had to have been about one-third greater than was actually provided (to allow for a balance on the current account, let alone the 2–3 percent of GDP deficit that the program originally envisaged and which would have been consistent with medium-term debt stability).[39] If this additional financing were to have been provided by the IMF alone, total access would have had to have been about 2½ times as large (around 1,200 percent of quota rather than 500 percent).

The magnitudes involved almost surely preclude official financing taking up the full amount of the slack. Moreover, there is the risk that the financing gap itself becomes endogenous, with greater outflows of private capital enabled by more official money.[40] This suggests that a pragmatic approach needs to be adopted with official money being used in conjunction with (and perhaps leveraging) private sector involvement—preferably, though not necessarily, on a voluntary basis.[41] This would reduce the

[37]Standard intertemporal models of the current account suggest that a country should finance a temporary shock but adjust to a permanent shock. Since the stock of external debt is finite, capital outflows may be viewed as a temporary shock (unless the country never regains the same level of market access), which would be appropriate to finance with official resources. However, if a wide class of domestic liabilities—in the limiting case, a large fraction of the M2 monetary aggregate—is subject to outflows, this might require implausible levels of official financing.

[38]Strictly speaking, this argument holds even if official financing is enabling greater capital outflows as long as the offset is not one-for-one. In such cases, however, it would be very difficult to justify greater official financing without simultaneously attempting private sector involvement as well.

[39]This also assumes that the full financing package would be used to offset capital outflows in 1998. In fact, capital outflows in 1997 had already amounted to some 8 percent of GDP.

[40]A further consideration concerns the source of the crisis: when the crisis results purely or primarily from contagion, there may be a stronger argument for providing large, official financing (and the CCL facility goes part of the way in providing such insurance). But, in practice, it is often difficult to distinguish between domestically driven and pure contagion crises; notably, the initial crisis in Indonesia in 1997 was largely viewed as being driven by regional contagion.

[41]The IMF's thinking on coordinated private sector involvement has evolved in light of experience. Thus, as part of the reformulated Brazil program, the authorities reached a voluntary agreement with commercial bank creditors to maintain their exposure to Brazilian banks at their end-February 1999 levels. In the more recent programs with Turkey (1999) and Argentina (2000), some form of coordinated private sector involvement has

risk that official resources are simply financing private capital outflows, and would limit the disruptively excessive current account adjustment. To serve this role, official financing must be large enough (in relation to the potential stock imbalances) and disbursed quickly enough that it credibly signals the international community's confidence in the program, and can make an appreciable difference to the extent of excessive current account adjustment that the country must undertake. As discussed above, identifying the potentially vulnerable stock is not always straightforward, but, notably, the programs with the largest projection errors—those in Asia—were also the ones where official financing covered the smallest proportion of the stock that might be considered most at risk, as proxied by short-term debt (Box 3.1).

Conclusion

The magnitude and sudden reversals of capital flows to capital account crisis countries have fundamentally altered the traditional trade-off between financing and adjustment. Catalytic effects of the programs generally failed to stem capital outflows, which were significantly larger than anticipated. In turn, these capital outflows forced adjustments of the current account well in excess of program expectations or the balances required for medium-term debt stability.

Once the crises broke, and given the nature of the balance sheet problems, it was probably impossible to avoid a major macroeconomic disruption. Capital outflows exacerbated this disruption, however, and reducing the excessive current account adjustment would have required a combination of larger official financing and greater private sector involvement. Financing packages were large, though in most cases not large enough to avoid excessive adjustment. Attempts at private sector involvement were generally cautious, for fear of exacerbating outflows as well as adding to contagion effects.

Taken as a whole, the experience of these countries suggests that, in capital account crises, neither large official financing packages nor coordinated private sector involvement on its own is likely to suffice. In many cases, coordinated large-scale private sector involvement would not be feasible, or at least would be severely disruptive and perhaps would have as costly an impact as the outflow that it would be trying to avoid. At the same time, large official financing risks simply feeding further outflows. Accordingly, in such situations, modalities need to be found for using official financing in conjunction with, and perhaps leveraging, coordinated private sector involvement.

But, above all, this discussion suggests that there are rather narrow limits to what the available financing tools can do to address an ongoing crisis. This, in turn, underscores that emerging market countries need to do more to protect themselves from the vulnerabilities and fragilities that trigger crises.[42] Prevention requires that countries develop and maintain a solid financial sector, pursue sound economic policies, avoid unsustainably large current account deficits and large stocks of short-term debt, and strengthen their national (including private sector) balance sheets. Countries must also maintain adequate sources of international liquidity to deal with crises. Larger foreign exchange reserves and credit lines from private and official creditors, while entailing costs of their own, are likely to be far less expensive than the painful adjustment required in their absence in the event of a crisis. The IMF enhances countries' incentives to engage in prevention through surveillance (including initiatives such as the Financial Sector Assessment Program), technical assistance, and, when needed, with financing that provides its seal of approval for the adoption of sound policies.[43]

---

been an integral part of program design from the outset. Moreover, the technical capacity to undertake private sector involvement has also improved. At the outset of the program in Korea, for instance, basic information on the extent and terms of credit lines to banks was lacking, thereby complicating the logistics of private sector involvement; such information systems have now been established in many emerging market countries.

[42]See Feldstein (1999) on the need for self-help.

[43]Kenen (2000) proposes tying prevention efforts—such as the implementation of international standards—to the terms of IMF support in the event of crisis.

IV Macroeconomic Frameworks and Outcomes

Larger than anticipated capital outflows meant that the original macroeconomic frameworks—which envisaged modest and orderly adjustment—soon had to be abandoned. Unprogrammed capital outflows resulted in corresponding current account adjustments; in turn, output contracted, reflecting a combination of demand and supply shocks.

Macroeconomic Frameworks in the Original Programs

As discussed above, the original macroeconomic frameworks envisaged relatively moderate improvements in the current account, ranging from half a percentage point of GDP in Brazil and Indonesia to about three percentage points in Thailand. Growth was expected to slow—on average by 3 percentage points—but the programs projected a contraction of output only in two countries (Brazil and Turkey).

Events proved otherwise. Continued turbulence in financial markets meant that capital outflows turned out to be larger and more persistent than anticipated. With limited reserves to intervene in most cases, the exchange rate took the initial brunt of the adjustment, far overshooting any pre-crisis estimates of overvaluation. Very quickly, however, current accounts began to adjust as well, and program projections were revised by significant margins (Figure 4.1).

In line with successive upward revisions of the projected current account balances, growth projections had to be adjusted downward as it became evident that economic activity was rapidly faltering.[44] In the event, the magnitude of the current account adjustment in most countries broadly matched the change in net financing flows from official and private sources, with reserve changes in most cases broadly in line with program projections. Unanticipated capital outflows, and hence the unanticipated current account adjustments, were particularly large in Korea, Mexico, and Thailand. In Korea, the adjustment in the current account was, in fact, larger than required as official reserves increased faster than programmed. By contrast, in Brazil, financing flows turned out somewhat more favorable than projected and the current account position remained essentially unchanged. See Table 4.1.

Current Account Adjustment

For a given current account adjustment—mostly reflecting capital outflows—there was a corresponding fall of imports and rise in exports.

The export performance of the Latin American countries and Turkey differed significantly from that of the Asian countries. Export receipts (in U.S. dollar terms) rose by almost 25 percent in Mexico, and by almost 30 percent in Argentina (in Turkey, exports grew by 15 percent, while they declined by 7 percent in Brazil). In contrast, despite the substantial real exchange rate depreciations, export receipts actually declined by 5 to12 percent in the Asian countries. This partly reflects the less favorable external environment—as growth in trading partners was weaker in the Asian crisis countries than in the other cases—and the regional nature of the crisis meant that these countries were competing against each other. But it probably also reflects, to a considerable extent, the disruption to supply associated with balance sheet adjustments in Asia, given the foreign debt exposure of the corporate and banking sectors. Some price behavior also counteracted the increases in export volumes. Finally, given the export performance, imports fell very sharply (particularly in Korea and Thailand), associated with a correspondingly sharp fall in real GDP.[45]

Output Dynamics

Initial program projections for output growth were clearly far off the mark in all the crisis cases

[44]The pattern of program projection errors in these countries differed markedly from most IMF-supported programs. See Mussa and Phillips (2001).

[45]Estimates of short-run activity elasticities on imports are somewhat smaller in East Asia than in Latin America, so that a given decline in imports is associated with a larger decline in real GDP.

Figure 4.1. Macroeconomic Projections and Outcomes in Capital Account Crisis Programs[1]

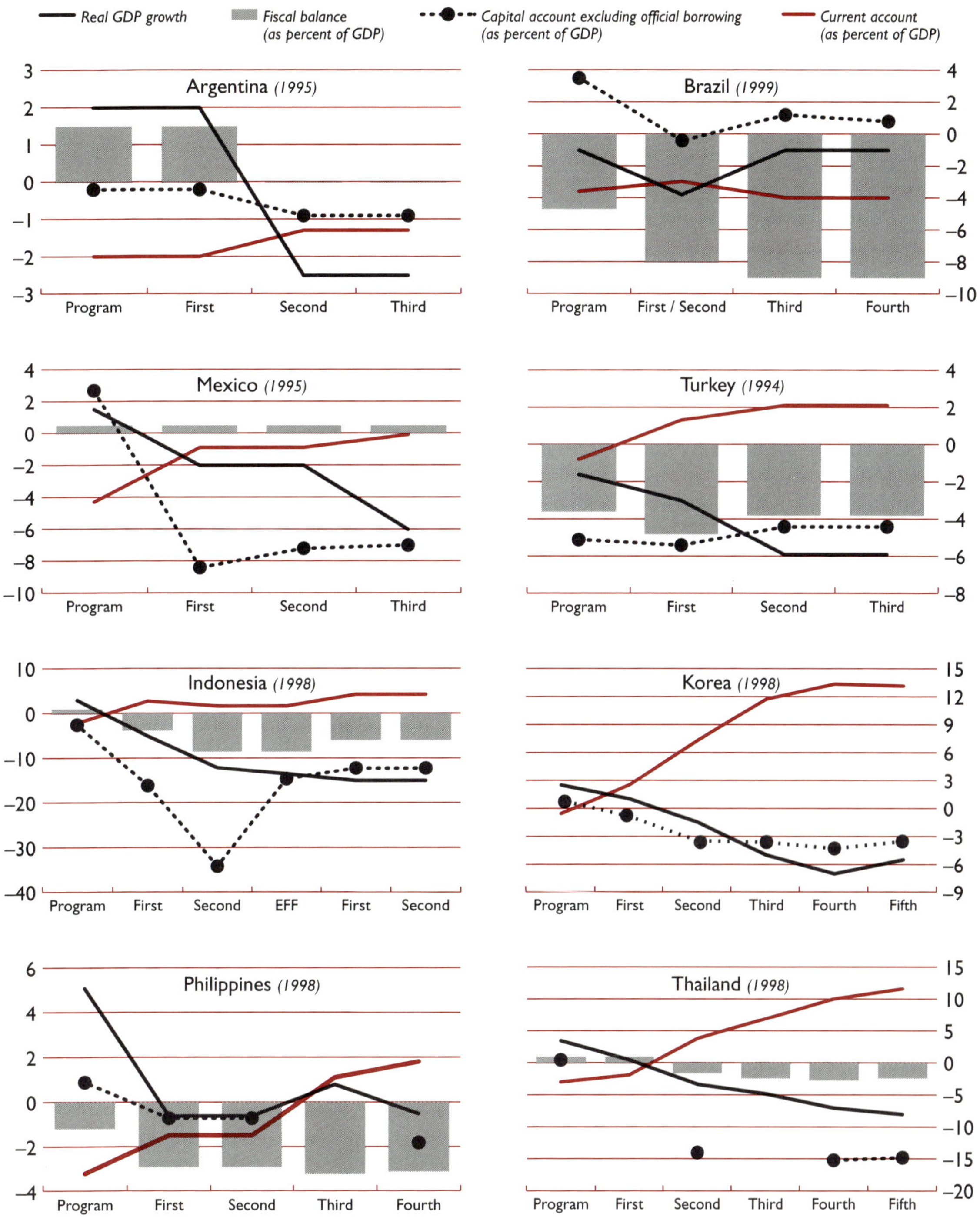

Source: IMF, MONA Database.
[1]Evolution of program projections for indicated year at the time of original program and subsequent reviews.

Table 4.1. Current Account Adjustment

	Current Account (As percent of GDP)		Growth (Percent per year)						
	Year *t*–1	Year *t*	Real GDP	Real exchange rate	Export value	Export volume	Import value	Import volume	Foreign activity[1]
Argentina	–4.3	–1.9	–2.8	0.6	28.6	22.6	–4.8	–10.0	4.2
Brazil	–4.3	–4.7	0.8	–34.4	–7.8	5.8	–17.5	–10.7	2.1
Indonesia	–1.7	4.2	–13.1	–54.7	–11.8	11.2	–22.1	–5.3	0.2
Korea	–1.7	12.7	–6.7	–28.2	–5.0	13.2	–33.2	–22.4	0.8
Mexico	–7.0	–0.6	–6.2	–31.1	24.3	12.1	–22.3	–26.4	2.7
Philippines	–5.3	2.4	–0.6	–22.2	–8.4	10.1	–21.5	–16.9	1.0
Thailand	–2.1	12.8	–10.8	–19.3	–8.8	6.5	–33.1	–21.7	0.6
Turkey	–3.5	2.8	–4.7	–25.6	15.4	15.2	–21.7	–21.9	1.5

Sources: IMF, *World Economic Outlook*; IMF, MONA database; and IMF staff estimates.
[1]Trade-weighted real GDP growth in partner countries.

examined.[46] One way to view this is simply as the counterpart to the larger-than-anticipated capital outflows and the corresponding forced current account adjustment. But it is also useful to examine the nature of these output declines from a variety of other vantage points, particularly with a view to understanding the appropriate policy response (which is discussed in Chapter V, below). This section examines the nature of the output declines using various approaches, each of which provides particular insights, but probably none of which fully captures the extraordinarily complex output dynamics in capital account crises.

Contributions to Growth

As a first step, the changes in output may be decomposed into "growth contributions." It bears emphasizing, however, that without a priori exogeneity assumptions, these decompositions cannot say what is "driving" the output dynamics and, in particular, whether it mainly reflects shocks to the demand or the supply side. One such exogeneity assumption has already been discussed: to the extent that the capital outflows forced a current account adjustment, this determined the contribution of net exports to real GDP growth. A second a priori reasonable exogeneity assumption concerns public consumption, since this is largely a policy variable.

Figure 4.2 shows growth contributions in the eight countries. Three observations are immediately evident. First, in the year of steepest output decline, net exports provided a large positive contribution to output growth. As discussed above, however, there is a significant difference between the Asian countries, where the contribution of net exports comes mostly from a decline in imports, and the other countries, where the contribution reflects export growth, as well as some decline in imports. Second, the contribution of public consumption, positive or negative, is minimal: the largest effect is in Indonesia, where the decline in public consumption "contributes" 1 percentage point of the 13 percent real GDP decline. Third, the contribution of the decline in gross fixed investment was much more important in Asia—where it ranged from about 7 percentage points in Korea, to 12 percentage points in Indonesia, and to 13 percentage points in Thailand—than in the other countries (the maximum was about 5½ percentage points in both Mexico and Turkey). This reflected, in part, the high initial levels of investment and the "overinvestment" that had taken place in Asia in the years running up to the crisis, and the subsequent asset price collapse, which together set the stage for a decline in investment. Finally, presaging the discussion below, it is worth noting that, particularly in Asia, inventory accumulation during the crisis was negative.[47]

[46]This feature was not exclusive to IMF forecasts. For instance, the IMF's program projections are compared with commercial "consensus forecasts" made for the Asian crisis countries; the former were not systematically more pessimistic (Lane and others, 1999).

[47]The charts graph the contribution of gross fixed investment. The actual real GDP decline was greater than the sum of the components shown because of the negative contribution of inventories.

Figure 4.2. Contributions to GDP Growth in Capital Account Crisis Programs
(In percentage points)

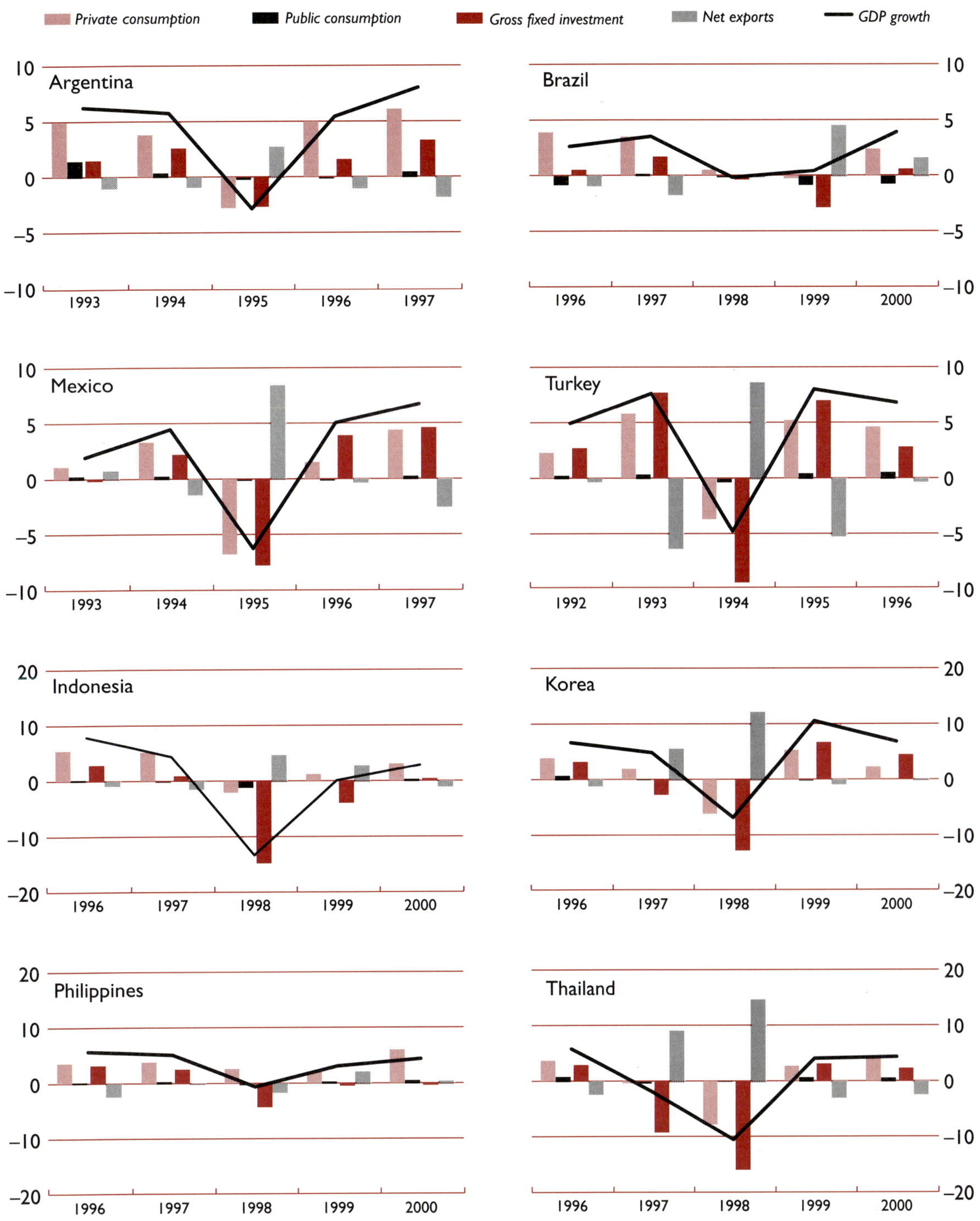

Sources: IMF, *World Economic Outlook;* and IMF staff estimates.

Box 4.1. Decomposition of Output Movements into Aggregate Supply and Aggregate Demand Shocks

The main text reports a decomposition of output movements into aggregate supply shocks and aggregate demand shocks. There are a variety of ways of undertaking this decomposition. One approach is to exploit the univariate time-series properties of the real output series using, for example, a Beveridge-Nelson decomposition to identify long-run versus short-run movements (where the former might be considered supply shocks and the latter demand shocks). An alternative approach, developed by Blanchard and Quah (1989), exploits information on multiple macroeconomic time-series (prices and real output).[1]

Consider a typical representation in price-quantity space of aggregate supply and aggregate demand. Although in the short-run, the aggregate supply function may be upward-sloping (SS), in the long-run, aggregate supply depends upon factor accumulation and technical progress (LL). Aggregate demand is downward-sloping in both the short-run and the long-run.

From the figure, it is apparent that an increase in aggregate demand (a rightward shift of DD along SS) will in the short-run raise both prices and output. In the long-run, however, this aggregate demand shock can only affect prices and not the level of output. A supply shock, by contrast, can affect both the level of output and of prices in the long-run (via a movement of the LL curve).

This suggests a particular identification scheme: *aggregate supply shocks are those shocks that can affect output in the long-run.* It turns out that this restriction on the long-run properties of the shocks is sufficient to identify the aggregate supply-aggregate demand shocks uniquely within a bivariate system.

The first step in the analysis is to verify that the first differences of output and prices (GDP deflator) are stationary. Augmented Dickey-Fuller tests reject the null of a unit root (except for Thailand, where rejection of the unit root for real GDP is marginal, and Argentina, where the data span is simply too short).[2]

Next, a reduced-form VAR in ΔQ and ΔP is estimated:

$$B(L)X_t = \varepsilon_t \qquad \text{var}(\varepsilon_t) = \Omega$$

where $X = \{\Delta Q, \Delta P\}'$ and $B(L)$ is a 2 x 2 matrix of lag polynomials. The VAR can then be inverted to obtain the moving average representation:

$$X_t = C(L)\varepsilon_t \text{ where } C(L) = B^{-1}(L) \text{ and } C_0 = I.$$

[1]Blanchard and Quah (1989).

[2]Data are quarterly, seasonally adjusted, and cover the following periods: Argentina (1995:1–1999:3); Indonesia (1985:1–1999:2); Korea (1985:1–1999:3); Mexico (1985:1–1999:3); Thailand (1993:1–1999:3); and Turkey (1987:1–1999:3). ADF tests with up to five lags (ΔQ and ΔP respectively): Argentina (–2.80, –3.03); Indonesia (–3.73**, –3.22*); Korea (–3.65**, –3.89**); Mexico (–3.86**,–2.99*); Thailand (–2.42, –3.67*); and Turkey (–3.87*,–3.19*).

Aggregate Supply and Demand

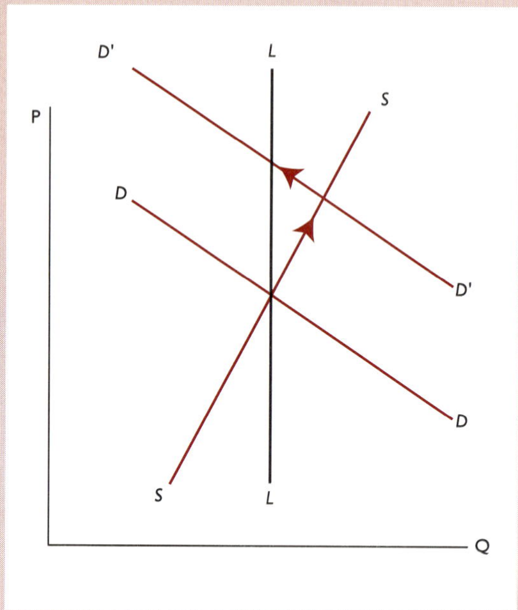

The shocks, ε, however, are a combination of supply and demand shocks. The objective, therefore, is to write X_t in an alternative representation:

$$X_t = A(L)\eta_t \qquad \text{var}(\eta) = I$$

where $\eta = \{\eta^s, \eta^d\}' = A_0^{-1}\varepsilon$ are uncorrelated, and have the interpretation of aggregate supply and aggregate demand shocks respectively.

Comparing polynomials in the lag operator, $A_j = C_jA_0$, for some (2 x 2) matrix A_0. Then, using the fact that $A_0'A_0 = \Omega$ gives three restrictions on the elements of A_0, leaving one element unrestricted. This element is pinned down by the economic restriction identified above, namely that a pure aggregate demand disturbance cannot have a long-run impact on the level of output. Once A_0 has been uniquely determined, the fundamental (i.e., aggregate supply and aggregate demand) shocks are given by $\eta_t = A_0^{-1}\varepsilon_t$.[3]

Finally, given the estimated aggregate supply and aggregate demand shocks, it is possible to generate the historical decomposition of the real output series. The first difference of output, and its decomposition into aggregate supply shocks and aggregate demand shocks, is plotted in Figure 4.3 of the text.

[3]The computer programs to undertake the estimation were kindly provided by Eswar Prasad.

Supply and Demand Shocks

As noted above, the growth contributions exercise cannot determine the extent to which the declines in output primarily reflect aggregate demand or supply shocks. In fact, there are both theoretical reasons and empirical indications that suggest that the initial steep output declines were at least partly associated with negative shocks to aggregate supply.

Although the precise propagation mechanism of the aggregate shock depends on the structure of the economy, the sharp exchange rate movements at the onset of the crises are likely to have disrupted aggregate supply in countries in which the foreign exchange exposure of the corporate and banking sectors was substantial. In addition, because of interfirm relationships, the sudden withdrawal of foreign savings from the economy would have had a cascading effect on the availability of finance, including for working capital, compounded by the effects of corporate sector bankruptcies.[48]

Although there is little direct evidence that the initial output declines were caused by aggregate supply shocks, there are a few empirical indicators. One such indicator comes from an econometric decomposition of real GDP growth into aggregate supply and aggregate demand shocks, based on a particular identification technique (see Box 4.1 and Figure 4.3). Focusing on the cases of Mexico and Indonesia, Korea, and Thailand, the decompositions suggest that much of the sharp output declines were initially associated with negative shocks to aggregate supply. Only in Turkey is there strong evidence of a negative demand shock accounting for about 8 of the 10 percentage point decline in real GDP in the second quarter of 1994. In Mexico, some 6 percentage points of the 7 percent decline in real GDP in the second quarter of 1995 is explained by the shock to aggregate supply, and about 1 percentage point by the decline in aggregate demand.[49] Likewise, in Korea and Indonesia, about three-quarters of the real GDP decline at the end of 1997 and the first quarter of 1998 is attributed to aggregate supply shocks.[50] This seems consistent with the view that, particularly in the case of the Asian crises, balance sheet weaknesses in the corporate and financial sectors combined with the sharp exchange rate movements and a withdrawal of external financing at the onset of the crises, resulted in widespread corporate distress with persistent adverse effects on the productive capacity of the economy.

The decompositions (particularly for Mexico, Thailand, Indonesia, and Korea) also suggest that there are important macrodynamics associated with the currency crises, whereby the initial aggregate supply shock is followed by a decline in aggregate demand with a one to two quarter lag. This seems intuitively plausible as well: the initial corporate sector distress translated into lower investment spending and increased redundancies and unemployment, which in turn depressed private consumption demand. In turn, this shifting dynamic of a supply shock followed by (and compounded with) a negative aggregate demand shock complicated the role of macroeconomic—especially fiscal—policy, as discussed below.

A second indication comes from the behavior of inventories. In particular, during the periods of the steepest falls in output, inventories declined—both in levels and in terms of contributions to growth (Table 4.2). This was particularly striking for the Asian crisis countries, where the decline in inventories amounted to some 10 percentage points of quarterly GDP during the quarters of steepest output decline. In Mexico, the change in inventories was positive, but the contribution to growth was negative. In each of these countries, the rate of decline in inventories either slowed or reversed after one to two quarters. Without further identifying restrictions, this behavior of inventories is consistent with a number of possible explanations, including a lower demand for inventories by firms in anticipation of lower demand for their output. Notably, however, in the most standard "production-smoothing" model of inventory management, this decline in inventories would be more consistent with a supply-side shock—such as an increase in production costs—than with a demand shock.[51] Such evidence

[48]See below on the debate regarding the "credit crunch" in East Asia. Calvo (1999) develops a model in which the sudden withdrawal of foreign saving cascades through the economy via interfirm financial and production relationships, causing a disproportionate negative supply response.

[49]Note that the shocks sum to the actual change in real GDP growth. Thus, the econometric technique decomposes the observed change in real GDP growth into a component associated with a movement of the aggregate supply function and a component associated with the movement of the aggregate demand function.

[50]For Thailand, the decomposition suggests an even larger share of aggregate supply shocks. However, the very short time series of quarterly data available probably makes the estimates unreliable. Note that the predominance of supply shocks begins with the very sharp output contractions. For the run-up to the crisis (early to mid-1997 in Thailand and Korea), the Blanchard-Quah decomposition identifies negative demand shocks, especially in Thailand, perhaps reflecting falling external demand for these countries' exports.

[51]In these models, a negative demand shock would be associated with an increase in inventories as firms "smooth production" by not cutting production by the full amount of the demand decline. On the other hand, faced by a shock to costs—or other disruption to production—firms reduce production and meet demand out of existing inventories, leading to a decumulation of inventories; see West (1990). It bears emphasizing, however, that such patterns are very sensitive to the precise timing of the shocks.

Figure 4.3. Blanchard-Quah Decompositions of Growth
(In percentage points)

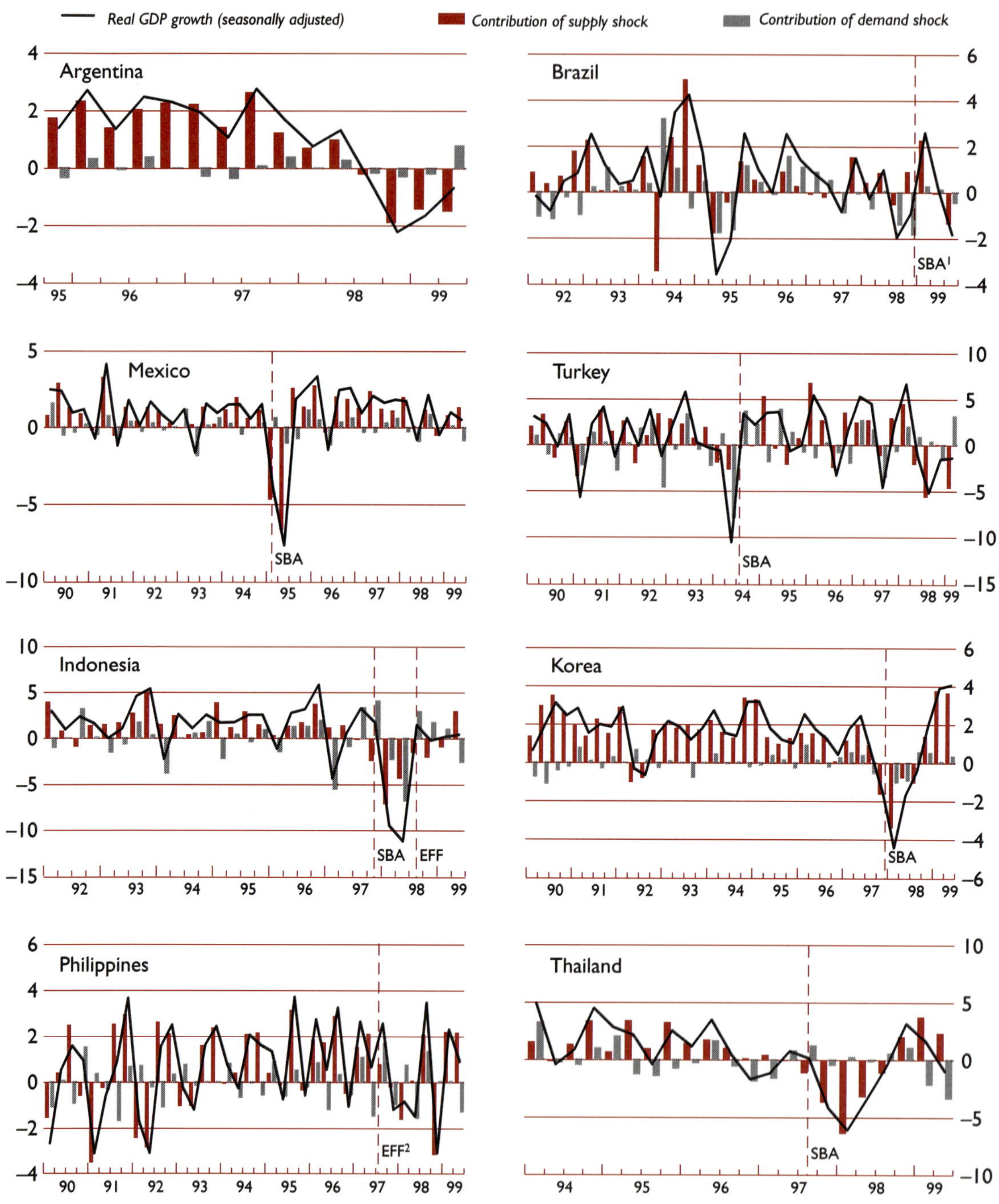

Source: IMF staff estimates.
[1]SBA refers to Stand-By Arrangement.
[2]EFF refers to Extended Fund Facility. In the case of the Philippines, the EFF was the Fourth Review and an extension of the EFF approved in June 1994.

Table 4.2. Behavior of Inventories

		Change in Stock Levels (As percent of GDP)	Quarterly Data, Seasonally Adjusted (Percent per quarter)		
			Change in stocks' contribution to GDP growth[1]	Change in stocks' contribution to GDP growth[2]	Memo item: Real GDP growth
Mexico (1995)	1994 Q3	2.8	0.1	2.0	–0.4
	1994 Q4	1.7	0.5	–0.4	0.7
	1995 Q1	3.8	–2.1	1.8	–3.9
	1995 Q2	0.3	–1.2	–1.5	–5.8
	1995 Q3	0.6	0.4	–0.1	0.8
	1995 Q4	–1.3	–0.3	–0.3	1.8
Indonesia (1997)	1997 Q3	1.3	6.1	3.8	3.6
	1997 Q4	–1.2	–0.5	–0.9	2.4
	1998 Q1	–0.9	–8.4	–4.6	–10.0
	1998 Q2	–6.5	–2.3	–4.1	–10.6
	1998 Q3	–2.7	9.0	7.0	1.8
	1998 Q4	–1.8	2.2	2.9	0.5
Philippines (1998)	1997 Q3	–0.8	–0.2	–0.4	–1.5
	1997 Q4	1.2	1.7	0.3	3.0
	1998 Q1	–0.9	–2.1	–1.5	–6.3
	1998 Q2	2.1	–1.2	–0.7	1.5
	1998 Q3	–1.4	1.3	1.5	–1.8
	1998 Q4	0.4	–0.1	–0.2	4.2
Korea (1997)	1997 Q3	–2.6	–0.9	–1.0	0.3
	1997 Q4	0.5	–1.9	–1.0	–0.9
	1998 Q1	–9.9	–5.2	–5.4	–5.3
	1998 Q2	–8.8	1.7	1.1	–1.6
	1998 Q3	–8.5	–0.2	0.0	0.6
	1998 Q4	–1.8	1.5	2.0	0.7
Thailand (1997)	1997 Q1	0.2	2.4	1.8	–3.7
	1997 Q2	–0.4	0.3	0.3	2.0
	1997 Q3	–1.4	–1.5	–1.2	–2.0
	1997 Q4	0.6	0.8	0.7	0.9
	1998 Q1	–2.2	–2.1	–2.2	1.2
	1998 Q2	–10.9	–6.5	–6.3	–12.4
	1998 Q3	–4.9	5.2	5.4	3.6
	1998 Q4	5.1	9.5	9.2	11.4
Turkey (1994)	1994 Q1	–1.5	2.5	0.1	–1.8
	1994 Q2	–6.7	11.4	–2.7	–9.9
	1994 Q3	1.0	1.2	–0.1	3.8
	1994 Q4	–6.7	2.4	2.2	2.7

[1]Computed residually from multiplicative X–11 seasonal adjustment of components of real GDP growth.
[2]Seasonally adjusted using additive X–11 seasonal adjustment.

must, of course, be interpreted with particular caution since a formal model of production-smoothing inventory behavior is not being tested here, and given the notoriously low quality of inventory data in most countries (and in Indonesia and Thailand, in particular). Nonetheless, it is perhaps of some relevance when considered together with other evidence.

V Policy Programs

The central role of private capital flows in capital account crises fundamentally altered the nature of the policy response. Macroeconomic and structural policies needed to be directed at restoring confidence and stemming capital outflows. For fiscal policy, this meant adjusting public sector imbalances when they were the root of the vulnerability; for monetary policy, it meant maintaining interest rates sufficiently high to compensate investors for higher perceived risk; for structural policies, it meant underpinning the fiscal adjustment where appropriate, and addressing weaknesses in the banking and corporate sectors.

The extent of the macroeconomic disruption triggered by the crisis clearly depended on the magnitude of the shift in the capital account. Therefore, as previously pointed out, the immediate objective of the programs was to restore confidence, halt the hemorrhage from the capital account, and ensure orderly adjustment in the current account. To achieve this, the underlying vulnerabilities that had led to the crisis needed to be addressed. Given the different sources of these vulnerabilities, this implied that the focus of the policy packages differed across countries.

In some countries, such as Brazil, Mexico, and Turkey, dealing with the fragilities in public sector finances was the most pressing issue, while in others, notably in Asia, structural reforms to address the fragilities in the financial sector were required. In all countries, monetary policy needed to be sufficiently restrained to ensure, at a minimum, that domestic monetary conditions did not give impetus to additional capital outflows and put further pressure on the exchange rate. (All but two of the countries, Argentina and Brazil, had floating exchange rates by the time the programs were adopted.) Moreover, maintaining monetary stability and preventing a sustained pickup of inflation in the wake of the large exchange rate depreciations that had already occurred was essential for the restoration of macroeconomic stability as well as market confidence. Finally, fiscal policy, besides addressing the fragilities in public sector finances, had a potential role to play in the external adjustment process by contributing to the increase in net domestic saving necessitated by the shift in the capital account.

This chapter discusses the three elements of the policy programs: fiscal policy, monetary and exchange rate policy, and structural policies. It examines how their respective roles were defined in the original programs, how they were adapted as the crisis evolved and the macroeconomic outlook changed, and how they affected the evolution of the crisis. The chapter draws some tentative conclusions about the roles of the different components of the policy programs in capital account crises.

Fiscal Policy

The crises presented fiscal policy with a twin challenge. On the one hand, to the extent that countries' vulnerabilities were rooted in the public sector, addressing these vulnerabilities was essential to creating a basis for confidence to return. At the same time, the public sector could contribute directly to the current account adjustment, easing the burden on private sector savings. On the other hand, a more relaxed fiscal stance could help offset weakening economic activity. Moreover, to the extent that such weakening activity was itself of concern to investors, too tight a fiscal stance might erode, rather than enhance, confidence. Thus, the two goals—dealing with underlying fragilities and facilitating macroeconomic adjustment—did not necessarily always point in the same direction. The potential conflict faced by fiscal policy was compounded by the uncertainty under which the original macroeconomic frameworks were formulated, given the inherent risks of the financing strategies. This section examines how fiscal policy approached these challenges.

Fiscal Adjustment in the Original Programs

Without exception, the original programs envisaged a strengthening of fiscal balances relative to the previous year. Both the rationale and the magnitudes of the planned adjustment varied across countries. Programmed improvements in overall fiscal bal-

Table 5.1. Evolution of Fiscal Performance Criteria and Indicative Targets[1]
(As percent of GDP)

	Previous Year[2]	Original Program	First Review	Second Review	Third Review	Fourth Review	Outcome
Argentina (1995)[3]							
Overall balance of nonfinancial public sector[4]	–0.5	0.7	–0.8	–0.8	. . .	. . .	–1.5
Indonesia (FY98/99)[5]							
Overall central government balance[4]	0.8	1.0	–3.2	–8.5	–8.5	–8.5	–2.1
Korea (1998)							
Central government balance (indicative target, 1997)	–0.5	1.0	–0.7	–0.9	–3.3	–4.2	–3.9
Thailand (FY97/98)							
Central government balance[4,6]	–1.1	1.1	1.0	–1.6	–2.4	–2.7	–2.6
Philippines (1997)[7]							
Public sector borrowing requirement[8]	–0.5	–0.3	–1.2	. . .	. . .	. . .	–1.4
Philippines (1998)							
Public sector borrowing requirement[8]	–1.4	0.5	–1.5	–3.8	. . .	. . .	–4.2
Mexico (1995)							
Overall balance of nonfinancial public sector (indicative target)[4]	0	0.5	0.5	0.5	0.5	. . .	0.9
Turkey (1994)							
Central government balance[4]	–9.0	–3.8	–3.8	. . .	. . .	. . .	–3.8
Primary balance	–1.2	6.4	6.4	. . .	. . .	. . .	3.8
Brazil (1999)[9]							
Public sector borrowing requirement[4,8]	–8.1	–4.7	–10.4	–10.4	–8.98	–10.8	–9.5
Primary balance[10]	0.1	2.6	3.1	3.1	3.1	3.1	3.1

Source: IMF staff reports.
[1]In some cases, the precise definitions of performance criteria differed in coverage from the concept labeled "performance criterion" here.
[2]Estimate as of time of original program approval.
[3]For Argentina (1995), "original program" refers to the Ninth Review of the Extended Fund Facility (EFF) approved in March 1992.
[4]Concept used for calculation of fiscal impulse measure, below.
[5]Fourth-Fifth-Sixth Review refers to Original Program, Second, and Third Reviews under the EFF approved in August 1998.
[6]There was also a performance criterion on banking system credit to the public sector and an indicative target on central government expenditure.
[7]For Philippines (1997), "original program" refers to the Fourth Review of the EFF approved in June 1994; December targets were indicative.
[8]A minus sign indicates a deficit.
[9]First and Second Reviews were combined.
[10]Performance criterion on overall public sector borrowing requirement and indicative target on primary balance of federal government, replaced by performance criterion on primary balance of consolidated public sector and indicative target on net debt of the consolidated public sector.

ances[52] ranged from 1–1½ percent of GDP in Mexico, Argentina, and Korea, to 2–2½ percent of GDP in Philippines and Thailand, 3½ percent in Brazil, and over 5 percent of GDP in Turkey (Table 5.1).[53] In Turkey, this was expected to be achieved through a large improvement in the primary balances, whereas in Brazil the primary balance was expected to strengthen less—by some 2½ percent of GDP—as lower interest rates were assumed to reduce financing cost.[54] The implied fiscal measures were typically larger than the planned changes in overall balances as all countries, with the exception of the Philippines, were expected to experience some decline in output growth, albeit much less than the decline that eventually materialized.

With starting conditions and definitions of fiscal positions varying across countries, the planned fiscal

[52]For country-specific definitions of fiscal balances, see Annex III.

[53]Excluding carrying cost of financial sector restructuring.

[54]In the original program, the public sector borrowing requirement (for the first half of 1999) was a performance criterion and the primary balance was an indicative target. This implied that in the event of higher interest rates than assumed in the program, a larger adjustment in the primary balance would be needed. However, the indicative target for the primary balance may have signaled that the projected adjustment was, indeed, all that was required. At the same time, an unintended implication of the performance criterion for the public sector borrowing requirement is that it gave the authorities an incentive to refrain from raising interest rates.

Table 5.2. Medium-Term Fiscal Sustainability
(As a percent of GDP, unless otherwise specified)

	Total Public Debt[2]	Inflation Rate (Average over period)[2]	Primary Balance[1]		*Memo Item* Financial Sector Cost[4]	
			Required[3]	Program[3]	Initial estimate	Latest estimate
Argentina (1995)	36.5	4.2	−1.5	2.1	. . .	. . .
Brazil (1999)[5]	48.3	3.2	2.8	2.6	. . .	. . .
Indonesia (1998)[5]	37.2	6.2	−1.5	2.2	0.5	2.8–3.9
Korea (1998)[5]	12.7	4.4	–0.8	1.0	0.8	1.8
Mexico (1995)	41.0	7.0	1.0	3.4	0.5	1.2
Philippines (1998)[5]	57.4	5.9	–0.2	4.2	. . .	. . .
Thailand (1998)[5]	4.6	5.6	−1.0	1.0	1.0	2.5
Turkey (1994)	35.0	66.1	−1.7	4.0	. . .	. . .

Sources: IMF, *World Economic Outlook* database and IMF staff estimates.
[1]Primary balance required to stabilize ratio of public debt-to-GDP, estimate for year *t* as of year *t*–1; excludes financial sector restructuring costs.
[2]Year *t*–1; debt data exclude financial sector restructuring bonds and quasi-fiscal losses.
[3]Year *t*.
[4]Includes only actual or imputed carry costs of financial sector restructuring.
[5]Date refers to year *t*, not to program approval year.

adjustments are difficult to compare. An alternative, and more meaningful, approach is to assess the programmed adjustment in each country against a well defined yardstick. A useful metric for such an assessment is the medium-term sustainability of the public sector. In general, gauging medium-term sustainability is not straightforward, but one operationally useful yardstick is the balance needed to stabilize the ratio of public debt to GDP.[55] Naturally, the level at which the debt ratio is being stabilized is also an important consideration. In some of the countries reviewed here, the initial level of public debt was already high, so a reduction in the debt ratio may have been desirable to provide flexibility against future shocks, or to free up future budgetary resources from interest payments. In other countries, the initial level of debt was sufficiently low that stabilizing the debt ratio may have been less important.

Starting from the public sector's flow budget constraint, and assuming a unit elastic demand for base money, yields the primary surplus required to stabilize the debt-to-GDP ratio at a given inflation rate.[56] Table 5.2 reports the minimum required surplus on the eve of the programs, assuming historical growth, real interest, and inflation rates (and excluding financial sector restructuring costs).[57] It bears emphasizing that these estimates embody a number of underlying assumptions and thus should be taken as broad indications rather than precise parameters. Moreover, the reported primary balances are those required to maintain a constant ratio of public debt to GDP over the medium term. Such surpluses are unlikely to stabilize the debt-to-GDP ratio in the short run if real interest rates are higher and real growth rates lower than the assumptions underlying the estimates—a situation typically encountered during financial crises.[58] More generally, the "required" primary balance should be viewed as referring to the

[55]See, for example, Chalk and Hemming (2000) for a discussion.

[56]The required minimum primary surplus is given by:

$$p = (i - \pi - g)b - \frac{\pi - g}{v}$$

where $(i - \pi)$ is the real interest rate, b is the ratio to GDP at which the level of public debt is to be stabilized, g is the real growth rate of GDP, and v is velocity of base money (nominal GDP divided by base money). The required primary surplus is thus increasing in the real interest rate, decreasing in the growth rate of the economy, and, for a given money velocity, decreasing in the inflation rate. Note that this includes seignorage as revenue, whereas part of base money will generally reflect increases in NIR.

[57]For each program, the required primary surplus as of the year-end closest to the program approval date is reported; Appendix III provides details of the calculations. By aggregating domestic and external public debt, the calculations implicitly assume that there will be no further real depreciation (which would raise the debt ratio and thus the required primary surplus) nor any real appreciation (which would lower the debt ratio and the required primary surplus correspondingly).

[58]Moreover, historical growth rates may have been unsustainably high.

structural primary balance—that is, abstracting from cyclical movements of the budget balance.

The estimates suggest that all programs, with the exception of Brazil, initially envisaged primary surpluses that exceeded the balances required for medium-term debt stability. In Brazil, the targeted primary surplus was almost identical to the "required" surplus; in fact, the Brazil program explicitly targeted a fiscal balance consistent with medium-term stability. In the other countries, there were several reasons for targeting larger fiscal adjustment than suggested by the criterion of stabilizing the debt-to-GDP ratio over the medium term.

In Turkey, the program explicitly aimed at a reduction of the public debt ratio to reduce the vulnerability of the fiscal position to interest rate shocks and a funding crisis. The government's decision to switch to money financing as it encountered increasing funding difficulties and rising real interest rates had been a trigger of the crisis.[59] The program targeted a lowering of the public debt ratio by 5 percentage points (from 45 percent of GDP at end-1994) which, together with a more ambitious inflation target, would have necessitated the programmed primary surplus of 4 percent of GDP.[60]

Likewise, in the Philippines, there was a longer-term strategy of reducing public debt, which had exceeded 85 percent of GDP in 1993, and had been steadily declining to 60 percent of GDP by end-1996. Moreover, with the depreciation of the exchange rate after the floating of the peso in July 1997, debt servicing costs increased[61] and there were doubts about the government's ability to access international capital markets to refinance its maturing external obligations in the unsettled environment caused by the Thai financial crisis. Both factors argued for stronger fiscal adjustment than medium-term stability of the public debt ratio would have suggested.

Acute financing problems were the main reason for targeting substantial fiscal adjustment in Mexico and Argentina. Medium-term public debt sustainability was not a concern, but governments in both countries faced a short-term funding crisis as they were unable to refinance their maturing external obligations. In addition, in Mexico, fiscal plans sought to accommodate the carrying cost of financial sector restructuring as financial institutions were encountering growing difficulties in the wake of the crisis and the floating of the exchange rate.[62]

The prospective cost of financial sector restructuring also argued for stronger fiscal positions in Indonesia, Korea, and Thailand. Even after taking into account initial estimates of the carrying cost of financial sector restructuring, however, the targeted primary balances exceeded the balances required to stabilize the public debt-to-GDP ratio by 3 percentage points of GDP in Indonesia and by about one percentage point of GDP in Korea and Thailand. In Indonesia, some additional margin—albeit probably less than 3 percentage points of GDP—seemed consistent with the government's policy in the pre-crisis years of running overall surpluses to lower the debt-to-GDP ratio, which was comparable to those in Argentina and Mexico and likely to rise as a result of the fiscal burden of financial sector restructuring. In Korea and Thailand, by contrast, public debt was very low and was viewed as likely to remain in a moderate range, even after the burden of financial sector restructuring was taken into account. In Korea, the objective was to keep the overall balance, including the estimated carrying cost of financial sector restructuring, at roughly the same level as that achieved in 1995–96; in Thailand, the program sought to reverse the weakening in the fiscal position that had occurred in the previous year. In terms of the underlying economic arguments, however, it is clear that the main rationale for fiscal adjustment in the Asian programs lay elsewhere.

Confidence Effects of Fiscal Adjustment

In all of the programs, the impact of fiscal adjustment plans on market confidence was an important consideration. Fiscal consolidation was expected to reassure markets. This seemed a reasonable assumption where fiscal issues were a problem and vulnerabilities rooted in public sector finances had contributed to the emergence of the crisis—either because public debt dynamics raised concerns about sustainability, as in Brazil and Turkey, or because the composition of public debt made the government vulnerable to a funding crisis, as in Argentina, Mexico, and the Philippines.[63] It was also reasonable to assume that markets would seek assurances that fis-

---

[59]Preannounced treasury bill auctions actually had to be canceled.

[60]For instance, to lower the debt-to-GDP ratio by 5 percentage points and achieve an inflation rate of 60 percent (roughly the inflation rate prevailing prior to the currency crisis) would have required a primary surplus of 4 percent of GDP.

[61]External obligations accounted for over half of total public debt.

[62]Typically, only the carry costs of the present value of the (implicit or explicit) fiscal burden of banking sector restructuring costs are included in the overall deficit. This is consistent with the logic of stabilizing the public debt ratio, albeit at the higher debt level implied by the additional stock of debt so created. Likewise, privatization receipts should be excluded from the overall balance and treated as a financing item.

[63]Giavazzi and Pagano (1990) explore the possibility that fiscal contractions can have expansionary effects on the economy.

cal issues would not become a problem as the costs of the crisis in the financial sector were surfacing.[64] This suggested that fiscal plans in the countries facing serious problems in the financial sector—Indonesia, Korea, Mexico, and Thailand—needed to allow for the carry cost of financial sector restructuring, even though initial estimates of these costs would inevitably be rather crude.

The confidence argument was explicitly articulated in the Mexico program, which noted that ". . . these steps [among others, consolidation of public finances] . . . would help bolster foreign investors' confidence . . ." and was echoed in several subsequent programs—most notably for Argentina, Thailand, Korea, and Indonesia. However, while there are strong reasons arguing for fiscal adjustment to address current or prospective vulnerabilities in public sector finances, it is less clear whether fiscal consolidation beyond what is required to achieve this helps strengthen confidence.

Did fiscal adjustment in fact bolster market confidence? This question is difficult to answer because confidence cannot be measured directly and changes in confidence, however defined, cannot necessarily be attributed to a specific policy, but reflect the impact of the whole policy and financing package. Bearing in mind these caveats, the behavior of private capital flows can be considered a useful indicator of market confidence in a capital account crisis and there appears to be some episodic evidence suggesting that fiscal policy did affect confidence in those countries where fiscal issues were widely viewed as the main source of vulnerabilities. This is particularly borne out by the experience of Brazil, where news about weaknesses in the provincial finances raised concerns about the viability of the program and prompted further capital outflows, which led to the abandonment of the exchange rate peg. Following the devaluation, and a more resolute fiscal stance, capital outflows were stemmed and a massive swing in the current account was avoided. Likewise, in Turkey, fiscal adjustment under the program appears to have been instrumental in restoring confidence in capital markets, with capital flows reversing soon after the adoption of the program.

There are also indications that determined efforts to strengthen the fiscal position helped restore confidence in Argentina and Mexico (although, of course, many other factors were simultaneously at play). In response to the Mexican financial crisis, Argentina experienced large withdrawals of bank deposits and sizable capital outflows during the first quarter of 1995. At the same time, it became increasingly apparent that, in the absence of policy changes, the overall fiscal deficit would widen significantly. Concerns about the size of the prospective deficit were underscored when the government had to cancel plans to issue Arg$2 billion of treasury bills as interest rates jumped sharply at initial auctions. The IMF-supported program approved in March 1995 aimed at achieving a fiscal surplus of 0.7 percent of GDP, which, together with official financing, would have been sufficient to amortize public sector debt falling due and fund two Trust Funds for financial system restructuring without recourse to the international capital market. The program was largely successful in restoring confidence. Capital flows were reversed relatively quickly and the government was able to tap the market sooner than expected. In the event, instead of having to generate a surplus of 0.7 percent of GDP, the program was able to finance a deficit of about 1.4 percent of GDP.

In Mexico, the link between fiscal policy and the restoration of market confidence was less clear. The original program, which envisaged an improvement in the overall fiscal balance of 1 percentage point of GDP, failed to restore market confidence and capital outflows continued in the first quarter of 1995. With capital outflows significantly larger than projected, at the first review the target for the primary balance was raised by a further 1 percent of GDP to offset higher interest payments and keep the overall deficit target unchanged. At the same time, monetary policy was tightened and the official financing package was strengthened. These measures stemmed private capital outflows. Clearly, the reversal of capital flows in the next quarter cannot be attributed to the tightening of the fiscal target alone. In particular, the clarification of the financing arrangement appears to have played an important role. Nevertheless, given Mexico's vulnerabilities, it is questionable whether an augmentation in the financing package in the absence of credible fiscal adjustment would have been sufficient to turn around capital flows.

Why did fiscal adjustment appear to help restore confidence in Brazil, Turkey, Argentina, and Mexico? In Brazil and Turkey, unsustainable public debt dynamics were widely perceived as the countries' main vulnerability, calling for a significant reduction of the fiscal deficit. In Argentina and Mexico, two factors may have been at play. First, even though the fiscal deficits in both countries were modest, the governments were facing, or were close to facing, a funding crisis, with potential difficulties in rolling over maturing obligations. As such, fiscal adjustment would reduce the vulnerability of the government to a funding crisis, and its announcement could be expected to bolster confidence. Second, both Argentina and Mexico, despite the modest imbalances

[64]Some authors have, in fact, argued that prospective fiscal deficits associated with the weaknesses in the financial sector were at the core of the Asian crisis (see Burnside, Eichenbaum, and Rebelo (1999)).

at the time of the programs, had a long history of fiscal deficits and high inflation. Accordingly, markets may have welcomed the reassurance that these countries were not reverting to the inflationary policies of the past.

In Asia, the experience was quite different. In all three countries, the programs failed to restore market confidence and private capital outflows continued for over a year after the onset of the crisis. In Indonesia, Korea, and Thailand, neither the initial tightening of fiscal policy nor the subsequent easing had a perceptible influence on market confidence. These countries' vulnerabilities were viewed as rooted primarily in the private sector and fiscal policy did not have much of a role to play in addressing them, other than ensuring that the fiscal cost of financial sector restructuring would be dealt with in a responsible manner. Fiscal policy neither faced unsustainable debt dynamics, as in Brazil and Turkey, nor an imminent funding crisis, as in Argentina and Mexico. Against this backdrop, the negative market reaction to the January 1998 draft budget in Indonesia, which failed to secure the originally programmed fiscal adjustment, probably needs to be seen as an expression of concern that support for the whole program was lacking rather than a verdict about the importance of fiscal adjustment in Indonesia.

In addition to the effect of the fiscal stance itself, the composition of adjustment and the accompanying structural measures can play a critical role in underpinning the sustainability of fiscal adjustment and thereby contributing to a restoration of confidence.

Fiscal Policy, External Adjustment, and Output Declines

Confidence effects aside, there is another, quite distinct, argument for undertaking fiscal adjustment in the face of a capital account crisis. For a given capital outflow, the larger the increase in public saving, the smaller is the increase in net private saving that is required to achieve the necessary adjustment in the current account. Fiscal tightening can thus ease the burden of adjustment falling on the private sector. Although the argument is, by definition, correct in terms of private saving, it does not necessarily follow that greater public sector adjustment eases the burden of adjustment in the private sector in terms of absorption. Fiscal adjustment, by reducing aggregate demand, can cause output to slow or even contract. Thus, while greater public sector adjustment reduces the required increase in private saving, it may do so at the cost of a loss of output and private absorption.

The need for an increase in public saving to assist the external adjustment process evidently depends on the position of the economy at the beginning of the crisis—whether it is close to full employment or well below—and how supply and private demand are expected to respond to the crisis. As noted in the previous section, the original programs typically assumed a moderate adjustment in the current account accompanied by some slowing of output growth. The sharp declines in output that occurred were not foreseen. Moreover, in most countries, with the possible exception of Brazil, it seemed plausible to assume that output on the eve of the crisis was close to potential. In Argentina, Mexico, the Philippines, and Turkey, growth had remained strong or accelerated in the year preceding the crisis. In Indonesia, Korea, and Thailand, growth was already slowing, but these countries had experienced several years of strong expansions. Against this background, it was not unreasonable to argue that an increase in public saving will reduce the burden of adjustment on the private sector, a view that was expressed in several program documents.

From the point of view of the original macroeconomic frameworks, the two principal goals of fiscal policy—addressing weaknesses in public finances to restore market confidence and contributing to macroeconomic adjustment—coincided. On the basis of the original projections, all programs, with the exception of the Philippines, envisaged a withdrawal of fiscal stimulus, ranging from half a percent of GDP in Indonesia to over 8 percent of GDP in Turkey (Table 5.3).[65]

The picture changed as it became increasingly evident that output was declining sharply, reflecting both adjustments on the supply side and a contraction of private demand. Given the prospect of a significant contraction of output, adhering to the original fiscal targets would have implied a more substantial withdrawal of stimulus, exacerbating the economic downturn. A tension between the two goals of fiscal policy was emerging.

The response to this tension differed. In countries where fragilities in public sector finances were widely viewed as the core of their vulnerabilities, the need to address these fragilities generally took

[65]Since the impact of fiscal policy on aggregate demand is likely to be multifaceted, any summary indicator, such as the fiscal impulse, inevitably suffers from some shortcomings; see, for instance, Chand (1992). Numerically, the fiscal impulse equals the change in the fiscal stance, which, in turn, equals the difference between the actual and cyclically neutral fiscal balances. In terms of stimulus to economic activity, the overall deficit is of relevance. In terms of adjustment effort, the primary balance is a better indicator. Corresponding calculations for the primary balance are given in Annex III; in general, these differ little from the figures reported here, except those for Brazil and Indonesia, where the primary fiscal impulse turned out to be about –2 percent of GDP, and Mexico, where the primary impulse was about –4½ percent of GDP.

Table 5.3. Fiscal Balances and Fiscal Impulse Ratios: Programs versus Outcomes

	Program					Actual				
	Real GDP	Fiscal balance	Cyclically neutral balance	Fiscal stance	Fiscal impulse	Real GDP	Fiscal balance	Cyclically neutral balance	Fiscal stance	Fiscal impulse
	(Percent change)	(As percent of GDP)				(Percent change)	(As percent of GDP)			
Argentina (1995)	2.0	0.7	1.0	0.3	–1.3	–2.8	–1.4	–0.4	1.0	–0.2
Brazil (1999)[1]	–1.0	–3.6	–6.6	–3.0	–2.9	0.8	–6.8	–5.9	0.9	0.9
Indonesia (1998)[1]	5.0	1.0	0.0	–1.0	–0.6	–13.1	–2.1	–1.3	0.8	0.0
Korea (1998)[1]	2.5	0.0	–1.3	–1.3	–1.5	–6.7	–4.2	–1.5	2.7	1.2
Mexico (1995)	1.5	0.6	–2.5	–3.1	–0.9	–6.2	0.0	–4.5	–4.5	–2.7
Philippines (1998)[1]	5.1	–1.0	0.1	1.1	0.5	–0.6	–2.6	–1.3	1.3	0.9
Thailand (1998)[1]	3.5	1.0	–0.8	–1.8	–3.1	–10.8	–2.5	–0.4	2.1	–1.4
Turkey (1994)	–1.6	–3.6	–11.6	–8.0	–8.3	–4.7	–4.0	–11.7	–7.7	–8.7

Sources: IMF, *World Economic Outlook*; IMF, MONA database; and IMF staff estimates.
[1]Dates refer to year *t* (or closest fiscal year), rather than to program approval year.

precedence over concerns about the contraction of economic activity. These countries tried to adhere to, or even strengthen, their original fiscal targets. As noted above, in Mexico, the planned primary surplus was raised by 1 percentage point of GDP at the time of the first program review to achieve the original target for the overall balance in the face of higher interest cost (Table 5.1). At the same time, growth projections were reduced by 3½ percentage points.

Similarly, in Turkey the original fiscal target was maintained as growth projections were revised downward. In the event, the target was achieved with a smaller adjustment in the primary balance than envisaged in the initial program, as interest rates came down sharply. In Brazil, with growth turning out somewhat stronger than originally projected, unanticipated output shocks were less of an issue.[66] The target for the primary surplus was raised at the first review to offset part of a sharp increase in interest cost, which nevertheless implied a significantly larger overall deficit than envisaged in the original program.[67]

In Argentina and the Asian program countries, in contrast, the unexpected contraction of output prompted a revision of the original fiscal targets. In Argentina, this was facilitated by a swift recovery of confidence in response to the initial adjustment measures: by the time of the first review under the extension of the EFF arrangement (September 1995), half of the deposits withdrawn during the spring crisis had returned. By contrast, in Asia, capital outflows were not quickly reversed and the deepening recession was increasingly seen as contributing to weak confidence. Since public finances were not perceived as a major source of vulnerability in these countries, there were no strong reasons to adhere to the original fiscal plans in a macroeconomic environment that was radically different from that envisaged in the initial programs. Beginning in early 1998, fiscal targets were thus eased successively as growth projections became more pessimistic.

As a result of the changing macroeconomic outlook and the ensuing modifications of fiscal targets, fiscal outcomes and the impact of fiscal policy on the adjustment process turned out significantly different from what had been originally envisaged. In Mexico, the fiscal adjustment that was undertaken entailed a withdrawal of stimulus well in excess of what had been planned; in Turkey, the contractionary impact of fiscal policy was also stronger than originally programmed. In all other countries, the withdrawal of fiscal stimulus was either smaller than initially planned (Argentina, Indonesia, and Thailand),[68] or fiscal pol-

[66]Following the abandonment of the real's currency peg and the sharp depreciation of the exchange rate in January 1999, the outlook was believed to have deteriorated significantly and growth projections were lowered at the time of the first review. With growing evidence that these fears were unlikely to materialize, growth projections were subsequently raised again.

[67]At the same time, the primary balance rather than the public sector borrowing requirement became a performance criterion.

[68]The stimulus was relatively small in Thailand, where the fiscal deficit turned out significantly smaller than programmed.

icy provided a positive stimulus (Brazil, Korea, and the Philippines).[69]

This suggests that in most crisis countries (notably in Asia), fiscal policy did not contribute to the output declines, and, in fact, offset part of it—albeit a relatively small part. Nevertheless, the question remains whether the initial fiscal tightening contributed to the negative output dynamics. Figure 5.1 graphs quarterly fiscal impulses and seasonally adjusted quarterly real GDP growth during the first two program years when the largest output declines occurred. In most cases, the decline in real GDP precedes the negative fiscal impulse. Indeed, rather than tight fiscal policy causing the output decline, the output decline "drives" the measured negative impulse. In Korea, the fiscal impulse was actually strongly positive in the last quarter of 1997, when real GDP growth (on a seasonally adjusted basis) was already negative.[70] Similarly, in Indonesia, the fiscal impulse is strongly positive in the last quarter of 1997 and the first quarter of 1998, before turning negative as discretionary expansionary measures did not keep up with the output decline. Similar patterns may be seen in Thailand and Mexico. Only in Turkey does the strongly negative fiscal impulse in the second quarter of 1994 coincide with the sharp output decline.[71] Sample correlations (during the crisis periods) between fiscal impulses and changes in output growth range from 0.82 and 0.55 in Turkey and Mexico, respectively, to 0.11 in Indonesia and Korea, and –0.16 and –0.30 in Thailand and the Philippines.

The Role of Fiscal Adjustment in Capital Account Crises

Although the fiscal plans in the original programs bore certain similarities, the outcomes in the first, full program year—the critical year in the short-term adjustment process—differed significantly. Two factors appear to account for the divergence: the importance of fiscal consolidation for the restoration of confidence and the unpredictability of the macroeconomic adjustment process triggered by the crisis. Fiscal adjustment was sustained where it was needed to alleviate vulnerabilities in public sector finances. In these countries, the underlying need for fiscal consolidation took precedence over concerns about its impact on aggregate demand in the face of an unexpectedly large decline in output and, indeed, appears to have contributed to the restoration of confidence. In contrast, in countries where fiscal problems were not seen as a factor contributing to the emergence of the crisis, fiscal targets were revised substantially as concerns about the impact of tighter budgets on aggregate demand ultimately prevailed.

The experience suggests two lessons regarding the role of fiscal policy in capital account crises. First, fiscal consolidation is critical for the restoration of confidence when fragilities in public sector finances are perceived as a source of a country's vulnerability. But conversely, it seems doubtful that fiscal adjustment as such—when it is not motivated by underlying weaknesses—helps strengthen confidence. A more tricky case concerns the possibility of *prospective* fiscal costs, such as those associated with bank recapitalization costs (beyond initial estimates of the carry costs). This may call, not so much for a short-term fiscal squeeze in the midst of a crisis, but rather for an articulation of a clear set of policy rules that will restore a viable debt path over the medium term, and whose credibility might be buttressed by conditionality.[72]

Second, the extraordinarily complex dynamics of supply and demand shocks—and uncertainty about the private sector's response more generally—means that, beyond confidence effects, the scope for short-term fine tuning may be limited. Thus, to the extent that fiscal adjustment is not dictated by medium-term considerations, it may be preferable to aim for fiscal targets that are broadly neutral from a cyclical point of view and allow automatic stabilizers to work if macroeconomic developments differ from the original program framework.

Aside from the aggregate fiscal stance, the composition of the targets may play an important role in mitigating the effects of the crisis, in particular by expanding and strengthening social safety nets (see Box 5.1).

Monetary and Exchange Rate Policy

Monetary policy had a critical role to play in restoring confidence and stabilizing capital flows. First, monetary policy had a direct bearing on the incentives for investors to hold domestic currency assets and could thus help mitigate the adverse shift in the capital account. Second, by ensuring nominal stability and preventing a sustained increase in inflation that would eventually feed into further exchange rate depreciation, monetary policy could

[69]In Brazil, part of the positive stimulus reflects the cost of higher foreign currency denominated debt interest payments.

[70]However, part of the positive impulse in the fourth quarter of 1997 may have reflected World Bank and Asian Development Bank loans which were channeled through the budget.

[71]Turkey is also the only case in which the Blanchard-Quah decomposition discussed in the previous section finds a large negative demand component to the output contraction.

[72]The use of such policy rules is discussed in Kopits (2000).

Figure 5.1. Quarterly Fiscal Impulses and Real GDP Growth
(Seasonally adjusted, in percent)

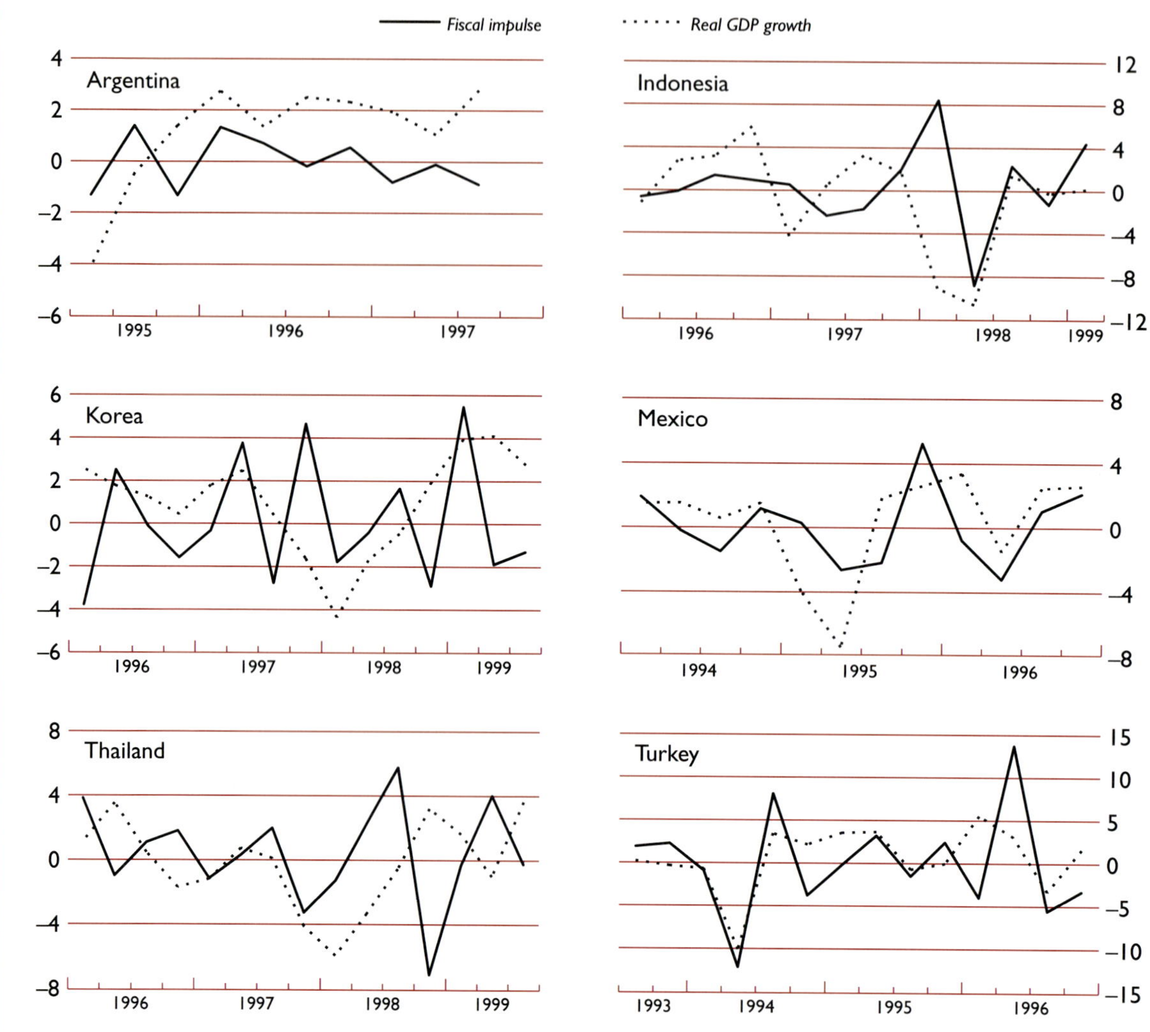

Source: IMF staff estimates.

make an important contribution to orderly macroeconomic adjustment, thereby helping to restore confidence. The latter role is particularly salient in countries with a history of high inflation, but it is nonetheless important in countries with no preexisting inflation problem, given the magnitude of the shocks involved.

The importance of a credible monetary policy stance was underscored by the fact that five of the eight countries considered had been forced to abandon their exchange rate pegs after the first waves of capital outflows and had thus lost previous nominal anchors. Brazil initially sought to maintain the peg but had to follow the same route soon after the program was approved, then establishing inflation targets as a new anchor. Only Argentina managed to maintain its exchange rate peg in the context of the existing currency board arrangement. Against this background, the programs invariably placed strong emphasis on maintaining a monetary policy stance that would keep inflation under control.

The two main objectives of monetary policy—ensuring appropriate returns on domestic currency assets to limit capital outflows and preventing a spiral

Box 5.1. Social Safety Nets

The recent crises triggered by large capital outflows underscored the need to cushion the impact of adverse economic developments. Sound macroeconomic and structural policies may create foundations of long-term sustainable growth, but they may also hurt some of the poor in the short-term. Examples are the removal of generalized price subsidies, an exchange rate devaluation that increases the price of tradable goods, the reduction of budgetary support to state enterprises, and so on. Most of the countries in our sample recorded increases in poverty, loss of physical assets among the poor, rising rates of malnutrition, and a shrinking middle class.

To mitigate the adverse short-term effects on the vulnerable groups, most IMF-supported programs incorporate outlays on temporary social safety nets or increased allocation to existing social programs to transfer income or protect consumption (Chu and Gupta, 1998). Safety nets—in addition to their redistributive effects—can help to garner the necessary political support for the adjustment and structural reforms.[1] Traditionally, safety nets included subsidies or cash compensations targeting particular social groups, improved distribution channels for or temporary price controls on essential commodities, severance pay and retraining for redundant public sector employees, and employment through public works programs. Most programs in countries in our sample included one or several instruments outlined above. Although it would have been preferable to have these instruments in place before the crises erupted, some countries had to install or expand safety nets only during the crisis. The pre-crisis transfer programs were very small, particularly in Asia.

In Indonesia, no explicit safety net was in place prior to the crisis and generalized price subsidies were used instead. Although the initial cost of these subsidies was relatively modest (about 3 percent of GDP in 1997/98), following the sharp depreciation of the domestic currency, this cost rose to more than 4 percent in 1998/99, mostly on account of higher fuel prices. The generalized food and fuel subsidies were eventually replaced by a targeted subsidy on lower quality rice, and through a combination of public works programs and cash assistance, respectively. In addition, microcredit programs were initiated and the government launched a "stay-in-school" campaign providing block grants to schools to help fund lunches for eligible children.

Korea had the most developed social safety net system in Asia, but the system had to be expanded substantially to cope with the crisis. The relatively small pre-crisis Livelihood Protection Program (LPP) was expanded to include cash benefits (up to $70 per month), tuition fee waivers, lunch subsidies for students, and a 50 percent reduction in family medical insurance contributions. Eligibility was based on a minimum income and asset tests. In October 2000, the LPP was replaced with a program linking cash and in-kind transfer to participation in labor programs. The formal unemployment insurance scheme remains relatively small and the jobless have benefited more from the public works program. Social protection spending increased threefold from 1997 to 1999.

In Thailand, the safety net was decentralized, with a range of inadequately linked programs. It included, among others, cash transfers to families and the elderly poor, in-kind transfers (mostly subsidized health care), and public works programs (Tambon Development Program and Poverty Alleviation Program). Most of these programs were expanded in 1998–99, with funding coming both from domestic resources and donors (Social Investment Project). In 1998, the Labor Protection Act increased the minimum severance pay, extended some social security benefits to small firms, and added old-age and child allowance schemes.

In Mexico, elements of a social safety net were in place for a number of years, but very few of these specifically targeted the poor. Recently, the authorities began shifting the programs from pure income transfers to transfers conditional on human capital investment. Examples of such programs include PROGRESA, which is conditional on children's school attendance and regular health care visits. In response to the 1994 crisis, a program of small-scale public works (PET) was instituted, providing up to three months of employment at 90 percent of minimum wage.

In Brazil, social security benefits and labor protection programs are the main safety nets. Although most programs are at the national level, some of them are run by local governments. Examples of the latter are *Bolsa Escola*, targeting cash transfers to low-income families on the condition of school attendance, and child labor eradication programs (PETI). As an innovation in IMF programs for Brazil, 22 core assistance programs, chosen in collaboration with the World Bank and the Inter-American Development Bank, have been protected from fiscal adjustment in 1999 and 2000.

In Argentina, the safety net comprises the public pension system, free education up to the secondary level, and a free public health system for the indigent and uninsured. The major programs targeting the poor and the unemployed include health care for the elderly (PAMI), housing programs (FONAVI), and a public works program (TRABAJAR). Similar to Brazil, social spending in the IMF-supported programs was protected in real terms.

[1]Of course, the economic distortions that come with redistributive policies ought to be recognized in the design of safety nets.

Table 5.4. Firm-Level Risk Measures: Country Medians, 1995–96

	Financial Leverage		Short-Term Debt Use	
Crisis Countries	Total debt to (Book value of) equity	Total debt to (Market value of) equity	Short-term debt to long-term debt	Short-term debt to net working capital
Argentina	0.36	0.33	0.80	0.45
Brazil	0.45	0.93	1.14	0.38
Indonesia	0.73	0.56	1.01	0.56
Korea	1.95	2.49	1.43	0.33
Mexico	0.53	0.34	0.46	0.24
Philippines	0.41	0.24	0.93	0.14
Thailand	1.05	0.92	1.46	0.19
Turkey	0.24	0.10	1.99	0.28
OECD average[1]	0.52	0.35	1.02	0.20

Source: Claessens and others, 1999.
[1]Excluding crisis countries.

of inflation and depreciation—called for monetary restraint. There were also important considerations arguing against excessive monetary contraction, however. Pursuing the two main objectives in a single-minded manner and allowing interest rates to rise to arbitrarily high levels risked worsening public debt dynamics (in Turkey and Latin America). Another risk of aggressive tightening was that it could aggravate weaknesses in the financial sector and highly leveraged firms, especially in Asia, where the corporate sector was highly leveraged with excessive reliance on short-term debt (Table 5.4). Indeed, "second-generation" models of balance of payments crises suggest that a perceived reluctance on the part of the authorities to raise interest rates (for these or other reasons) may have triggered the crises in the first place, as markets challenged the parity in a self-fulfilling speculative attack.[73]

However, in cases where (as in Asia) the balance sheets of financial institutions and corporations had substantial foreign currency exposures, allowing the exchange rate to depreciate further would entail a further deterioration in these balance sheets. Adverse effects on the public sector balance sheets would also occur in cases where (as in Brazil) the government had issued substantial foreign currency debt. Moreover, an accommodative monetary stance could have entailed a spiral of depreciation of the nominal exchange rate, as against a temporary spike in interest rates.

In practice, the choice between high interest rates and the exchange rate depreciation was one of degree: *given* the capital outflows from the economy and corresponding decrease in real savings, it would have been difficult, if not impossible, to avoid *some* combination of higher real interest rates and a more depreciated real exchange rate (Figure 5.2). Certain combinations of higher real interest rates and real exchange rate depreciations may be preferable to others, however, depending on the relative importance of vulnerabilities to exchange rate and interest rate risk. Still, assessing the tradeoffs among these combinations was often difficult: while information on the public sector's exposure to these risks was largely available, that on the private sector's exposure was much more limited. In these circumstances, to the extent that both exchange rate and interest rate exposure mattered, neither a staunch defense of the exchange rate at any cost nor a complete abandonment of the exchange rate was likely to be optimal. In most countries, monetary policy thus tried to strike a balance between exchange rate and interest rate adjustment.

Was monetary policy under the programs too tight or too loose in light of these considerations? In order to address this question, three issues are addressed in the following sections: How was monetary policy implemented? How successful was it in achieving its main objectives—stabilizing capital flows and controlling inflation? And how large was the negative impact of monetary tightening on output?

[73]Flood and Marion (1998) provide a useful survey of these models. A "third-generation" model in which corporate balance sheet vulnerabilities make the currency susceptible to a crisis is presented by Aghion, Baccehetta, and Banerjee (2000).

Figure 5.2. Changes in Real Interest Rates and Real Exchange Rates

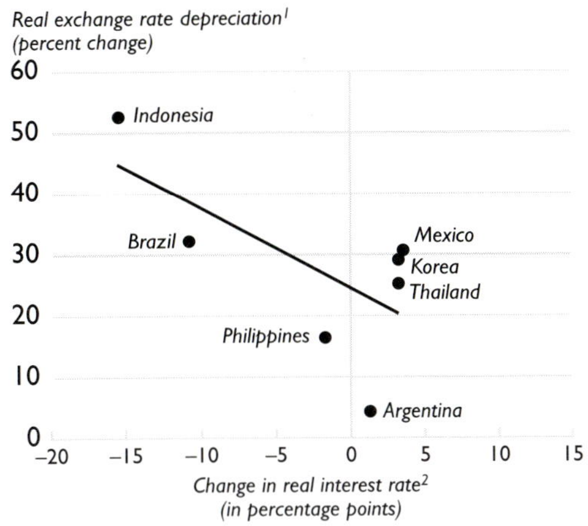

Sources: IMF, International Notice System; and IMF staff estimates.

[1]Average real effective exchange rate during 12 months following program approval minus average real effective exchange rate during 12 months prior to program approval (percent change).

[2]Average real overnight interest rate during 12 months following program approval minus average real overnight interest rate during 12 months prior to program approval. Real interest rates based on estimates of contemporaneous inflation, a three-month moving average of monthly consumer price index changes (previous month, current month, and one month ahead, as available).

Monetary Policy Implementation Under the Programs

To monitor monetary policy implementation, all of the programs—with the exception of Indonesia and the Philippines—included the traditional quantitative performance criteria: a floor on net international reserves (NIR) and a ceiling on net domestic assets (NDA) of the central bank.[74] Implementation of the monetary programs was mixed, however. In most of the cases—with the notable exceptions of Indonesia, Mexico, and Turkey (Table 5.5)—the program ceilings were respected,[75] but these quantitative ceilings provide only a rough check to help ensure that reserves are not squandered in futile sterilized foreign exchange market interventions and to prevent monetary expansion from fueling a sharp acceleration of inflation. Particularly in the tumultuous environment prevailing in financial markets in these countries at the height of the crisis, these quantitative limits were insufficient to guide the response of monetary policy to changing market conditions on a day-to-day basis. Monitoring of monetary policy under the programs therefore needed to rely on indicators that were observable at high frequencies and bore a direct relationship to market conditions.

In this context, interest rates came to play an increasingly important—if often nonspecific[76]—role in program monitoring. The use of nominal interest rates for program monitoring has well known limitations, however, particularly in cases where rising nominal rates primarily reflect exchange rate premia or of inflationary expectations rather than monetary tightening. In Indonesia, for instance, at end-1997 nominal interest rates rose to 60 percent—by far the highest in the region—at a time when the money supply was expanding at a *monthly* rate of 30 percent. Thus, while the increased focus on interest rate developments helped guide monetary policy with regard to the programs' external objectives, they did not provide an alternative to the nominal exchange rate anchor that most of the countries had lost when they abandoned their exchange rate pegs. Accordingly, quantitative limits may still have served as an important check on monetary expansion.

Inflation Control

How successful was monetary policy in keeping inflation under control? In general, remarkably so given the magnitude of the shocks experienced.

Inflation in the crisis countries averaged some 13 percent per year in the year prior to the crisis, rising to 30 percent in the year of the crisis, before declining to 20 percent by the following year (Table 5.6). This inflation performance is all the more remarkable

[74]In the Philippines and Indonesia, there was a ceiling on base money instead of central bank NDA. This allowed for large scale sterilized intervention in support of the currency—quite intentionally, in the original Indonesia program, as the weakness of the exchange rate was viewed as being mostly the result of contagion, and therefore to be resisted. But it may have also contributed to capital outflows because the automatic tightening from the capital outflows was vitiated by expansions in central bank credit. In the event, in Indonesia, the increase in central bank liquidity (in support of the collapsing banking system) eventually breached the base money ceiling anyway.

[75]In Mexico, there was a significant overrun of central bank NDA at end-1995, associated with late disbursements of agricultural subsidies and the early payment of minimum wage increases. In Indonesia, the end-1997 stock of base money was some 15 percent above the program ceiling, reflecting massive liquidity support to banks in the midst of the banking crisis, not all of which had been "sterilized" by reserve losses.

[76]For instance, as widely reported in the press, in the Korean program there was an understanding in early 1998 that the authorities would not reduce interest rates until the exchange rate had substantially appreciated back to 1,400 won per U.S. dollar, but there was no specific commitment to *raise* rates further if necessary to achieve such appreciation.

Table 5.5. Monetary Conditionality[1]

	Original Program				Revised Program			
					Program	Outcome	Program	Outcome
Argentina (1995)	Mar-95	Jun-95	Sep-95	Dec-95			Dec-95	Dec-95
Cumulative change in net domestic assets of the central bank (performance criteria ceiling in millions of pesos)	2,690	3,370	2,870	2,315			2,210	1,961
Cumulative change in net international reserves (NIR) of the central bank (performance criteria floor in millions of U.S. dollars)	–2,790	–1,990	–1,190	–390			–190	–8
Cumulative change in NIR of the central bank (indicative floor in millions of U.S. dollars)	–5,340	–5,940	–4,785	–2,290			–2,745	–1,752
Brazil (1999)[2]		Dec-98	Mar-99	Jun-99	Dec-98	Dec-98	Jun-99	Jun-99
Net domestic assets (stock, in millions of Reais)		–9,506	–7,376	–6,130	–9,506	–5,838	487	–7,981
NIR of Brazilian Central Bank (BCB) (floor on stock in millions of U.S. dollars)		20,000	—	—	20,000	34,300	—	—
Net sales of foreign exchange by BCB (ceiling in millions of dollars)[3]		—	—	1,500	—	—	1,500	1,483
Indonesia (1997)		Dec-97	Mar-98	Jun-98	Dec-97	Dec-97	Jun-98	Jun-98
Base money (performance criteria stock, billions of rupiah)		42,723	42,744	44,240	40,500	46,700	—	—
NIR of Bank Indonesia (performance criteria floor in billions of U.S. dollars)		17	16	14	17	18	14	15
Net domestic assets of Bank Indonesia (performance criterion, First Review onwards)		—	–30.5	–29.4	—	—	–74.8	–74
Base money (trillions of rupiah; indicative target First Review onwards)		—	61.8	62.2	—	—	68.6	71.1
Liquidity support (trillions of rupiah; indicative target First Review onwards)		—	116.5	128	—	—	163.1	165.8
Korea (1997)[4,5,6]		Dec-97	Mar-98	Jun-98	Dec-97	Dec-97	Jun-98	Jun-98
Net domestic assets of the Bank of Korea (performance criteria stocks, in billions of won)		10,950	17,875	6,745	26,571	25,819	4,080	–5,382
Reserve money (indicative target)		23,270	23,580	24,000	23,271	22,519	23,540	20,798
Broad money (indicative target)		709,775	—	—	709,775	710,895	—	—
NIR (performance criteria stocks, in billions of U.S. dollars)		11.2	3.8	11.9	–3.0	–3.0	13.9	18.7
Mexico (1995)	Mar-95	Jun-95	Sep-95	Dec-95			Dec-95	Dec-95
Change in net domestic assets of the monetary authorities (performance criteria ceiling in millions of Mexican pesos)	3,750	1,700	250	10,000			10,000	27,600
Changes in credit to the private sector and commercial banks by the national development banks and trust funds (performance criteria ceiling in millions of Mexican pesos)	5,800	16,750	21,400	30,750			30,750	3,100
Change in NIR of the monetary authorities (target, in millions of U.S. dollars)	–1,500	–1,000	–500	—			—	–2,800
Philippines (1997)[7]	Sep-97	Dec-97	Mar-98	Jun-98	Dec-97	Dec-97	Jun-98	Jun-98
Base money (ceiling, stocks in billions of pesos)	239	274	301	315	306	298	312.4	286
NIR (floor, in millions of U.S. dollars)	7,500	8,000	7,384	7,631	7,276	6,622	7397	8249
Thailand (1997)	Sep-97	Dec-97	Mar-98	Jun-98	Dec-97	Dec-97	Jun-98	Jun-98
Net domestic assets of Bank of Thailand (performance criteria, stocks in billions of baht)	–525	–507	–503	–525	–133	–166	–73	–96
Indicative target for reserve money (stocks, in billions of baht)	456	489	499	489	489	455	468	445
Change in NIR of Bank of Thailand (performance criteria floor in millions of U.S. dollars)	500	3,400	8,300	11,200	1,500	5,761	8,800	11,432
Indicative range for overnight interest rates	12–17	12–17	11–16		15–20	24.7	—	—

Turkey (1994)	Jun–94	Sep–94	Dec–94	Dec–94	Dec–94
Net domestic assets of the Central Bank (stock, in billions of lira)	305,500	295,000	293,000	293,000	305,536
NIR of the Central Bank (cumulative change, in millions of U.S. dollars)	–350	300	1,000	1,000	3,424
Indicative limit for the nominal exchange rate of the Turkish lira[8]	35,000	35,700	38,000	35,000	38,726

[1]Initial perfomance critieria or indicative targets related to monetary sector or net international reserves.

[2]The performance criterion also required no new exposure in forex futures or forward markets. Fourth Review introduced consultation mechanism on inflation.

[3]Performance criteria introduced at first review.

[4]LOI of December 24, 1997, required that call money rates be raised to 30 percent, or above if needed, to stabilize the exchange rate and sterilize activated amounts of 11.3 trillion won worth of liquidity support to keep overall liquidity sufficiently tight to maintain interest rates at adequate levels.

[5]LOI of First Quarterly Review (Feb-98) required that "Monetary Policy will be conducted flexibly with the aim of maintaining stability in the foreign exchange market . . . call rates will be cautiously allowed to ease, in line with continued exchange rate stabilization. A further lowering of interest rates is envisaged only after the foreign exchange market has durably stabilized."

[6]Targets and criteria for March 1998 and June 1998 were set during the First Quarterly Review.

[7]December 1997 figures pertain to the authorities' indicative targets.

[8]The LOI required that "monetary policy will be geared to preventing the nominal exchange rate from depreciating beyond the following path."

Table 5.6. Inflation Program Projections and Outcomes
(Period average, in percent)

	Actual $t-1$	Program t	Actual t	Program $t+1$	Actual $t+1$
Argentina (1995)	4.2	3.6	3.4	. . .	0.2
Brazil (1999)[1]	3.2	2.2	4.9	2.2	7.0
Mexico (1995)	7.0	19.0	35.0	7.0	34.4
Turkey (1994)	66.1	58.6	106.3	20.0	93.7
Indonesia (1998)[1]	6.2	10.0	58.0	9.0	20.7
Korea (1998)[1]	4.4	5.2	7.5	. . .	0.8
Philippines (1998)	5.9	8.0	9.7	6.0	6.6
Thailand (1998)[1]	5.6	5.0	8.1	4.3	0.3
Median	5.8	6.6	8.9	6.5	6.8
Average	12.8	14.0	29.1	8.1	20.5

Sources: IMF, *World Economic Outlook*; MONA database; and IMF staff estimates.
[1]Date refers to year *t*, not to year of program approval.

given the very sharp nominal exchange rate movements that occurred (Figure 2.1).

These averages, however, mask some important differences among the programs. In general, inflation was in line with what might be expected, given monetary and exchange rate developments, with some exceptions. In Argentina, the only program here in which the fixed exchange rate (currency board) was maintained, inflation actually declined slightly in 1995, while in Korea and Thailand, despite the large nominal depreciation, inflation rose only modestly, from about 5 percent per year in 1997, to 8 percent in 1998, before declining to below 1 percent by 1999. Turkey made little headway in reducing inflation. In Brazil, where inflation stabilization had succeeded only four years prior to the program after numerous unsuccessful attempts, there was a serious concern that the currency devaluation might reignite inflationary expectations. In the event, the move to an inflation targeting framework to reestablish a nominal anchor helped to underscore the authorities' commitment to keeping inflation under control, and inflation rose by less than 1 percentage point (to about 4.6 percent). Mexico saw large increases in inflation, partly reflecting exchange rate pass-through, but also, as noted above, overruns in monetary policy, while Indonesia provides a vivid illustration of how a previously stable economy can lurch into a vicious cycle of inflation, depreciation, and loss of monetary control.

Expected Returns and Capital Outflows

To what extent did monetary policy succeed in stabilizing capital outflows and nominal exchange rates? Although the view that monetary restraint is needed to counter an adverse shift in the capital account has long been widely accepted, it has recently been challenged in the context of the three programs in Indonesia, Korea, and Thailand. Some commentators have argued that higher domestic interest rates, far from reversing capital flows, had a perverse effect in these countries, exacerbating the capital outflows and resulting in further exchange rate *depreciation*. In this view, higher interest rates, by bankrupting domestic firms, resulted in a widening of the country (default) risk premium.[77] This criticism has stimulated an extensive debate on the relationship between interest rate increases and capital flows and the exchange rate.

As noted in Chapter II, the dynamics of the capital flows differed markedly between the Latin American countries (especially Argentina and Brazil) and Turkey, on the one hand, and the East Asian countries (especially Thailand, Indonesia, and Korea), on the other. Whereas capital outflows were relatively short-lived in the Latin American programs (typically lasting one quarter following the onset of the currency crisis), they were more prolonged (and larger in mag-

[77]See, for instance, Furman and Stiglitz (1998), for a summary of the evidence on the interest rate-exchange rate relationship, see Lane and others (1999), p. 46. One issue concerns the initial exchange rate overvaluation. To the extent that real exchange rates are viewed as being overvalued, high dollar rates of return may no longer be effective in stemming capital outflows as devaluation expectations take hold. As discussed above, however, the very sharp nominal and real depreciations experienced at the onset of these crises meant that any initial overvaluation (which had, by most measures, been greater in Latin America and Turkey than in the Asian countries) was soon eliminated.

nitude) in East Asia. Can this contrasting experience be related to the monetary policy stance?

A precise correlation between capital flows and domestic interest rates is difficult to establish—not least because other factors, such as fiscal policy, political developments, and the credibility of the programs, were at play. Moreover, the response of capital flows to interest rate differentials may be expected to depend on the nature of those flows. To the extent that capital flows take the form of foreign direct investment or equity flows, they may be relatively unresponsive to higher interest rates.[78] Likewise, if outflows consist mostly of the cutting of banks' foreign currency lines of credit, higher domestic interest rates may be of limited use and, as discussed in Chapter III, more direct forms of private sector involvement may be called for.

Although there may be limitations to using higher interest rates to attract capital (depending, among other things, on the nature of the capital flows), at least some components of capital flows should be responsive to interest rate differentials. In this regard, Figure 5.3, which compares private capital flows and ex post monthly dollar rates of return on domestic assets relative to the London interbank offered rate (LIBOR), is revealing. In Indonesia, the Philippines, and Thailand, these interest differentials were negative for several quarters during the period mid-1997 to mid-1998. Put in this context, capital outflows of the magnitude and duration experienced in these countries were scarcely surprising: investors were not even being compensated for currency depreciation, let alone the risk of holding assets in a financial system that was in the midst of a crisis. By contrast, in Argentina and in Turkey, interest rate differentials were generally positive and capital outflows less persistent than in Asia. Comparing ex-ante dollar rates of return (based on surveys of exchange rate expectations), it is noteworthy that dollar interest rates (relative to LIBOR) were often negative—especially in Korea (fourth quarter of 1999) and Thailand (third quarter of 1997)—whereas they were consistently positive in Brazil (Figure 5.4).

The available empirical evidence on the relationship between ex post relative returns and private capital flows in the eight countries is clearly somewhat tenuous. In a number of instances, ex post positive returns on domestic assets were not sufficient to prevent capital outflows.[79] Nevertheless, there were few episodes where negative interest differentials actually coincided with capital *inflows*, suggesting that a lax monetary policy stance is unlikely to be helpful in stabilizing capital flows.

Some commentators, particularly in the Asian context, have turned this argument on its head, suggesting that higher interest rates—by leading to widespread bankruptcies—actually resulted in further capital outflows and exchange rate *depreciation*. Existing empirical evidence does not give much support for this view (Box 5.2). In fact, the spread between onshore U.S. dollar and rupiah interest rates in Indonesia suggests that high domestic interest rates reflected expected exchange rate depreciation rather than a higher default risk premium, as the critics of a tight monetary policy would argue.[80] If higher interest rates were indeed contributing to domestic bankruptcies and, therefore, reflected greater bankruptcy risk, then both local and foreign currency interest rates should rise in tandem. In fact, however, onshore U.S. dollar interest rates in Indonesia rose only slightly. Dollar interest rates did increase to about 15 percent in April–June 1998 at the height of the political and security concerns, but even then, the increase in rupiah interest rates was significantly higher.

To summarize, in capital account crises, monetary policy—in the form of higher expected rates of return—can play a crucial role in stemming capital outflows and thus avoiding massive swings in the current account (with the attendant consequences for economic activity). In Argentina (and, to a lesser extent, the other Latin American countries), such interest rate increases were indeed successful in stemming capital outflows. In Asia, there is little evidence of a perverse effect (whereby higher interest rates contributed to capital outflows and greater exchange rate depreciation), and relative U.S. dollar rates of return on domestic assets were not positive for several months after the onset of the crises.

Impact on Economic Activity

Tightening monetary policy in the midst of a crisis, even to the extent that it was necessary to stabilize capital flows and keep inflation under control is likely to have had a negative impact on economic activity. This impact, of course, needs to be compared with the relevant counterfactual: if failing to tighten adequately had resulted in sustained large capital outflows and a vicious circle of exchange rate depreciation and inflation, these developments likely would have had more devastating consequences. Nevertheless, it is legitimate to ask whether

[78]For instance, in Indonesia the Balanced Budget Law had contributed to stifling the development of a domestic government bond market, leaving relatively few instruments with which to lure investors into domestic currency assets.

[79]Comparing capital flows and ex post U.S. dollar returns on domestic assets is somewhat problematic because the change in the exchange rate is, of course, influenced by the capital flows.

[80]Of the Asian countries, Indonesia is the only one with substantial onshore dollar deposits.

Figure 5.3. Private Capital Flows and Ex Post Dollar Rates of Return[1]

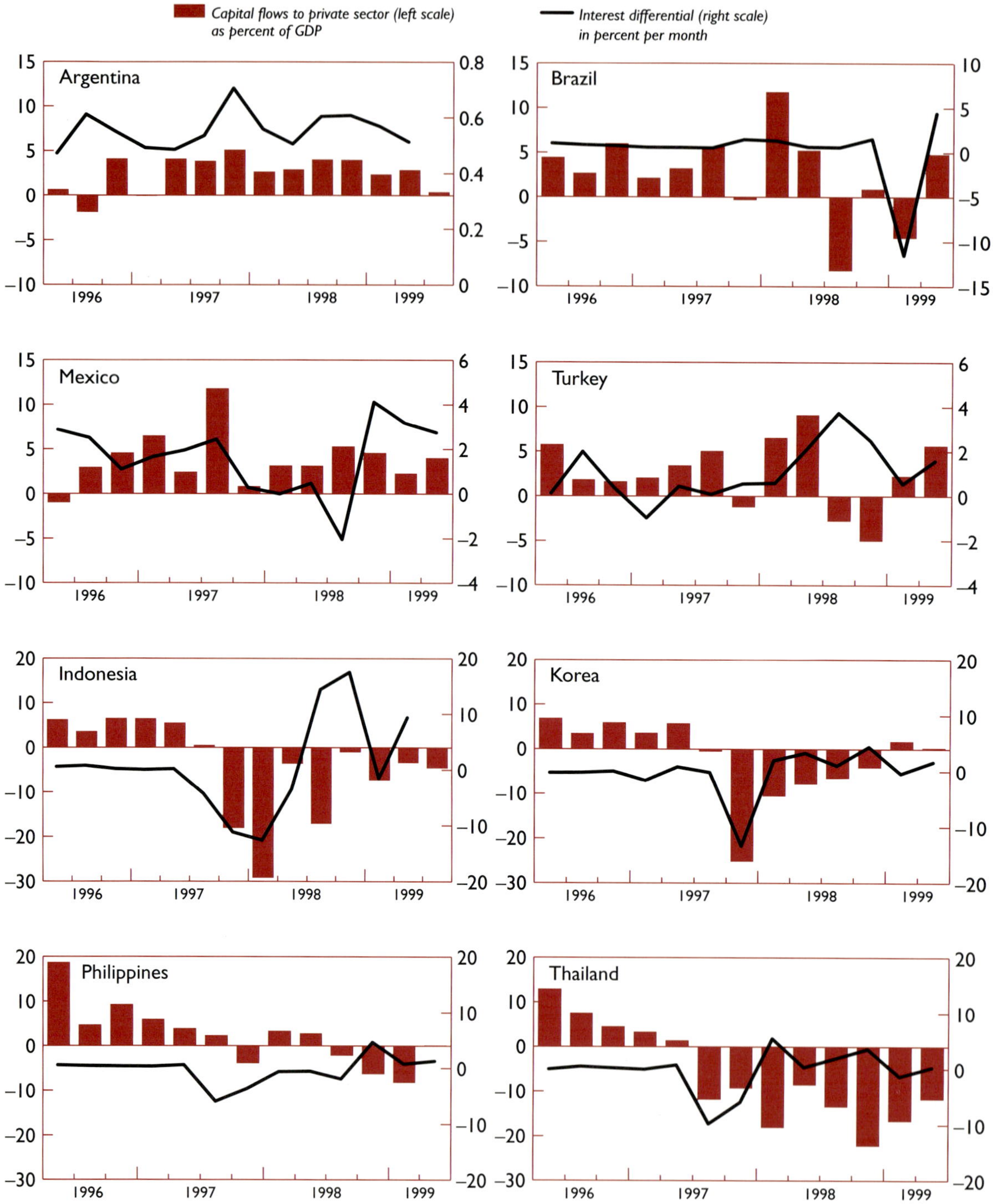

Sources: IMF, *World Economic Outlook*; and IMF staff estimates.

[1]Capital flows are in percent of GDP. Ex post uncovered interest differentials in U.S. dollar terms relative to the London interbank offered rate (LIBOR) in percent per month.

Figure 5.4. Private Capital Flows and Ex Ante Dollar Rates of Return[1]

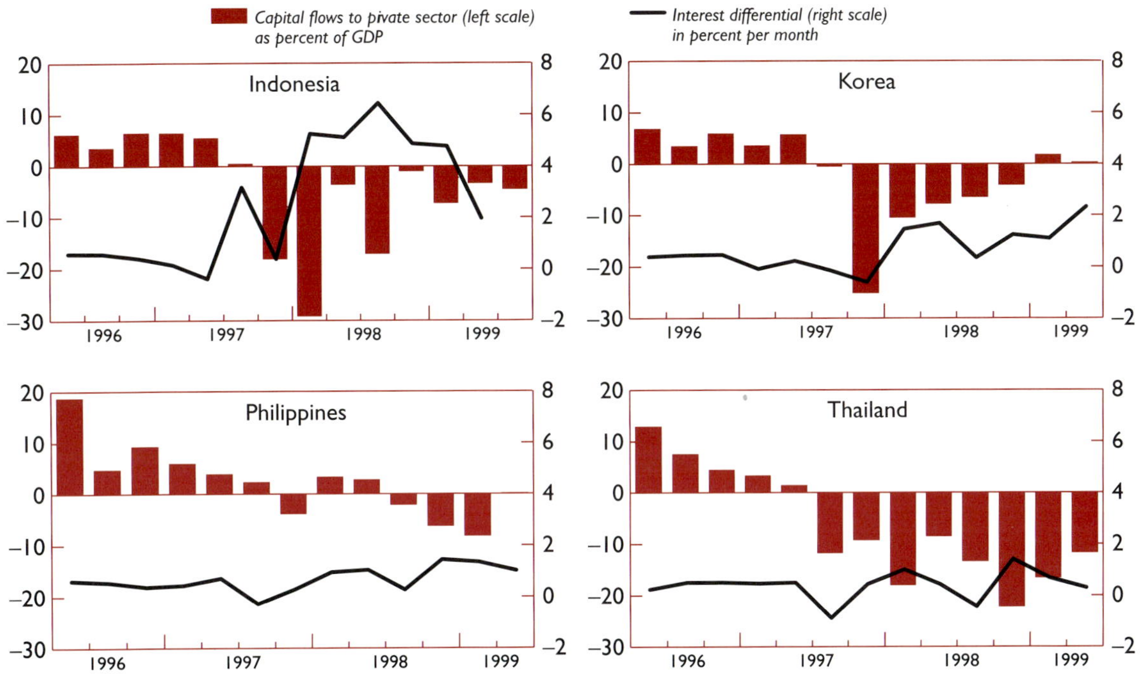

Sources: IMF, *World Economic Outlook*; and IMF staff estimates.
[1]Capital flows are in percent of GDP. Ex ante uncovered interest differentials in U.S. dollar terms relative to the London interbank offered rate (LIBOR) in percent per month.

monetary and credit conditions contributed significantly to the observed output declines.

Figure 5.5 graphs nominal and real (overnight and lending) interest rates.[81] Although some caution is required in comparing the levels of interest rates across countries (particularly lending rates, where definitions and applicability differ widely), judging by the developments in real lending rates in the first year after program approval, credit conditions do not appear to have been excessively tight. In Indonesia, real lending rates were strongly negative for most of the year; in Brazil, they declined steadily after a moderate initial increase and fell well below the pre-crisis 1997 average from mid-1999 onward. In Korea, Mexico, and Thailand, real lending rates at first turned negative as inflation rose in the wake of the large initial exchange rate depreciations. In Korea, this movement was followed by a sharp but relatively brief rise in real interest rates and then a significant decline from mid-1998 onward. In Thailand, in contrast, the rise in real lending rates was more gradual and sustained. Real lending rates also rose in Mexico after the initial decline. In all three countries, as well as the Philippines, real lending rates in the first year after program approval were, on average, barely higher than in the preceding year. By contrast, in Argentina real lending rates rose sharply at the beginning of the program and stayed well above pre-program levels throughout the year.

In the Asian countries and Mexico, real interest rates were not closely correlated with the periods of the steepest output declines in late 1997 and early 1998: indeed, these declines occurred well before the increase in real interest rates. If tight monetary conditions resulted in increased quantity rationing, however, developments in real lending rates may not tell the full story. There is evidence that relatively low (or negative) real interest rates in these countries were associated with *credit rationing* (see Box 5.3). This appears to have reflected mainly a lack of sufficient bank capital and an unwillingness to lend in a

[81]These real interest rates are deflated by the consumer price index. Since producer prices generally rose by more, wholesale price index-deflated real interest rates were lower.

Box 5.2. The Interest Rate-Exchange Rate Nexus in Currency Crises: A Review of the Literature

A number of recent studies have tried to assess empirically whether higher interest rates are useful in supporting the exchange rate (that is, the "traditional" effect) or whether they instead have an opposite, "perverse" effect. Rather than examining the long-run relationship between monetary policy and the exchange rate, these studies focus on patterns inside selected short episodes.

The results of these studies are inconclusive and indeed quite mixed. In general, they fail to find overwhelming evidence of the traditional effect. This is not surprising, however, given the inherent policy endogeneity problem: that is, interest rates are likely to be raised precisely during episodes of currency depreciation, as both variables respond to shifts in market sentiment. On the other hand, there is also no clear pattern of evidence across studies of a perverse effect of interest rate policy.

Furman and Stiglitz (1998) identify a set of 13 episodes, in nine emerging markets, of "temporarily high" interest rates (episodes during which interest rates rose by more than 10 percentage points for at least five days, then fell back). Using a simple regression analysis, they find that both the magnitude and duration of such interest rate hikes are associated with exchange rate *depreciation*. While Furman and Stiglitz note that this evidence is not definitive, and that its interpretation is fraught with difficulties concerning endogeneity, they conclude that it at least questions the usefulness of raising interest rates.

Kraay (2000) focuses instead on episodes of speculative attacks on currencies and uses a more sophisticated and complex methodology. He identifies a set of 121 attacks that were successful, in the sense that there was an uncharacteristically large monthly depreciation; he also identifies (with greater inherent difficulty) a set of 192 unsuccessful attacks. The essential finding is that increases in central bank discount rates are neither necessary nor sufficient for staving off a speculative attack. Indeed, no relationship is found between central bank discount policy and the success or failure of speculative attacks. When Kraay tries to control for the endogeneity of interest rate policy, the results are similar, although, as he notes, they are preliminary and could reflect the difficulty of specifying appropriate instrumental variables to control for policy endogeneity.

Goldfajn and Gupta (1999) ask a somewhat different question, one probably more relevant for the East Asian countries during their IMF-supported programs. They consider cases *following* an exchange rate crisis in which the real exchange rate has become clearly undervalued, so that considerable real appreciation is likely to follow. They then study whether tighter monetary policies—in terms of higher-than-average real interest rates—are associated with the corrective real appreciation occurring mainly through currency appreciation rather than through higher inflation.

In general, Goldfajn and Gupta find that tight monetary policy does raise the probability of "success"; that is, achieving the corrective real appreciation via currency appreciation. When the sample is restricted to

period of heightened uncertainty, rather than a lack of sufficient liquidity, however. As such, there may have been little scope to address this problem through expansionary monetary policy.

For most countries, developments in real credit aggregates[82] tell a broadly similar story to real lending rates (Figure 5.6).[83] In Indonesia and, to a lesser extent, in the Philippines, real credit rose sharply after the programs were approved and began to decline only in the second half of the first program year. In Brazil and Thailand, real credit increased initially as well, but these increases were considerably smaller, of shorter duration, and were followed by steady decline; in Korea and Mexico, real credit fell steadily throughout the first program year although the decline in Mexico was much steeper than in Korea. Real credit growth during the first program year was positive only in Argentina.

There appears to be a somewhat better correspondence between real GDP growth and real money and credit aggregates than with real interest rates. Appendix IV reports impulse response functions of real GDP growth (seasonally adjusted) to shocks in real money and real credit growth (seasonally adjusted), respectively, from a fourth-order vector autoregression.[84] The estimates suggest that the positive effects of an expansion in real money or real credit is generally quite short-lived, lasting a quarter or two, and

[82]The analysis of real money and real credit growth rates is complicated by a number of factors and caveats. In particular, sharp exchange rate movements can affect the behavior of these aggregates to the extent that foreign currency deposits or loans are important. In 1998, the share of foreign currency loans in total domestic credit amounted to about 7 percent in Korea, 25 percent in the Philippines, and less than 1 percent in Thailand.

[83]Although nominal growth rates of money and credit are a better indication of the monetary policy stance, in terms of the impact on the real economy, presumably, it is the behavior of real aggregates that matters.

[84]The ordering of the vector autoregression (VAR) assumes that real money (real credit) is exogenous with respect to output growth; in consequence, the VAR estimates may well overstate the effect of monetary policy on output growth.

cases where the banking sector is fragile, however, tight monetary policy seems to reduce the probability of success (although as the authors note, this latter result is based on very few cases and is not robust).

Goldfajn and Baig (1998), rather than defining and identifying crisis episodes from a broad sample of countries, focus on the very recent experience of five Asian countries, from mid-1997 through May 1998. Using daily data, they analyze the relationship between nominal interest rates and nominal exchange rates during the recent Asian crisis. A vector autoregression does not find a significant relationship—in either direction—for any of the five Asian countries. On the other hand, a panel regression using *changes* in interest rates and exchange rates yields a traditionally-signed coefficient over all the sample spans examined, although this is statistically significant only in some subperiods. Country-by-country regressions find a significant traditionally-signed coefficient in some periods for Indonesia, Korea, and the Philippines (the only significant coefficient with the opposite sign is found for Malaysia, and this is in one subperiod only). Goldfajn and Baig thus conclude that their study finds no evidence that higher interest rates lead to weaker exchange rates; if anything, there are periods where higher rates lead to stronger exchange rates.

Gould and Kamin (2000) examine the link between exchange rates and interest rates using weekly data. They attempt to control explicitly for the endogeneity of interest rates by entering variables proxying for the risk premia in the regression. The paper finds no effect of interest rates on exchange rates in either direction, which the authors suggest may be due to the difficulty of identifying such an impact in weekly data, especially in a short sample.

Tanner (2000) examines the relationship between domestic credit growth and exchange market pressure (i.e., the sum of exchange rate depreciation and reserve outflows scaled by base money). Using data for Brazil, Chile, Mexico, Indonesia, Korea, and Thailand, he finds that contractionary monetary policy tends to reduce exchange market pressure, consistent with the traditional view.

Basurto and Ghosh (2001) argue that the effect of an interest rate increase on the exchange rate should depend on whether the increase is perceived as temporary, and on how the decline in the interest rate is expected to be reversed (through an increase in the money supply or through lower inflation reversing the decline of real money balances). They also argue that, in terms of monetary aggregates, monetary policy was not especially tight in East Asia, and that high nominal interest rates, particularly in Indonesia, were a reflection of inflationary expectations rather than of tight monetary policy. Using an explicit monetary model of exchange rate determination to control for monetary policy, therefore, they examine whether higher real interest rates contributed to a widening of the risk premium (perhaps through the expectation of bankruptcies). With the exception of a brief episode in early 1998 in Korea, they find no such evidence.

the impact multiplier is no greater than 0.3–0.4, and generally lower.

Applying these estimated elasticities out of the sample to the *non*-Asian crisis countries suggests that the observed declines in real GDP growth were broadly commensurate with the tightening monetary and credit conditions.[85]

In Asia, by contrast, the declines of real GDP growth in the first two quarters of 1998 generally exceeded the fall in real money or real credit growth rates (with the implied "elasticity" well above the estimated 0.3–0.4).[86] This suggests that either tightening monetary conditions had an unusually large (but difficult to estimate) effect during the crisis in Asia or, more simply, that monetary developments themselves can account for only a small fraction of the observed output declines. Moreover, declines in real money or real credit generally led, or were contemporaneous with, declines in real GDP in Turkey and Latin America; in Asia, by contrast (especially in Indonesia, Thailand, and the Philippines), the sharp decline in real GDP growth led declines in real money or real credit (Figure 5.7).

To summarize, in a capital account crisis, monetary policy must focus on stemming capital outflows and preventing spiraling exchange rate depreciation and inflation. This was done relatively more successfully in Latin America than in East Asia, perhaps because the Latin American authorities were less

[85]Thus, in Argentina, real money growth declined by about 13 percentage points in the first quarter of 1995, and the output decline was 4 percentage points in the second quarter of 1995. In Mexico, real money growth declined by 21 percentage points (and real credit growth by 23 percentage points in the second quarter of 1995), while real GDP growth declined by 4 percentage points. In Turkey, real money growth declined by 10 percentage points and real credit growth by about 20 percentage points, while real GDP growth fell by almost 10 percentage points.

[86]In Indonesia, real money and real credit growth were strongly positive in the first and second quarters of 1998, reflecting liquidity support to the banking system. The very high nominal money growth rates could not be supported, however, and the bout of subsequent inflation resulted in strongly negative real money/credit growth rates in the second half of 1998.

Figure 5.5. Nominal and Real Overnight and Lending Rates

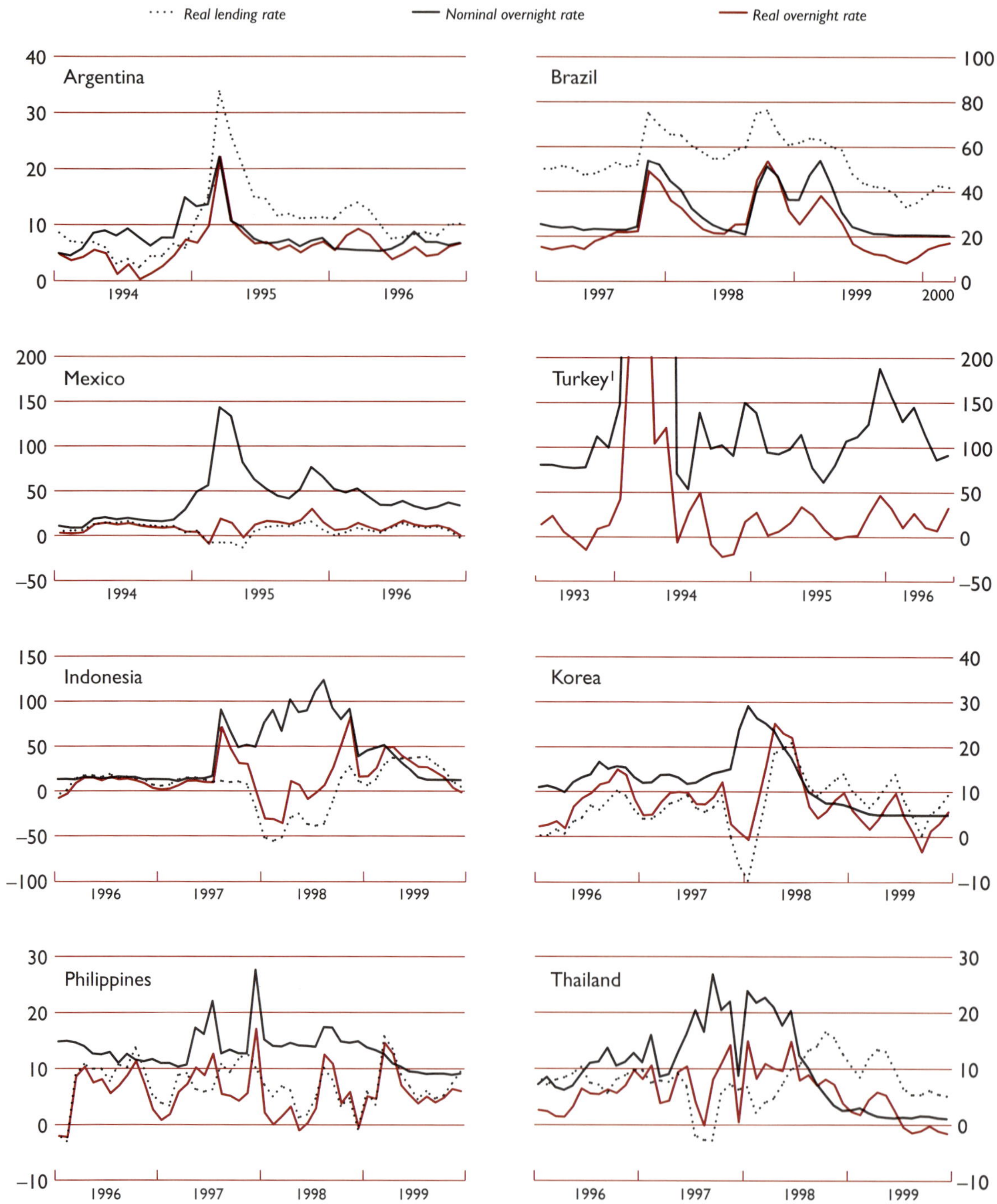

Sources: Data provided by the national authorities; IMF, *International Financial Statistics*; and IMF staff estimates.
[1]Nominal overnight rate in March 1994 was 3,119 percent per year.

Box 5.3. Credit Markets and Quantity Rationing in the Asian Crisis Countries

There has been considerable debate on whether a credit crunch developed in Asia in the aftermath of the crises.[1] Ghosh and Ghosh (2000) note that, while real lending rates were quite low, and even negative, in the Asian countries at the onset of the crises, credit conditions may nonetheless have been tight because of *quantity rationing*.

In order to capture such rationing, Ghosh and Ghosh apply an explicit disequilibrium model to estimate the supply of, and demand for, real credit during the crisis period. The demand for credit is assumed to depend on the real lending rate, and a vector of indicators intended to capture actual and expected economic activity (including real GDP growth, the moving-volatility of growth, the stock market index, and inflation). Credit supply is assumed to be a function of the real spread and real GDP growth (reflecting banks' willingness to lend) and banks' *lending capacity*. Lending capacity, in turn, depends on banks' liquidity (total liabilities minus reserves minus cash-in-vault) and their capital capacity (the maximum amount of loans that can be supported with existing capital while respecting capital adequacy requirements).

The estimates suggest that tightening credit conditions at the onset of the crises resulted in quantity rationing to the tune of 10–20 percent (i.e., estimated real credit demand was some 10–20 percent higher than estimated real credit supply). Thereafter, however, the decline in economic activity and weakening aggregate demand resulted in a fall in credit demand as well. By the beginning of the second quarter of 1998, credit supply was no longer the binding constraint and there was no more quantity rationing (real interest rates had also risen, especially in Korea). (As emphasized in the paper, individual firms (especially small and medium-sized enterprises) may have continued to face credit rationing.)

Decomposing the factors behind the quantity rationing "credit crunch," Ghosh and Ghosh find that about 10 percent of the decline in estimated credit supply is accounted for by the banks' "willingness to lend" variables, and the rest by a fall in banks' lending capacity. The reduction in lending capacity, moreover, largely reflected a lack of adequate capital rather than insufficient liquidity (although, in Indonesia, there was a decline in liquidity for a period as well). As such, it is unlikely that further injections of central bank liquidity to the banking system would have done much to ameliorate the credit crunch.

[1]The term "credit crunch" is often used broadly to mean a situation in which credit is "tight," rather than necessarily quantity rationing. See Dollar and Hallward-Driemeier (1998), who use survey data on 1,200 Thai manufacturing firms in end-1997 and early 1998; Domaç and Ferri (1998), who examine the relationship in Korea between increases in the spread between bank lending rates and treasury bond rates and industrial production; and Claessens, Djankov, and Ferri (1998), who assess the impact of the currency and interest rate shocks (between early 1997 and September 1998) on the liquidity and the solvency of a sample of East Asian firms.

The analysis suggests an important crisis dynamic which is consistent with the results reported above on aggregate supply and demand shocks. At the onset of the Asian crises, weakness in the banking system resulted in credit rationing, contributing to the supply shock. With the subsequent downturn in aggregate demand (and real interest rates now reflecting the withdrawal of real resources available to the economy), the demand for credit also fell, and credit supply was no longer the binding constraint. See the bar charts for Indonesia and Korea in the figure below.

Indonesia: Estimated Credit Demand and Supply

(In constant rupiah, 1995 = Rp100)

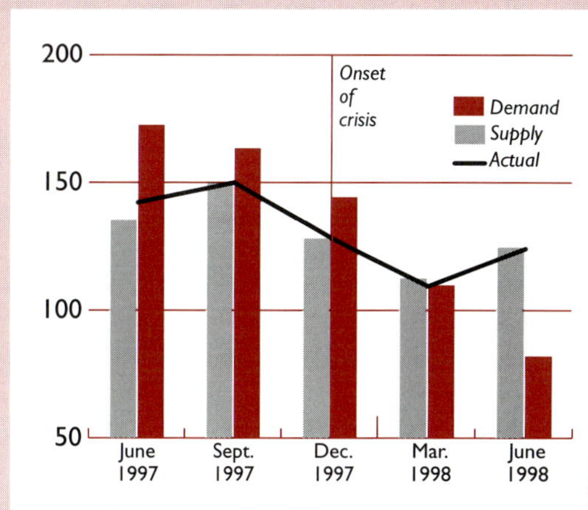

Korea: Estimated Credit Demand and Supply

(In constant won, 1995 = 100)

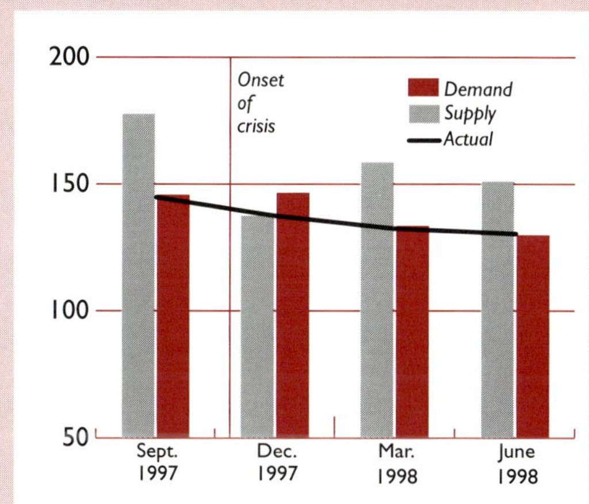

Figure 5.6. Broad Money and Banking System Credit in Real Terms[1]

Sources: Data provided by the national authorities; IMF, *International Financial Statistics*; and IMF staff estimates.

[1]Broad money and domestic credit at actual exchange rates, deflated by the consumer price index. Index, January 1994=100 for Argentina, Mexico, and Turkey; index, January 1998=100 for Brazil; index, December 1996=100 for Indonesia, Korea, the Philippines, and Thailand. For Indonesia, since March 1999, the domestic credit data reflect transfers of nonperforming loans to Indonesia Bank Restructuring Agency (IBRA).

Figure 5.7. Real GDP, Real Credit, and Real Money
(Quarterly growth rates, seasonally adjusted, in percent per quarter)

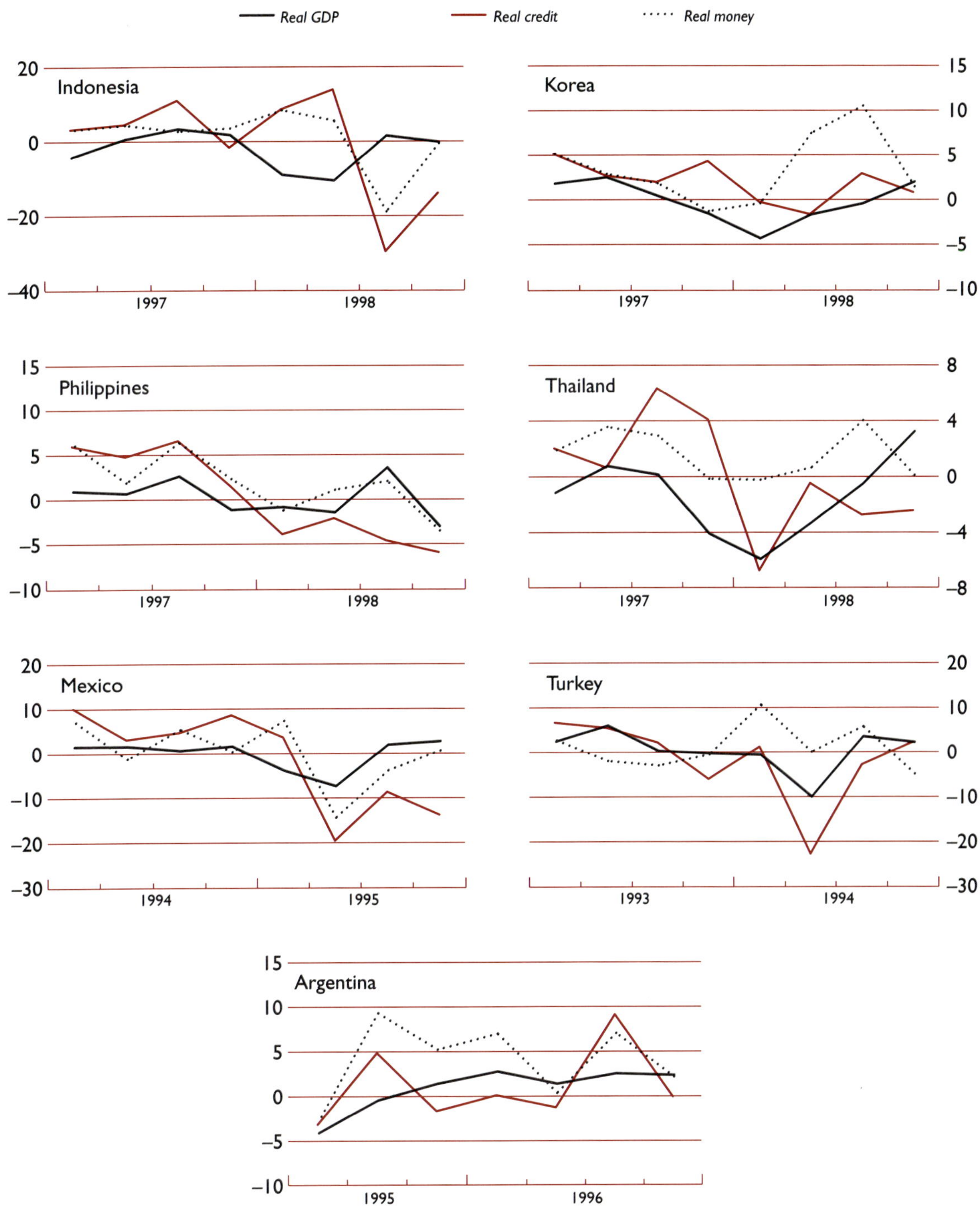

Source: IMF staff estimates.

reluctant to raise interest rates more aggressively. Moreover, given capital outflows, some combination of higher real interest rates (or credit rationing) and real exchange rate depreciation was unavoidable; there is little evidence to suggest that tighter monetary policy itself was responsible for the observed output declines in Asia.

Structural Policies

Structural policies also could play a major part in the response to capital account crises both by restoring confidence and by addressing underlying weaknesses. In the absence of credible measures to address underlying structural weaknesses, monetary and fiscal policies alone are unlikely to restore confidence and renew capital inflows. In fact, in the case of structural policies, the confidence effect is arguably more important, at least in the short run. Whereas monetary and fiscal policies have an immediate or medium-term impact on the economy, structural measures, by their very nature, normally require time to take effect. In the short run, therefore, their impact is largely limited to restoring confidence. This confidence effect puts structural reforms very much at the center of capital account crisis programs.[87]

Nonetheless, there are important trade-offs in determining the structural agenda in capital account crisis programs. On the one hand, reforms that merely "paper over" underlying weaknesses, or that are not perceived as credible, are unlikely to do much to engender confidence.[88] Indeed, as underscored by the experience with bank closures in Indonesia, attempts at reform that are half-hearted, or lack credibility more generally, may well exacerbate the loss of confidence and deepen the crisis. Moreover, there may be domestic political economy considerations that make it easier for the authorities to tackle difficult structural reforms in the aftermath of a crisis than in calmer times.[89] On the other hand, a desire for comprehensiveness may dilute and undermine the reform effort, strain the authorities' implementation capacity, and unnecessarily antagonize interest groups, thereby eroding public support for the program. In practice, the dividing line is not always clear-cut, and programs have no doubt erred on both sides—not tackling underlying weaknesses sufficiently aggressively in some cases, while trying to take on too many reforms at once in others.

Figure 5.8 compares the formal structural conditionality in capital account crisis programs to conditionality in other programs supported by stand-by or extended arrangements (with programs in transition economies shown separately).[90] Two features of the data are immediately apparent. First, with the exception of Indonesia, there was significantly less structural conditionality in capital account crisis programs than in other IMF-supported programs (particularly IMF-supported programs in the transition economies). Second, by and large, conditionality in capital account crisis programs *was* focused on the specific structural weaknesses of the countries.

Thus, in Turkey (1994), the core of the structural measures centered on improving the state of the public finances and the health of the banking sector. In addition to "traditional" tax and spending measures found in most IMF-supported programs, budgetary discipline was to be improved by an overhaul of the social security system, limiting transfers to state enterprises, and an ambitious privatization program (of which, however, only privatization was subject to formal conditionality). A blanket guarantee on all domestic and foreign currency deposits helped avert a full-scale run on the banking system, allowing the authorities to focus on improving supervision and regulation.[91]

In Brazil (1998), likewise, structural reforms centered on improving long-term public finances, especially those of the provinces. At the national level, the budgetary process was to be guided by the Fiscal

[87]There is now a large body of literature on macroeconomic factors underlying currency crises; see, for example, Kaminsky and Reinhart (1999), and Berg and Pattillo (1999). Most of this literature, however, does not focus on structural factors as such. For a discussion of the role of structural factors in currency crises, see Mulder, Perrelli, and Rocha (2001); and Ghosh and Ghosh (2001).

[88]Since structural reforms may need time to be instituted, a key concern is the credibility of announcements about future policy intentions.

[89]See Alesina and Drazen (1991), and Drazen and Grilli (1993).

[90]The term "conditionality" is used broadly here to include prior actions (or conditions for completion of a review), structural performance criteria, and structural benchmarks. In addition, particularly in the Asian programs, structural reforms were often specified in policy matrices, which did not have formal status, although they may have been perceived as part of IMF conditionality; see "Structural Conditionality in Fund-Supported Programs" for a discussion.

[91]The question of whether blanket guarantees should be extended in the midst of crises is not uncontroversial, however. Such guarantees may help avert a full-blown run on the banking system by providing some of the fiscal sector's strength to the banking system. If, however, the financial sector losses are sufficiently large to threaten the public balances, the guarantee may lack credibility. Blanket guarantees also raise important issues about possible moral hazard. Moreover, once such guarantees have been extended, it may be difficult to find an opportune moment to remove them. Thus, the Turkish blanket guarantee, introduced as a temporary measure in 1994, remains in place as of 2001.

Figure 5.8. Structural Conditionality[1]
(Structural measures per year of program)

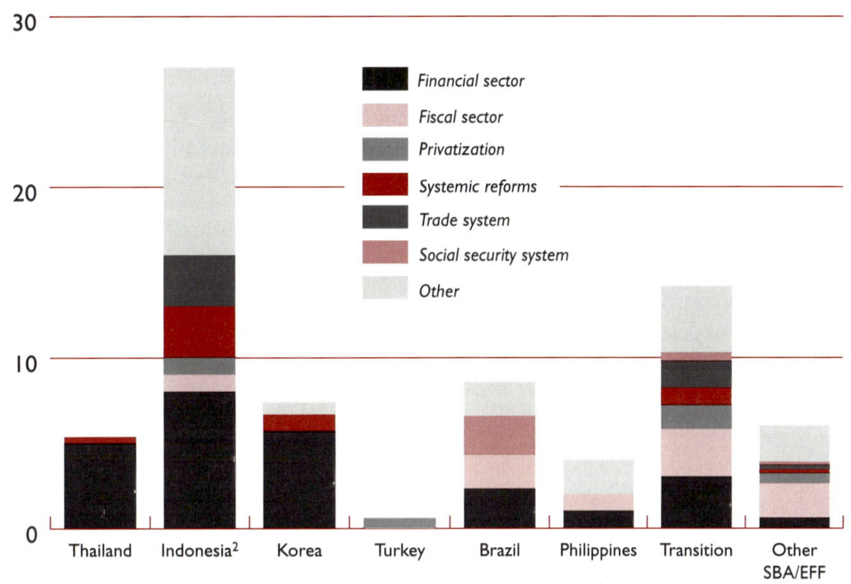

Source: IMF, MONA database; IMF-supported country program documents.
[1]Performance criteria, structural benchmarks, and conditions for completion of review; three sectors of conditionality (public enterprise restructuring, social safety net, and agriculture) did not contain any measures in the capital account crisis countries. The programs in Argentina and Mexico contained no structural conditionality.
[2]First year of the three-year Stand-By Arrangement (SBA), which was subsequently replaced by an Extended Fund Facility (EFF).

Responsibility Act (a structural benchmark under the program), bolstered by the introduction of a nationwide value-added tax and, on the expenditure side, reforms of the social security system and social spending programs.

Mexico (1995) and Argentina (1995) differed from the other programs reviewed here, in that financial sector weaknesses were not viewed as being the cause of the crises but rather its side effect. Particularly in Mexico, the crisis was mostly macroeconomic in nature—an overvalued exchange rate and an unsustainable current account deficit—and the program, which did not include any structural conditionality, reflected this.[92] Although the banking sector developed significant difficulties—with nonperforming loans growing by 50 percent during the period December 1994–March 1995—the financial sector crisis followed the currency crisis. Costs of financial sector restructuring in capital account crisis countries are reviewed in Box 5.4.

Brazil, Turkey, and Mexico all offer examples where, arguably, the implementation or design of the structural reforms did not go sufficiently far in

[92]Nor was there any formal structural conditionality in the Argentina (1995) program, where the main structural vulnerability concerned the banking sector. By late-1994, the share of nonperforming loans exceeded 10 percent of banks' portfolios. This made banks vulnerable both to contagion from the Mexican financial crisis and the monetary tightening needed to defend the currency board arrangement. The result was a liquidity squeeze on weaker banks that threatened to spread to apparently solvent institutions as well. The authorities responded to the growing banking crisis with a series of measures: reserve requirements were lowered and remunerated; swap and rediscount facilities were introduced or extended; trust funds were established to foster privatization of provincial banks and help with their capitalization and restructuring; a "safety net" was established to redistribute liquidity within the system; and a privately managed deposit insurance scheme was introduced. These measures proved sufficient to abate the banking crisis and restore confidence; by late-1995, risk premia had declined, monetary policy was gradually loosened, and by early-996 bank deposits had recovered to their pre-crisis levels.

Box 5.4. Costs of Financial Sector Restructuring

Capital outflows put heavy burdens on domestic banking systems, especially when associated with currency depreciations. The deposit base shrinks as agents run away from domestic currencies and the loan portfolio deteriorates as a result of the economic contraction induced by the falling currency. Recapitalization costs of crisis-affected banks depend on deterioration of the loan portfolio, the speed of currency stabilization, and capital endowment and loan loss provisioning in the banking system.

In Argentina, Turkey, and Brazil the recapitalization costs were modest, owing to relatively sound banking systems prior to the crisis and a fast return of confidence. In Argentina, the banks lost some one-fifth of their deposits and one-third of banks were taken over, forced to merge, or went bankrupt. The share of nonperforming loans increased by 15 percent, but thanks to large efficiency gains during 1991–94, proper loan loss provisioning, and functioning banking supervision, the overall health of the banking system was sustained with little explicit cost. The situation in Turkey was similar: the fast return of currency stability and business confidence limited the cost of bank recapitalization, which was done mostly through interest rate spreads and high yields on government paper. The extent of the damage to bank portfolios was not clear from the official data, mostly because of underreporting of nonperforming loans. In Brazil, the return of confidence was also rapid and private banks were relatively unaffected. The damage to state-owned financial institutions was much larger, however, and the outstanding bonds financing their restructuring amounted to 6 percent of GDP in mid-2000.

In contrast, in the remaining countries, the recapitalization costs were much larger, owing to weak banking systems, lack of prudential regulation, and protracted periods of currency instability. In Mexico, the share of nonperforming loans more than doubled and the total cost of bank recapitalization was revised to about 15 percent of GDP. The damage to bank portfolios was even higher in the four Asian countries: the peak-crisis estimates of the share of nonperforming loans were twice as high as the early-crisis estimates in Korea, the Philippines, and Thailand, and three to four times as high in Indonesia (see the table). The estimates of recapitalization cost—with the exception of the Philippines—dwarf the Mexican case and the domestic budgets are likely to bear the brunt of those costs.

Asian Crisis Countries: Nonperforming Loans and Recapitalization Cost
(As a percent of total loans)

	Indonesia	Korea	Philippines	Thailand
Early-crisis estimates (1998)				
J.P. Morgan	11.0	17.5	5.5	17.5
Goldman Sachs	9.0	14.0	3.0	18.0
Peak-crisis estimates (1998/99)				
J.P. Morgan	30–35	25–30	8–10	25–30
Goldman Sachs	40+	25–30	n.a.	35–40
Recapitalization costs[1]				
J.P. Morgan	19.0	30.0	0.0	30.0
Standard and Poor's	20+	20+	n.a.	34.0
Fiscal costs of recapitalization[1]				
Low scenario	. . .	7.2	0.9	8.0
Medium scenario	. . .	15.7	0.9	15.1
High scenario	. . .	31.7	2.8	30.0

Source: Berg (1999).
[1]As a percent of GDP. Recapitalization costs in Indonesia have been revised upward repeatedly. They are now estimated to be at around 47 percent of GDP, assuming that future asset recoveries approach 10 percent of GDP.

addressing the underlying weaknesses. In Mexico, for instance, inclusion of financial sector reform measures under the program might have speeded up the reform process. In Brazil, the initial announcement of the program helped calm markets and stem capital outflows. Subsequently, however, as Congress failed to pass key legislative changes (including increases in social security contributions and several tax increases), and there were increasing doubts about provincial finances, confidence was eroded, and by early 1999 Brazil faced a full-blown capital account crisis.

In Turkey, even though the announcement of the structural program served to stem capital outflows—and helped restore inflows—implementation of the structural reform agenda soon petered out, perpetuating structural weaknesses (especially in the fiscal accounts) that eventually necessitated another IMF-supported program. Likewise, in Mexico, it is at least debatable whether the program missed an important opportunity to undertake a comprehensive reform of the financial sector, which subsequently suffered from protracted difficulties.[93]

The Asian programs provide a sharp contrast in terms of the scope and depth of the structural measures (Box 5.5), and indeed have been criticized on grounds that the structural reform agenda was overly ambitious.[94]

The programs in Thailand and Korea were similar in that most of the *formal* structural conditionality pertained to financial sector reforms (Figure 5.6). These reforms—which included measures for bank restructuring and resolution, improvements in financial supervision and prudential regulation, the establishment of frameworks for debt workouts, and other closely related measures—were clearly integral to addressing the underlying weakness that had caused the crises. As such, even if the precise pace, sequencing, and modalities of the reforms may be debated, it would be difficult to argue that the reforms themselves were unnecessary or unfocused.[95] Beyond these formal conditions, however, both programs included a large number of ancillary measures. While many of these were supportive of the financial and corporate sector reform efforts (or were related to enhancing social safety nets), others—though worthwhile reforms in themselves—were of peripheral importance to the immediate crisis.[96]

The Indonesia 1997 stand-by is exceptional among the programs reviewed here in terms of the number and the scope and of structural measures subject to some form of conditionality (Figure 5.8). One reason for this broad brush approach was that the original program was primarily intended as a precaution against contagion (rather than dealing with an immediate crisis), and sought to reform the financial sector and deregulate the economy more generally. Events soon overtook the program, however, and the state of the banking system deteriorated dramatically as markets concluded that the authorities were not genuinely committed to undertaking reforms, with widespread runs even on solvent banks amid growing political uncertainty and confusion about the coverage of deposit guarantees.[97] Massive liquidity support had to be provided by the central bank to preserve the payments system, derailing monetary policy. Subsequently, the focus of the structural reform agenda had to be sharpened, concentrating on rehabilitating the core banking system, strengthening the social safety net, and restructuring corporate debt in the context of improved governance both of the corporate sector and of the country more generally.

Inevitably, the question arises whether the reform strategy, especially in the Asian countries, was appropriate. One view holds that it is wrong to start restructuring financial institutions and strengthening the regulatory framework in the midst of a crisis. Specifically, it is argued that the hasty closure of financial institutions weakens confidence, while tightening regulatory standards worsens the credit crunch. On this view, governments should have tried to buttress confidence through unconditional liquidity support, and should have started dealing with the underlying problems only once a degree of calm in the financial markets had been achieved. In fact, the introduction or enforcement of capital adequacy requirements (CARs) was phased in; in Korea and Thailand, 8 percent CAR standards were already in place, but loan classification and loan loss provisioning standards were relatively lax. Classification rules were tightened in two steps in Korea; while in Thailand, the implementation of stricter loan classification began only in mid-1998 (to be completed over the next year and half). In Indonesia, loan classification and provisioning was tightened in October 1998; at the same time, CARs were temporarily lowered. But there is still a question of whether a slower pace of reform would have been better.

Although it is difficult to prove the counterfactual, putting off financial restructuring until quieter times was probably not a realistic option. In the absence of immediate actions to assess and address the weakness in the balance sheets of financial institu-

[93]Anne Krueger and Aaron Tornell (1999) note on pp. 28–34 that "a major lesson from Mexico is that . . . delay (in cleaning up the bank's portfolios) is likely both to prevent recovery . . . and to lead to an even larger problem."

[94]See, for instance, Feldstein (1998) and Goldstein (2001).

[95]Lindgren and others (1999) provide a detailed discussion of the various financial sector reform strategies adopted in the Asian crisis countries.

[96]For instance, among the ancillary measures (that were not subject to formal conditionality), the Thai program envisaged "allow[ing] Thai citizens married to foreigners to own land" as part of the market opening effort. In a similar vein, the Korean program included measures on import liberalization ("phase out the Import Diversification Program, currently covering 16 items"). It should be noted, however, that the total number of measures that were largely irrelevant to the present crises was very small.

[97]At the start of the Indonesian program, 16 small banks were closed. Although their closure was needed, depositors were left with concerns that they might not be adequately protected in the event that other nonviable institutions were subsequently closed.

Box 5.5. Structural Measures in IMF-Supported Programs in the Asian Crisis Countries

The Asian capital account crisis programs were notable for their much greater structural content than those in Latin America and Turkey.

Thailand

In Thailand, owing to weak supervision and prudential regulation, together with a sharp decline in asset prices, the share of nonperforming loans more than doubled between end-1996 and March 1997. The national authorities soon recognized that many, if not most, Thai finance companies were insolvent or at least severely undercapitalized. The reform strategy consisted of closing bankrupt institutions, issuing a blanket deposit guarantee to calm markets, and eventual restructuring and rehabilitating of Thai financial institutions with the establishment of the Financial Sector Restructuring Agency. Financial sector reform was the centerpiece of the IMF-supported program, with several structural performance criteria, including: preventing deposit interest rate competition by insolvent banks; provision for taking over non-viable institutions; introduction of new loan classification rules; and, subsequently, on closing insolvent banks, and fully recapitalizing undercapitalized institutions in the course of 1998.

By the Second Review of the IMF program, in early 1998, it was clear that this ambitious timetable was not achievable. In particular, financial institutions were having difficulty raising sufficient capital and the legal system was incapable of speedy treatment of bankrupt cases. The program was therefore broadened to include strengthening of the legal and judicial system, and two new performance criteria—on introduction of new loan classification and provisioning guidelines, and on the signature of Memoranda of Understandings with all financial institutions regarding their recapitalization plans.

Subsequent reviews resulted in further broadening of the structural reform agenda, particularly in corporate sector restructuring and privatization procedures, bank consolidation, and a variety of legal issues. The critical mass of measures was implemented by end-1998, and by early-1999, bolstered by the pick-up in economic activity, major banks had begun the process of their recapitalization. Moreover, the simplification of legal procedures allowed for fast progress in resolving corporate sector insolvencies.

Korea

In Korea, banks' excessive exposure to the weakening *chaebols* (industrial conglomerates), their reliance on short-term foreign borrowing, and poor prudential regulation and supervision all made the economy vulnerable to a shift in sentiment following the Thai crisis.

The IMF-supported program, approved in late 1997, focused on financial sector restructuring, corporate governance, and capital account liberalization—as well as labor market reforms and trade liberalization. As in Thailand, it soon became clear that the original program underestimated the initial crisis and its implementation schedule was too ambitious. By the time of the First Quarterly Review, an agreement with foreign creditor banks had been reached, allowing the program to focus on addressing underlying structural weaknesses. Foremost was the need for bank restructuring and recapitalization, and the improvement of prudential supervision and regulation. The capital account was liberalized, mainly to remove distortions that had promoted short-term, unhedged foreign borrowing and to allow greater foreign participation in Korean financial markets.

Structural components of the program were further modified at the Second and Third Reviews, although their main thrust remained similar (the IMF paid special attention to the reform of commercial banks, while the World Bank focused on corporate sector restructuring). In light of the greater-than-expected economic downturn, the social safety net also received greater prominence. By early 1999, with the recovery well under way; short-term structural measures—such as the first phase of bank and corporate sector restructuring—had been undertaken. A number of longer-term measures (including bank restructuring that required substantial financial injections, and institution-building) still remained outstanding, however.

Indonesia

In Indonesia, major structural weaknesses centered on excessive regulation in domestic trade, banks were saddled with nonperforming loans, and large, unhedged borrowing in foreign currency. As in other Asian countries, the growth of nonperforming loans was caused by rapid expansion of the financial sector, poor supervision and regulation, unrestricted "connected-lending," and excessive property sector exposure. However, the extent of problem loans was difficult to assess because of non-transparent ownership and cross-holdings of equity and loans.

The original program, approved in early November 1997, and intended mainly as a precaution against contagion, sought to reform the financial sector and deregulate the economy more generally. Financial sector goals included transparent bank rehabilitation through the budget, revision of prudential regulations, and elimination of restrictions on bank lending. Deregulation of the economy was to be achieved by eliminating import and marketing monopolies and the expansion of activities open to foreign participation. To this end, a plethora of performance criteria and benchmarks were established, mostly dealing with state owned banks, tariff reduction, and increases in utility prices.

By the time of the First Review in April 1998, the state of the banking system had deteriorated dramatically, as markets concluded that the authorities were

Box 5.5 *(concluded)*

not genuinely committed to undertaking reforms, and confusion about the coverage of deposit insurance resulted in widespread runs even on solvent banks. A three-tiered approach to the banking crisis was adopted: blanket deposit insurance for two years; establishment of the Indonesian Bank Restructuring Agency; and the proposal of a framework for corporate restructuring. These steps, the thrust of which was basically unchanged from the original program, were detailed in a series of prior actions, performance criteria, and structural benchmarks. In addition, to help offset some of the price effects of the proposed structural reforms, the social safety net was strengthened.

Political uncertainty and program delays eroded confidence further; the exchange rate plummeted in mid-1998, partly because the announcement effects of the external debt restructuring under the Frankfurt agreement had short-lived benefits, and the crisis was reaching calamitous proportions. Although the longer-term goals of the program remained much the same, the immediate focus shifted to rehabilitating the core banking system and providing a social safety net.

The initial focus of the Extended Arrangement, approved in August 1998, was bank restructuring, social safety net issues, and corporate governance. By the time of the Second Review in October 1998, some progress in bank restructuring had been achieved, although estimates of the costs had risen to about 30 percent of GDP, while other reforms continued to lag.

By mid-1999, with a nascent recovery under way, program discussion centered almost exclusively on structural issues. Progress on recapitalization of private banks was encouraging, but losses of the state owned banks—accounting for more than three-quarters of all deposits—continued to mount. Measures in the critical areas of loan classification, asset recovery, and corporate restructuring were still overdue. In the ensuing months, progress was slow.

Philippines

Unlike the other Asian countries, the Philippines already had an IMF arrangement in place at the time of the crisis. While the Extended Arrangement, originally approved in 1994 as a precautionary program, included a number of structural measures, key vulnerabilities in the financial sector—excessive exposure to the property sector, weak prudential regulation, and reliance on short-term foreign currency borrowing—remained unresolved. Fortunately, in contrast to some other countries, the asset bubble was in a relatively early stage. The second, six-month extension of the EFF outlined two main measures for strengthening the banks: exposure to the real estate sector would be limited to 20 percent of banks' portfolios, and the maximum value of real estate collateral was lowered from 70 percent to 60 percent. Foreign exchange exposure risk was limited by requiring that 30 percent of the value of foreign liabilities be kept in short-term liquid assets. The subsequent stand-by arrangement sought to strengthen financial sector supervision and prudential regulation.

tions, unconditional liquidity support or comprehensive guarantees would have created enormous moral hazard, and likely would have resulted in further deterioration in balance sheets. In the case of Mexico, it is at least plausible that an earlier resolution of the banking system problems would have lowered the ultimate cost of financial sector restructuring. Moreover, as the experience in Indonesia illustrates, massive liquidity support would have been difficult to sterilize, resulting in a loss of monetary control. Finally, given that at least the broad dimensions of the problems in the financial system were well known, the failure to act at an early stage would have raised doubts about the governments' resolve to deal with the underlying problems—and this would likely have weakened confidence at home and abroad.

In turn, financial sector restructuring and dealing with problem loans often required corresponding changes in the corporate sector and, in some instance, reforms of the labor market (Korea) and the legal system (Thailand). Nevertheless, in retrospect, it is certainly questionable that all of the measures included in the broad structural reform agendas were critical to the program. Striking the right balance is a difficult task, particularly in capital account crises where the rather nebulous concept of "restoring confidence" is so critical to the program's success. The issue is being examined, however, in the context of the IMF's review of structural conditionality. The main lesson seems to be that, like fiscal and monetary policies, structural reforms should be directed at specific weaknesses of the economy—and not simply at "restoring confidence" in general.

VI Conclusions

The capital account crises in emerging markets confronted both the affected countries and the IMF with a new set of challenges. The central feature of all these crises was the rapid reversal of capital inflows, bringing about a large and abrupt current account adjustment with pervasive macroeconomic consequences. This presented a striking contrast to the typical situation in which countries turn to the IMF for support, in which macroeconomic imbalances associated with policy slippages result in a more gradual deterioration on the external side, and these imbalances are corrected gradually as policies are adjusted.

Although the reversal of capital outflows was a common feature of all the crises, the factors that account for the reversals differed, and these factors needed to be reflected in the policy response. To varying degrees, concerns about the sustainability of precrisis exchange rate pegs (either formal or de facto) played a role, but the changes in market sentiment that precipitated the reversals were ultimately rooted in the growing evidence of underlying vulnerabilities in public or private sector balance sheets. In the Asian crisis countries, vulnerabilities were rooted in the financial and corporate sectors, associated with the interaction of unhedged foreign currency exposures, maturity mismatches, and asset price bubbles. In Mexico, the risky public debt management strategy was of central importance. In Turkey and Brazil, fiscal policy faced an uphill battle against adverse public debt dynamics. In addition, in all cases, political uncertainties played a role, in part because they undermined confidence that the authorities would be able to tackle the underlying problems.

Once they started, these capital account crises displayed very distinctive patterns of macroeconomic events—which differed from those of other countries that have turned to the IMF for support. The reversal of capital flows was typically abrupt, and was associated with wide overshooting of the exchange rate. In many cases, dynamic instability associated with self-reinforcing processes came into play: for instance, in Asia, given the unhedged foreign currency exposures, currency depreciation generated widespread insolvency that further undermined confidence and led to more currency depreciation. The crises generally had large effects on economic activity: the recessions were in most cases associated with a collapse of private domestic demand, but there is also evidence, at least initially, of major supply-side effects—attributable, among other things, to the drying up of financing for imported inputs. In most cases, the recessions turned out much more severe than predicted, reflecting the larger-than-anticipated capital outflows—suggesting that beyond a confluence of exceptional factors in each case, the catalytic effect of official financing, on which the programs were predicated, was systematically over estimated. At least in some cases, the recovery of spontaneous market access, bringing reserve accumulation, a recovery in exchange rates, and an easing of the current account, has typically also been relatively swift.

Given the nature of these crises, the principal objective of the IMF-supported programs was to stem the capital outflows and mitigate their effects by addressing the vulnerabilities that had triggered the adverse market reactions and putting in place adequate financing. Macroeconomic policies played an important role, but only to the extent that they could contribute to this. In a setting where macroeconomic imbalances were typically not the root cause of the crisis, the traditional financial programming approach, with its emphasis on the correction of monetized deficits, had relatively little mileage in determining the policy response.

This basic logic was reflected in several aspects of the programs that were implemented—but in each case, there are questions of whether it was reflected enough:

- The financing packages were exceptionally large by international standards. They were also exceptionally front-loaded, particularly after December 1997 when the Supplemental Reserve Facility (SRF) was created. The size and front-loading sacrificed some policy conditionality for availability to deal with market forces. This made sense under the circumstances: large financing available up front was essential in restoring confidence and mitigating the effects of the outflows. But the amounts actually available, especially at the early stages of the programs, were nonetheless in most cases small in relation to the total commitments or to the actual (let alone potential) capital outflows.

- Attempts at private sector involvement—moral suasion by creditor central banks, agreements among major bank creditors, de facto standstills—were generally modest. Moreover, in most cases, concerted private sector involvement was eschewed at the outset on the grounds that it might exacerbate capital outflows, as well as concerns about possible contagion. In Korea the introduction of private sector involvement was a turning point, setting the stage for recovering stability in the markets, although the direct impact on the capital account was small in relation to overall capital flows.

- Structural reforms were an essential part of the solution in many of these cases. The main purpose of these reforms was to address the vulnerabilities that had contributed to the shift in market sentiment. In the Asian crisis countries, the programs sought both to address the financial system weaknesses that were at the heart of the crisis and to clean up the wreckage of insolvency that had resulted from the exchange rate and interest rate movements associated with the crisis itself. In Mexico, reforms were needed to restore the health of the banking system, although they were not included in the IMF-supported program and were mainly addressed with the help of bilateral assistance. In Brazil, the primary objective of structural reform was to underpin fiscal sustainability—and, indeed, doubts about the authorities' commitment to undertake these reforms was a major reason for the loss of market confidence. But, notably in the case of Indonesia, the structural reform agendas were not sufficiently well focused, especially in the early stages of the crisis.

- Given the large exchange rate movements associated with these crises, which significantly overshot any reasonable estimate of equilibrium levels, monetary policy faced a challenge of maintaining or regaining nominal stability. Monetary policies were thus tightened at some stages in all of these cases, but in many cases with significant hesitation. (In the case of Indonesia, monetary tightening was preceded by a period of several months of unbridled money and credit expansion with deeply negative real interest rates, in the context of a collapsing banking system.) Once monetary policy was tightened in a determined way, market conditions stabilized, and the period of high real interest rates was typically short-lived; nominal stability was preserved or restored. But at the same time, in most of these crises, monetary policies were handicapped by the loss of a nominal anchor, as they were driven off a previous exchange rate peg: Brazil responded by introducing formal inflation targeting soon after floating the real, but in other cases the authorities relied on a less formal price stability objective.

- Fiscal policies played a different role in different countries. In some cases—such as in Brazil, Argentina, and Turkey—establishing fiscal sustainability in the face of adverse debt dynamics or a fragile public debt structure was essential to build confidence. In other cases, notably the Asian crisis countries, fiscal sustainability was not a major issue, and efforts at fiscal adjustment (which were short-lived in Indonesia and Korea) were unsuccessful in boosting confidence. Taken together, the evidence suggests that fiscal adjustment is an essential part of the solution if, and only if, fiscal unsustainability is a major part of the problem to begin with. Fiscal adjustment that is unnecessary from a medium-term perspective is unlikely to have a favorable confidence effect. Finally, the macroeconomic analysis in the paper suggests that the crises were characterized by a shifting mix of supply and demand shocks, as balance sheet imbalances worked themselves out; in this setting, the scope for fiscal fine-tuning may be limited.

- Markets proved unforgiving of any lapses in program implementation or policy indecision. In a number of cases, firm political commitment to the reform process crystallized only after initial hesitations resulted in renewed bouts of capital outflows.

In reviewing these crises, it is difficult to see how they could have been managed without considerable pain once they had broken out. The crises were characterized by an over-adjustment of external current accounts in relation to what was needed for any reasonable means of sustainability. This over-adjustment was associated with severe macroeconomic disruptions. To avoid these consequences, substantially more financing—in the form of private sector involvement, official packages, or both—would have been needed. The scope to deliver such financing is quite limited, however. It is difficult to contemplate official financing packages several times the size of recent ones, while extensive work on private sector involvement suggests that, short of draconian measures that could jeopardize a country's market access for years to come, there is no simple way to stop the exit of capital once a crisis breaks. Moreover, even if available financing were abundant, resolving the underlying balance-sheet disequilibria would still involve some dislocation. It would be far better, if at all possible, to address these imbalances before a crisis breaks out. In short, these crises make a compelling case for improving prevention.

Beyond the importance of crisis prevention, the experience of these countries suggests a number of lessons for program design in the context of high capital mobility—such as the appropriate roles for monetary, fiscal, and structural policies. Yet their experience also underscores the difficulty of robust program design when stock imbalances can trigger sudden and massive capital outflows.

The capital account crises that broke in the mid and late-1990s have often been termed the first of the "twenty-first century" crises; no doubt they will not be the last. They posed particular challenges for the provision of financing and for the design of macroeconomic and structural policies. In many cases, they also severely tested the political commitment of the authorities to be resolute in undertaking reforms. Whether their lessons for crisis management and program design have been learned remains to be seen.

Appendix I Country Sample

The sample of programs included as capital account crisis programs consists of:

	Arrangement	Original Program Length (In months)
Argentina (1995)[1]	EFF	12
Brazil (1998)	Stand-by	36
Indonesia (1997)	Stand-by	36
Korea (1997)	Stand-by	36
Mexico (1995)	Stand-by	18
Philippines (1997)[2]	EFF	6
Thailand (1997)	Stand-by	34
Turkey (1994)	Stand-by	14

[1]Extension of the EFF originally approved in 1992.
[2]Extension of the EFF originally approved in 1994.

In the main report, reference is also made to a sample of "other" program countries. This sample consists of the following programs:

	Arrangement	Original Program Length (In months)
Algeria (1994)	Stand-by	12
Barbados (1992)	Stand-by	16
Belarus (1996)	Stand-by	12
Brazil (1992)	Stand-by	19
Bulgaria (1994)	Stand-by	12
Cameroon (1994)	Stand-by	18
Central African Republic (1994)	Stand-by	12
Chad (1994)	Stand-by	12
Dominican Republic (1993)	Stand-by	9
Ecuador (1994)	Stand-by	25
Gabon (1994)	Stand-by	12
Hungary (1993)	Stand-by	15
India (1992)	Stand-by	20
Jamaica (1991)	Stand-by	12
Jordan (1992)	Stand-by	18

	Arrangement	Original Program Length (In months)
Lithuania (1995)	EFF	36
Malawi (1995)	Stand-by	7
Moldova (1995)	Stand-by	12
Niger (1994)	Stand-by	12
Panama (1992)	Stand-by	22
Pakistan (1994)	EFF	36
Papua New Guinea (1995)	Stand-by	18
Peru (1996)	EFF	33
Poland (1991)	EFF	36
Romania (1997)	Stand-by	13
Russia (1995)	Stand-by	12
Ukraine (1995)	Stand-by	12
Uruguay (1992)	Stand-by	12
Vietnam (1994)	Stand-by	12
Republic of Yemen (1996)	Stand-by	15

Appendix II Financial Fragilities and Official Financing

It has often been asserted that the capital account crises of the 1990s constituted largely unexpected events. With the benefit of hindsight, however, there is now some evidence suggesting that, at least to some extent, the buildup of the financial vulnerabilities that made these crises possible reflected the consequences of a critical decision made by each of the governments of the countries affected: to finance, rather than adjust to, the effects of an exogenous shock through external borrowing or a rundown of international reserves. If this was indeed the case, an important question arises: Were countries that waited too long before acknowledging the need for adjustment and thus exposed their countries to a potential capital account crisis of a larger magnitude, rewarded with larger official aid packages?[98] In order to address this issue, this appendix provides an analysis of the behavior of two simple indicators of vulnerability, to determine whether they exhibit any clear trends in the run-up to the crises. The results of this analysis are then related to the size of the official packages granted to each of these countries.

The first of the two indicators examined below is a currency crisis index, which intends to measure exchange market pressures. This index is a weighted average of cumulative reserve losses and exchange rate depreciation, measured from a fixed starting point. The weights are given by the inverse of the variances of these two variables over a relatively long period.[99] The second indicator, the ratio of international reserves to short-term debt, is a measure of financial fragility, which has been found to be a key determinant of liquidity and currency crises in recent theoretical work (i.e., Chang and Velasco, 1998) and has been found to be highly correlated with the probability of capital account crisis in empirical studies. It is important to stress here that the focus of the analysis is not on the systematic ability of these indices to forecast a crisis. Instead, this appendix provides an ex post analysis (particularly since some of the data used to construct these indices were not available at the time of the crises) of the indices for each country, with the purpose of detecting any trends prior to the crisis, which may be interpreted as an indication of specific policy actions pursued by the governments involved.

Figures A2.1 and A2.2 show the behavior of the two vulnerability indices over a five-year span: four years prior to the countries' adoption of IMF programs and one year after.[100] By construction, the specific values taken on by the exchange market pressure index shown in Figure A2.1 are not very meaningful, but increases in the index reflect downward pressures on the exchange rate (i.e., losses of reserves or a depreciation of the national currency).[101] Specific values aside, it was possible to detect a steady increase in the index for at least six months prior to the adoption of IMF programs in three countries: Brazil, Mexico (where the index increases significantly for about a year prior to the program, with the exception of a single month: October 1994), and Thailand (where the index increases for nine consecutive months prior to the program).[102] Despite not representing a strict case

[98]The assumption here is, of course, that some unobservable "shock" hit these economies at some point before the crises, triggering a policy response from the national authorities. Traditionally, the perceived nature of the shock would dictate the optimal response: if it was temporary, it should be financed; if it was permanent, it should lead to adjustment. However, the applicability of this framework to a world of capital mobility and imperfect information has been questioned by Frankel (1999).

[99]This is the methodology employed by Sachs, Tornell, and Velasco (1995) in their analysis of the global effects of the Mexican financial crisis.

[100]The exchange market pressure index is available on monthly frequency, and the financial fragility index on a quarterly basis. In the latter case, the "program date" represents the actual quarter during which the program took place.

[101]In particular, in the case of Argentina, the estimated weights used in the construction of the index are extremely skewed, with exchange rate movements receiving a weight of more than 99 percent (reflecting the fact that the fluctuations in the peso/dollar exchange rate have been minimal during the period 1990–99). As a result, the index moves within a significantly smaller range of values than in the other countries.

[102]In the cases of Mexico and Thailand, these results are consistent with well-documented attempts by these countries to prevent initial capital outflows to be reflected in monetary contractions, which led to further losses in foreign reserves. See, for example, Fane and McLeod (1999) for Thailand; and Sachs, Tornell, and Velasco (1996), and Calvo and Mendoza (1996) for Mexico. In contrast, in Brazil, reserve losses were not sterilized and interbank rates rose significantly.

Figure A2.1. Crisis Index[1]

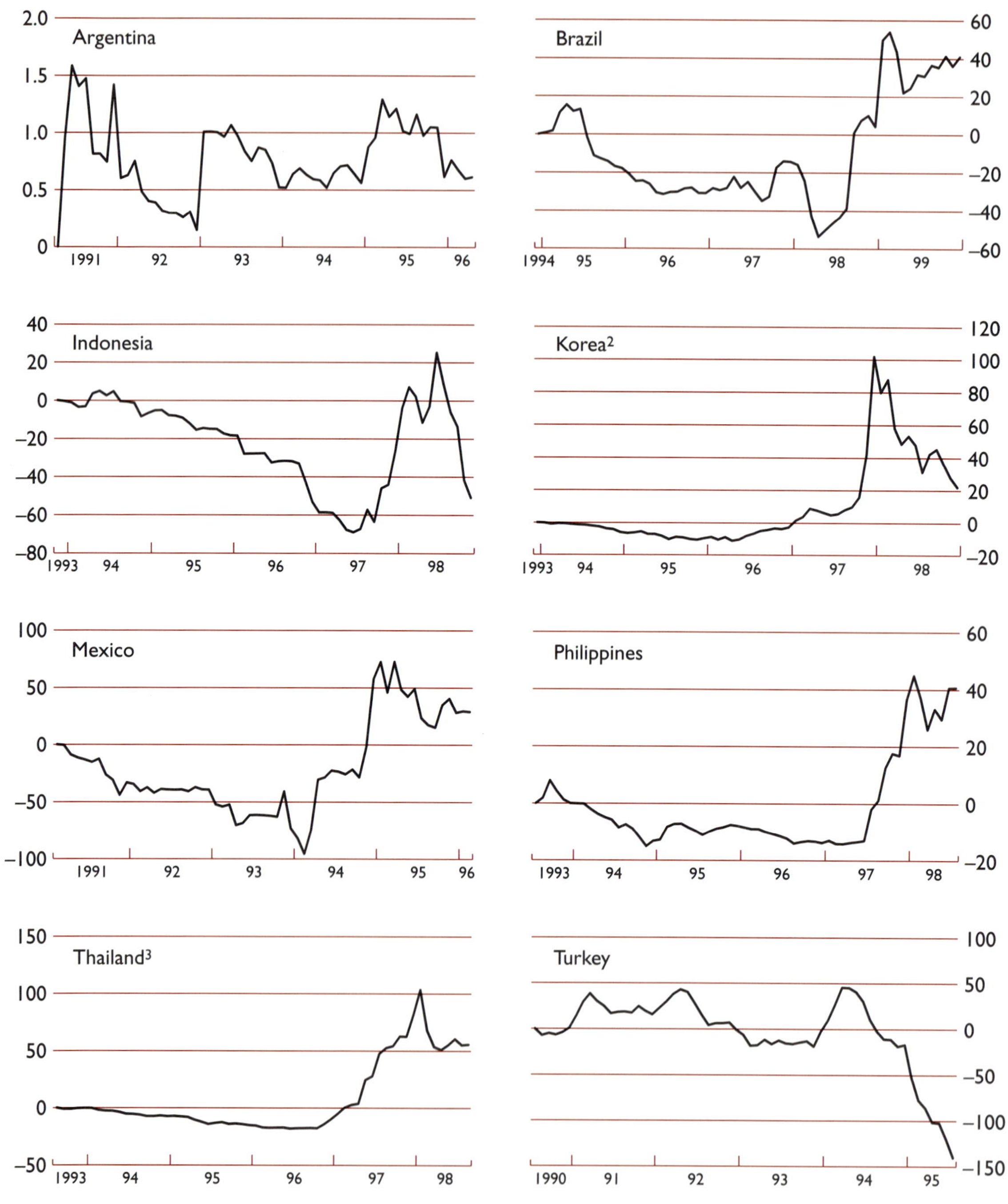

Sources: IMF, *International Financial Statistics*; national sources; and IMF staff estimates.

[1]Weighted average of (i) the cumulative percentage change in the level of gross reserves (with a negative sign) and (ii) the exchange rate, beginning four years before the adoption of the IMF program under study. The weights used were the precision of each of the series (computed over the period January 1991–December 1999) divided by the sum of the precisions. This methodology follows Sachs, Tornell, and Velasco (1996).

[2]Reserves are net of deposits at foreign branches of local banks.

[3]Reserves are net of forward operations of the Central Bank of Thailand.

Figure A2.2. Indicators of International Liquidity

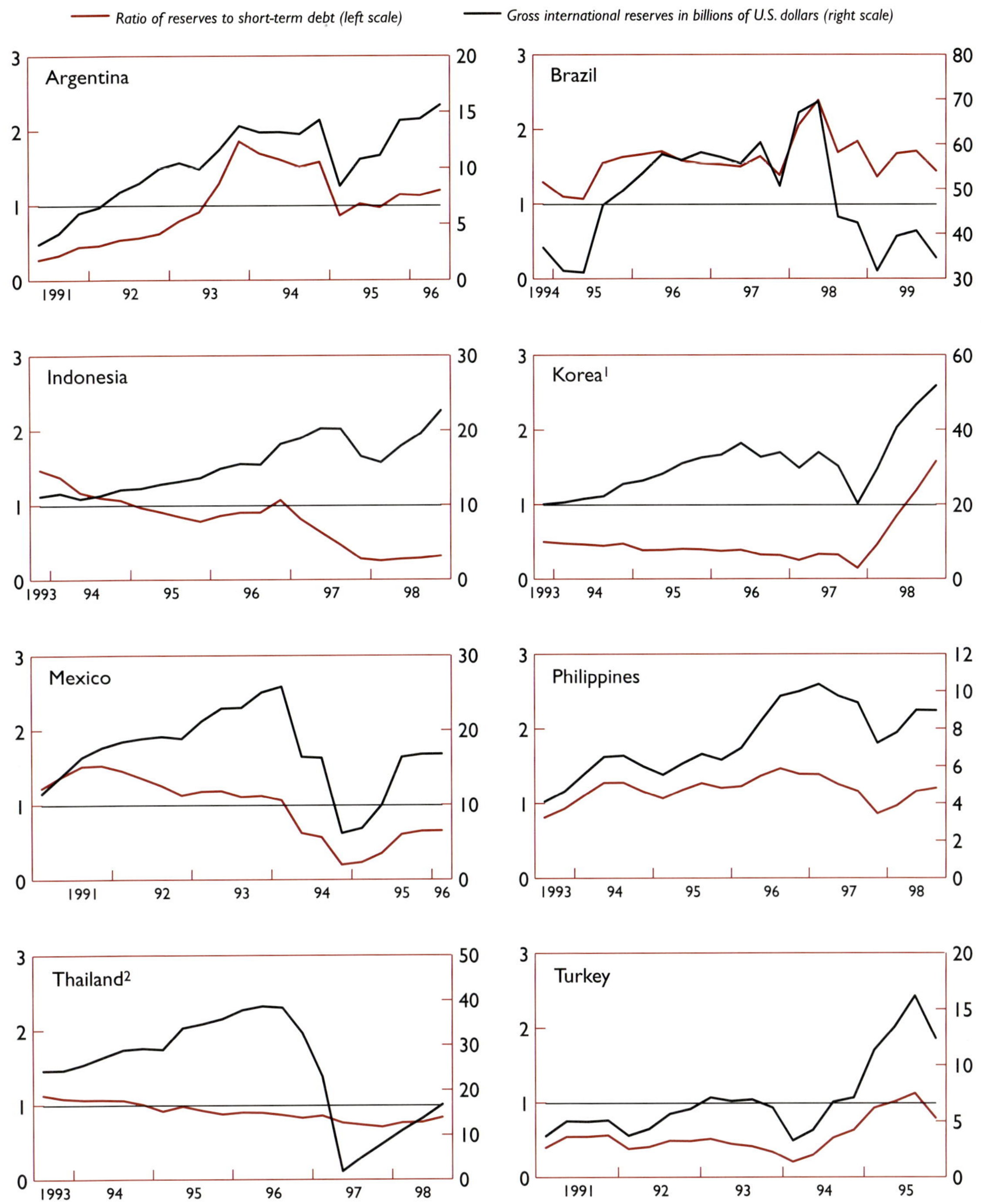

Sources: IMF, *International Financial Statistics* and *World Economic Outlook* database; national sources; and IMF staff estimates.
[1]Reserves exclude deposits at overseas branches and subsidiaries of domestic banks.
[2]Reserves are net of forward operations of the Central Bank of Thailand.

of a six-month deterioration in the pressure index, one could add Turkey to the list (the index deteriorates steadily only between November 1993 and April 1994, and improves for three months prior to the adoption of the program). In that case, the deterioration in the index coincides with a drastic and well-documented change in policy regime that the literature has identified as a key determinant of the currency crisis of April 1994: a switch in the source of financing of Turkey's large fiscal imbalance, from bonds to money creation, which led to a reduction in domestic interest rates and a depletion of reserves, as predicted by the "first generation" of currency crises models.[103] In the other four countries, the deterioration in the pressure index is either less protracted (Argentina and Korea) or both less protracted and less pronounced (Indonesia and the Philippines).

Notably, of the four countries for which a steady deterioration of the pressure index was detected (including the case of Turkey), all except Brazil have been usually regarded in the literature as cases where the crises were, in some way, self-inflicted rather than the result of contagion.[104] The crises in Turkey, Mexico, and Thailand certainly did not come in the aftermath of other currency crises in emerging markets and, moreover, the Mexican and Thai crises have been identified as the sources of regional contagion, as currencies in neighboring countries came under heavy pressure almost immediately after the peso and the baht were allowed to float. The Brazilian currency may have been ripe for a currency crisis during 1998 as a result of the cumulative effect of inconsistent policies over a relatively long period of time, as was discussed in Chapter II (more on this below). However, it would be difficult to ignore the possibility that the stability of the real may have been threatened also by external pressures stemming from Asia and, subsequently, from the Russian crisis of August 1998. On the other hand, the other four countries for which no steady deterioration in the index was found have been typically considered victims of contagion: Argentina, as a result of the Mexican crisis, and Indonesia, Korea, and the Philippines, following the Thai crisis (see, for example, Edwards, 2000).[105]

Figure A2.2 shows the ratio of gross international reserves to short-term debt, an indicator of a country's international liquidity. (Figure A2.2 also shows the evolution of reserves in billions of dollars.[106]) As mentioned earlier, this index is intended to capture a different dimension of the dynamics leading to currency crises (the vulnerability to financial panic) and, therefore, it provides information not contained in the exchange rate market pressure index. Not surprisingly, the evolution of this index tells a very different story from that obtained from Figure A2.1.

In the case of the reserves-to-short-term-debt ratio, there would seem to be a natural numerical benchmark (one) against which one could compare the value of the index at different points in time, although, in practice, this is far from a settled issue.[107] Despite its shortcomings, however, the evolution of this index reveals some distinctive patterns. There is a first group of countries (Korea and Turkey) for which the index stayed consistently and significantly below one during the four years prior to the crisis. There is a second group of countries (Indonesia, Mexico, and Thailand) for which the index stayed in the neighborhood of one for a relatively long period of time (at least two years) and then dropped significantly below one exactly three quarters prior to the adoption of an IMF program. Finally, there is a third group of countries where the index either (i) never dropped below one prior to the adoption of an IMF program (Brazil and the Philippines) or (ii) dropped slightly below one, but only briefly at the time of the crisis (Argentina).

To the extent that one can associate financial fragility and thus the potential for financial panic with situations in which the index fell below one for more than a single quarter, the analysis of the previous paragraph would seem to suggest that, irrespective of the quality of their other policies, Turkey and Korea had been in a danger zone for several years prior to their crises. Indonesia, Mexico, and Thailand seem to have been on the edge of the danger zone for quite a while, before clearly entering it and remaining there for a full three quarters before they

[103]For a description of the change in regime mentioned above and the motives behind it, see, for example, Agénor, McDermott, and Üçer (1997); Üçer, Van Rijckeghem, and Yolalan (1998); and Özatay (2000).

[104]This is not to say that the final trigger of the crises in those countries may have involved some form of self-fulfilling prophecy. But the fact remains that, according to the index examined above, the exchange rates of those countries were under pressure for several months before a crisis erupted and they agreed to a program with the IMF.

[105]Again, there is no presumption in this statement to the effect that these victims of contagion were "innocent" victims, as their vulnerability to contagion may have also resulted from the pursuit of inconsistent policies.

[106]Data on gross reserves were available on a quarterly basis, but data on short-term debt were interpolated from annual data extracted from the IMF *World Economic Outlook* database. Reserves were netted out of forward operations by the central bank in the case of Thailand, and central bank deposits at foreign branches of local banks in Korea's case.

[107]Although a ratio of one emerges as a straightforward benchmark because it reflects complete reserve coverage of short-term debt, there is no economic reason to set one as a policy target for such a ratio. Not only is short-term debt an incomplete measure of a country's gross borrowing needs, but the determination of a specific "critical" threshold for any measure of financial fragility is essentially an empirical matter.

adopted an IMF program. Although in Mexico and Thailand the drop in the index seems to be driven by a fall in reserves, suggesting that their central banks were actively engaged in defending their currencies through intervention in the foreign exchange market, in Indonesia the drop in the index reflects entirely a buildup of short-term debt, as foreign exchange reserves were actually rising.[108] In the absence of a more complete analysis of these countries' other macroeconomic and structural policies, it is hard to determine the extent to which having the index staying close to one (as opposed to significantly above one) may in itself have reflected a potentially dangerous situation. This would imply that, like Turkey and Korea, this group of countries also spent several years in a financially dangerous zone, before experiencing their crises.

Finally, neither Brazil nor the Philippines appears to have been near the danger zone, while in Argentina the temporary drop in the index reflects the effects of the crisis itself, and the authorities' willingness to allow the automatic adjustment mechanism built in their currency board arrangement to operate. Nonetheless, it must be stressed that even though Brazil did not enter the danger zone until after the program with the IMF was signed, it experienced a large loss in gross reserves (over $30 billion, or nearly one-half of its holdings, between February and November of 1999) and a strong, albeit less dramatic, fall in the reserves-to-short-term-debt ratio, as capital outflows during the period caused some reduction in the stock of short-term debt.

Based on the analysis presented so far, it would appear safe to say that, prior to the adoption of an IMF program, three of the countries in our sample (Mexico, Thailand, and Turkey) were subject to strong exchange rate market pressures, while being in a financially dangerous zone and exhibiting an increasing degree of financial fragility (as a result of deliberate intervention in foreign exchange markets) for at least half a year. Although Korea clearly stayed in the financially dangerous zone for a long time, Korea's case is somewhat different in that it appears to have experienced exchange market pressures (including a sizable loss of reserves) over a shorter period of time in the run-up to its crisis. Brazil experienced exchange rate pressures and loss of a significant amount of reserves over a period of at least six months, but it did so while still preserving a relatively safe degree of reserve coverage of its short-term debt. The indices provide much weaker evidence that the other countries (Argentina, Indonesia, and the Philippines) engaged in a systematic policy of deferring adjustment over a protracted period in the face of an adverse external shock.

Given these results, and the analysis of the official financing provided to the crisis countries in Chapter III, there does not appear to be a clear correlation between the size of the official packages and the extent to which the countries may have been attempting to defer an unavoidable adjustment in domestic policies. Although the Mexican package was among the largest on the basis of various benchmarks, the Thai and Turkish packages were small relative to the others, especially in relation to short-term debt. There is no clear pattern either in the case of the countries that did not try to postpone adjustment for a relatively long time: Indonesia's package was among the largest according to most measures except short-term debt, while the Argentine and Philippine programs were small. The Brazilian and Korean packages were on the large side but were not among the largest two. In other words, this appendix does not find empirical evidence in favor of the hypothesis that countries that may have engaged in a systematic postponement of adjustment were rewarded by larger official packages in the context of IMF programs.

[108]Notably, in all of these cases, public information about the current evolution of usable reserves (Mexico and Thailand) and short-term debt (Indonesia) was limited, a fact that may have prevented these countries' crises from having erupted earlier.

Appendix III Calculation of Fiscal Sustainability and Fiscal Impulse Ratios

Medium-Term Sustainability

In the text, "medium-term sustainable" fiscal balances are reported. These are the primary balances which, *given historical growth and interest rates*, are sufficient to stabilize the initial public debt ratio. Even if the primary balance equals this "medium-term sustainable balance," the actual debt-to-GDP ratio is likely to rise for at least two reasons. First, during a currency crisis, real GDP growth is likely to be lower, and real interest rates higher, than their historical norms. Second, there may be financial sector restructuring costs which explicitly or implicitly add to the stock of public debt. In the text, the estimated *carry costs* of financial sector restructuring are reported separately.[109] (Conversely, however, there may be privatization receipts that lower the stock of public debt.) Finally, it bears emphasizing that, since the calculations embody a number of underlying assumptions, they should be considered indicative rather than precise estimates.

In general, the widest concept of public sector for which there are available time series data on primary balances and domestic and external debt was used in the calculations. These correspond to:

- Argentina: Consolidated public sector
- Brazil: Public sector (federal, state, and public sector enterprises)
- Mexico: Nonfinancial public sector
- Turkey: Overall public sector (consolidated budget, local authorities, state economic enterprises)
- Indonesia: Central government
- Korea: Consolidated central government
- Philippines: National government
- Thailand: Consolidated nonfinancial public sector.

[109]Thus, abstracting from variations in interest rates and GDP growth rates, a primary balance equal to the "medium-term sustainable balance" plus the carry costs of financial sector restructuring would be consistent with stabilizing the public debt ratio at the higher level of debt (i.e., inclusive of the financial sector restructuring costs).

In undertaking the calculations, three-year backward averages are used for GDP growth and interest rates.[110] The estimated medium-term primary surplus at the year-end closest to the program approval date is reported in the text.

Annual and Quarterly Fiscal Impulse

The text reports programmed and actual annual fiscal impulses.

Programmed Fiscal Impulse

The programmed fiscal impulses are based on the original program projection of revenues and expenditures for the following concepts:

- Argentina: Consolidated public sector overall balance
- Brazil: Public sector (federal, state, and public sector enterprises) borrowing requirement
- Mexico: Nonfinancial public sector overall balance
- Turkey: Central government overall balance, cash basis
- Indonesia: Central government overall balance
- Korea: Consolidated central government overall balance
- Philippines: National government overall balance
- Thailand: Central government overall balance

An HP-filter is fitted for the log of real GDP using annual data from 1980 through year t–1, to calculate potential output which, particularly for the Asian countries, differs significantly from the full sample

[110]Effective interest rates are computed as the ratio of interest payments on the average stock of debt. For the Latin American countries (and Turkey), explicit monetary corrections are used; these are not available for the Asian countries (where, in any case, preprogram inflation rates were generally much lower). This implies that (for the Asian countries), the required "medium-term sustainable" primary surplus could be even lower than those reported.

Table A3.1. Primary Fiscal Balances and Fiscal Impulse Ratios: Programs versus Outcomes

	Program					Actual				
	Real GDP	Primary balance	Cyclically neutral balance	Fiscal stance	Fiscal impulse	Real GDP	Primary balance	Cyclically neutral balance	Fiscal stance	Fiscal impulse
	(Percent change)	(As percent of GDP)				(Percent change)	(As percent of GDP)			
Argentina (1995)	2.0	2.1	2.4	0.3	–1.6	–2.8	0.1	1.1	1.0	–0.2
Brazil (1999)[1]	–1.0	1.8	–0.2	–2.0	–2.0	0.8	2.5	0.3	–2.2	–2.2
Indonesia (1998)[1]	5.0	2.3	0.0	–2.3	–0.7	–13.1	1.1	–1.3	–2.4	–2.0
Korea (1998)[1]	2.5	1.8	–1.3	–3.1	–2.8	–6.7	–3.1	–1.5	1.6	0.6
Mexico (1995)	1.5	3.4	–2.5	–5.9	–1.1	–6.2	4.4	–4.5	–8.9	–4.5
Philippines (1998)[1]	5.1	4.2	4.8	0.6	–0.7	–0.6	2.1	3.8	1.7	0.5
Thailand (1998)[1]	3.5	1.2	–0.1	–1.3	–3.1	–10.8	–2.3	0.3	2.6	–1.3
Turkey (1994)	–1.6	6.4	–2.7	–9.1	–9.3	–4.7	3.7	–2.8	–6.5	–7.3

Sources: IMF, *World Economic Outlook*; IMF, MONA; and IMF staff estimates.
[1]Dates refer to year *t* (or closest fiscal year), rather than to program approval year.

("actual"). Program projections are also used for real GDP and expenditure and revenue. A base year for the revenue and expenditure ratios, r^0 and e^0 is chosen such that the absolute value of the output gap is small. As a percent of GDP, the program fiscal balance is given by $b^p = r^p - e^p$; while the cyclically neutral balance is given by $bc^p = r^0 - e^0(y^{pot}/y^{prog})$ where y^{pot} is potential output based on an HP-filter to log real GDP for the sample 1980 to t–1. The program fiscal stance is then $fs^p = bc^p - b^p$, and the program fiscal impulse is $fi^p = \Delta fs^p$.

Actual Fiscal Impulse

The actual fiscal impulse is calculated in the same way, except that the HP-filter is applied to the entire sample period, 1980–99; actual outcomes are used for the revenue and expenditure ratio: $b^a = r^a - e^a$; and the actual GDP outcome is used for the cyclically neutral balance: $bc^a = r^0 - e^0(y^{pot}/y^a)$, where y^{pot} is potential output based on an HP-filter to log real GDP for the entire sample. Then the actual fiscal stance is $fs^a = bc^a - b^a$, and the actual fiscal impulse is $fi^a = \Delta fs^a$. These are reported in Text Table 5.3, while the corresponding primary balances (i.e., excluding interest reports) are given in Table A3.1 above.

Quarterly Fiscal Impulse

Text Figure 5.1 also reports quarterly fiscal impulses. These are calculated in an analogous fashion, except that the real GDP series is seasonally adjusted using multiplicative *X*–11, and the HP-filter is applied to the logarithm of the seasonally adjusted series to obtain potential output. Rather than choose a single base year, quarter-specific revenue and expenditure base ratios, r_i^0 and $e_i^0 i=1. . ., 4$ are calculated as the average of the quarter-specific revenue and expenditure ratios over the full sample (since, by definition, average potential and actual real GDP should be equal).[111] Quarterly impulses are then defined as the quarter-to-quarter change in the fiscal stance, and graphed against the quarter-to-quarter change in (seasonally adjusted) real GDP. In some cases, a somewhat narrower fiscal concept was used for the quarterly impulses due to data availability limitations.

[111]If a single base period approach were adopted instead, different years might need to be used according to whether actual and potential real GDP were close in that particular quarter.

Appendix IV Vector Autoregression Estimates of Real Money and Real GDP Relationship

The text makes reference to impulse response functions of real GDP growth to real money growth or real credit growth; these are reported in Table A4.1 below.

Table A4.1. Impulse Response Functions[1]

	Impulse Response of Real GDP Growth to 10 Percent Shock to Real Money Growth[2]				Impulse Response of Real GDP Growth to 10 Percent Shock to Real Credit Growth[3]			
	Q1	Q2	Q3	Q4	Q1	Q2	Q3	Q4
Argentina	2.8	1.4	1.1	2.1	1.2	–0.2	–0.7	–0.2
Mexico	0.2	–0.2	0.1	0.0	0.8	–0.1	0.0	–0.2
Turkey	0.2	–0.8	–0.7	2.2	2.9	0.3	0.8	–0.7
Indonesia	0.6	–0.8	–1.7	0.3	–0.1	0.0	–0.7	–1.1
Korea	2.4	2.8	0.4	1.1	2.4	2.3	–0.3	–0.2
Philippines	1.6	–0.4	0.2	0.4	0.9	0.5	0.3	–0.9
Thailand	3.6	3.1	–1.6	–1.1	3.3	–1.4	–2.0	–3.5

Source: IMF staff estimates.

[1]Vector autoregressions with four lags over 1985:1–1999:4, as available.

[2]Assumes 10 percentage point increase in real money growth in the first quarter.

[3]Assumes 10 percentage point increase in real credit growth in the first quarter.

Appendix V Chronologies of Events in Countries' Capital Account Crises

Argentina (1995)

The capital account crisis in Argentina was short-lived, mainly because the banking system was strong enough to withstand a period of high interest rates and because the authorities acted expeditiously.

In 1991, Argentina launched a comprehensive set of reforms aimed at ending a protracted period of high inflation and restructuring its economy in a fundamental way. A key element of the program was the adoption of a currency board through the introduction of the "Convertibility Plan" in March 1991 and the enactment of the necessary supporting legislation. In addition, the government adopted a trade reform; abolished all price controls; deregulated wholesale and retail trade; privatized ports and public utilities; and reformed the financial sector. These efforts were supported initially by a Stand-By Arrangement (SBA) approved in July 1991 and subsequently by a three-year Extended Fund Facility (EFF) approved in March 1992.

Between 1991 and 1994, real GDP growth averaged close to 9 percent, while consumer price inflation declined from hyperinflationary levels to 3.9 percent at end-1994. Growth was driven by a large expansion in demand, particularly in investment, leading to a five-fold increase in imports and a deterioration in the current account, which moved from near balance in 1991 to a deficit of about 4 percent of GDP in 1994. The fiscal accounts recorded a significant improvement through 1993, but worsened in 1994, reflecting the shift of employees' social security contributions to the private pension system and a worsening in the provincial finances. Nonetheless, by end-1994 the magnitude of the fiscal imbalance was not alarming: the overall public sector deficit in 1994 was 2.3 percent of GDP and the public sector debt was 32 percent of GDP.

The reforms also led to a very fast process of remonetization: fueled by rapid growth in bank deposits financed with capital inflows, the M3 monetary aggregate-to-GDP ratio grew from 6 percent in 1990 to 19 percent in 1994. At the same time, bank credit to the private sector rose at an average rate of 12½ percent a year in real terms. Financial deepening was accompanied by improvements in productivity in the banking industry. As part of the reforms carried out since 1991, the government eliminated arrears and restored access to domestic and international capital markets, including through a Paris Club agreement and a Brady Bond restructuring in 1992. Since 1993, the government was able to place long-term notes in domestic and external markets for more than $8 billion (3 percent of GDP).

Through September 1994, Argentina had made all of its scheduled purchases under the EFF on time, but the program went off-track in the second half of 1994, and the Mexican crisis of December 1994 spilled over swiftly into Argentina. Interest rates rose sharply and the Argentine stock and bond markets fell. The pressure continued in early 1995 and, by the end of the first quarter of 1995, the central bank lost one-third of its gross reserves and the domestic deposit base shrank dramatically. The associated liquidity crunch led to another surge in interest rates (the interbank rate peaked at 70 percent), a sharp fall in asset prices (stock and bond prices fell by about one-half from end-1994 to March 1995), and declining profitability of financial institutions.

Contagion from the Mexican financial crises highlighted the fragilities of the 1991 currency board arrangement, particularly the absence of a formal deposit insurance scheme and of a lender of last resort. Despite the limited powers contemplated for it by that law, the central bank announced a series of measures. The central bank accommodated the outflow by gradually lowering reserve requirements on U.S. dollar and peso deposits. In addition, bank deposits in the central bank were dollarized in an attempt to give confidence to the markets and a fund was set up to purchase nonperforming loans of distressed financial institutions. In February, the central bank charter was modified to give the central bank additional powers to assist troubled financial institutions. Despite all these measures, deposit withdrawals and reserve losses continued, and, as a result, the central bank's ratio of reserves to monetary liabilities approached the statutory limit of 80 percent, which effectively eliminated the margin for further central bank support to the financial system.

On March 23, 1995, the authorities provided the details of an IMF-supported adjustment program. The program had two main objectives: first, to reinforce the public finances and demonstrate unequivocally the government's ability to service its maturing obligations and, second, to deal with a fragile financial system in the absence of a lender of last resort, by setting two trust funds to provide resources for restructuring the financial system. The IMF supported the program with an extension of the 1992 three-year EFF to a fourth year, including an augmentation of SDR1,537.1 million (100 percent of quota). Although the program was approved only on April 6, 1995, there was a positive market reaction to its March announcement, when interbank and prime rates fell significantly. Moreover, in April 1995, Argentina was able to place two $1 billion bond issues, with domestic and international investors, respectively.

Despite a reflow of deposits and a continued decline in interest rates during the remainder of 1995, credit to the private sector remained tight as banks struggled to rebuild their liquidity positions and increased lending to the government. This contributed to a significant decline in economic activity, particularly in the second and third quarters of the year. The compression of domestic demand combined with strong external demand led to a quick, albeit small, improvement in the external current account: the deficit narrowed from 3.7 percent of GDP in 1994 to 1.3 percent in 1995. Economic activity bottomed out in the last quarter of 1995, and GDP fell by some 3 percent in 1995.

The thrust of the economic program was maintained throughout 1995. Despite the difficult economic and social situation, the authorities observed the discipline imposed by the currency board arrangement. As a result, by year-end more than 90 percent of deposits withdrawn during the crisis had been recovered, peso and U.S. dollar denominated prime interest rates were close to their pre-crisis levels, and spreads on Argentina's sovereign debt narrowed considerably. Although there was some fiscal underperformance vis-à-vis the IMF targets, a tight fiscal stance was maintained in cyclically adjusted terms. A strong recovery of economic activity followed in 1996–97.

A few characteristics differentiate Argentina from other country cases of capital account crises. First, its banks were healthy prior to the crisis: risk-based capital asset ratios and liquidity ratios were high at 18 percent and 20 percent, respectively. Second, debt management had become a policy priority early in the reform process and the authorities avoided any bunching of amortization payments. Third, crisis management was expeditious and had an immediate and positive impact on market confidence.

Brazil (1997–99)

By the mid-1990s, stabilization programs, including the 1994 *Real Plan*—an exchange rate-based stabilization program—had succeeded in ending Brazil's chronic high inflation. Private capital inflows had picked up, including substantial foreign direct investment and portfolio flows, and the current account deficit had widened. The Brazilian economy did slow down appreciably as contagion from Asia and Russia spread worldwide during 1998. Still, positive growth was registered in 1998, and the 1999 V-shaped recession was mild and short-lived in comparison with the contraction in Mexico during the "tequila crisis"[112] and the experiences of Asia and Russia in the late 1990s.

A variety of factors can explain why Brazil's experience was less painful than those of Mexico, Asia, and Russia. On the face of it, Brazil was vulnerable on many fronts—certainly more so than Mexico in 1994–95. Of greatest concern were Brazil's fiscal and current account deficits, growing public and external indebtedness financed at short maturities, and a rigid and less than fully credible crawling peg exchange rate regime. The public sector continued to be plagued by an expensive and actuarially unbalanced public pension system, excessive government payrolls, and an inefficient taxation system. After an initial primary surplus of 5.3 percent of GDP in 1994, the balance worsened to a deficit of 1 percent of GDP in 1997, financed mostly at short maturities. The fiscal deterioration was accompanied by an appreciation of the real exchange rate by about 20 percent between April 1994 and end-1997. The external current account deficit widened from approximate balance in 1994 to a deficit of 4 percent of GDP in 1997.

Brazil's vulnerabilities became evident following the outbreak of the Asian crisis when reserves fell by nearly $8 billion in October 1997 alone. To stem the outflow of reserves, the central bank doubled interest rates to about 45 percent in October, and the government adopted a fiscal package with an annual yield estimated at about 2½ percent of GDP. The outflow of reserves stopped and capital inflows resumed in the last two months of 1997, reducing the loss of reserves for the year as a whole to $8 billion.

Doubts about the authorities' resolve to implement the previously announced budget cuts in an election year and the presentation of relatively loose budget proposals for 1999, together with the persistence of a substantial current account deficit, signaled that Brazil remained vulnerable to external shocks in the fall of 1998, when the Russian default

[112]The financial crisis that followed the December 1994 devaluation of the Mexican peso.

shook financial markets. In response, the authorities again tightened fiscal and monetary policies—interest rates were raised to 40 percent—to stem the outflow of reserves.

Brazil approached the IMF and other international financial institutions for support at a relatively late stage in November 1998. The Board approved the three-year SBA on December 2, 1998. The program was premised on the notion that confidence would return—and the fixed exchange rate regime could be maintained—through ample official financing and a strong policy package. In view of the imbalances in the public finances, the IMF-supported program had at its core a fiscal package sufficient to stabilize the debt-to-GDP ratio and forestall unsustainable debt dynamics. To this end, the official financing package envisaged under the SBA amounted to $41.8 billion, including $18.1 billion from the IMF.

The early December 1998 agreement had a calming effect on markets and led to easing of the pressures on reserves. Subsequent policy implementation faltered, however, as the central bank reacted to the easing of market pressures by beginning a rapid, premature reduction in interest rates, from 40 percent in November to 29 percent in December. Fiscal policy implementation suffered setbacks as well, aggravating earlier concerns: Congress defeated an important component of the fiscal package in early December and delayed other measures, while the state of Minas Gerais announced that it would not honor its debt to the federal government. As a result, outflows continued as foreign bank creditors refused to roll over their maturing credit lines, and the currency was subject to intense pressures in late 1998 and early 1999. After some interest rate increases and a one-day experiment with a wider band for the currency, the central bank was forced to float the real on January 15, 1999, and to seek to renegotiate and reinforce the IMF-supported program.

The exchange rate regime change required modifications to the monetary framework underpinning Brazil's IMF-supported program. Although these negotiations were under way in early 1999, the central bank continued to lose reserves ($8.5 billion during January–February) as the high interest rate policy proved insufficient in the absence of stronger measures to stem capital outflows. The reserve loss was stemmed in March 1999 following an agreement with the IMF on a revised monetary framework and the bailing-in of foreign creditors. Specifically, Brazil adopted inflation targeting to replace the nominal anchor lost when the exchange rate was allowed to float. A semi-voluntary form of private sector participation was secured when commercial bank creditors agreed in mid-March to maintain their interbank credit lines with Brazilian banks at their end-February level.

The strengthened program was successful in restoring confidence quickly, and the performance of the Brazilian economy in 1999 was significantly better than expected. The central bank was able to gradually reduce interest rates from a peak of 45 percent to 21 percent in mid-July. After an initial period of overshooting, the currency stabilized at around R$1.75 to the U.S. dollar and voluntary capital flows resumed in April. Real GDP grew by slightly less than 1 percent in 1999, in contrast with the 4 percent decline projected originally. The unemployment rate declined slightly, but wage pressures were moderated considerably by slack labor markets, and consumer inflation was moderate in 1999–2000. The fiscal position also improved in 1999, as the program's fiscal targets were met or exceeded. Progress was also registered in structural fiscal reforms, including significant steps in the reform of the social security system.

The authorities followed a policy of relatively clean float, limiting intervention in the foreign exchange market to counter disorderly market conditions. They also met understandings reached with the staff to not reduce interest rates while intervening in the foreign exchange market and to promptly consult with the staff about appropriate policy responses in the event of substantial pressure on net international reserves.

Despite its numerous vulnerabilities, Brazil enjoyed several advantages that are responsible for the soft landing of 1998–99. These advantages included steadily growing inflows of foreign direct investment, large foreign exchange reserves, and a relatively healthy banking system. Judicious policy implementation in the fall of 1997 also seems to have played a role in restoring confidence and averting a full-blown crisis during the initial phase of contagion.

Indonesia (1997–98)

Indonesia demonstrates consequences of an unresolved capital account crisis. Although the country's starting macroeconomic position was probably more favorable than that of other Asian countries, the long-term costs of the crisis have been drastic owing to domestic political turmoil and general procrastination.

The currency, the rupiah, came under pressure in July 1997, soon after the float of the Thai baht. Although the pre-crisis current account deficit was modest at around 3 percent of GDP, export growth remained high and the fiscal balance stayed in surplus. Indonesia's short-term private sector external debt grew rapidly, however, and evidence of weaknesses in the financial sector raised doubts about the government's ability to defend the currency. Following the float of the rupiah in mid-August 1997, the exchange rate was initially relatively stable, albeit volatile, but began to fall sharply in October—the cumulative depreciation soon became the largest in the region (about 30 percent from July 1997).

In early November 1997, the IMF approved a three-year Stand-By Arrangement equivalent to $10 billion (490 percent of quota) and additional financing commitments and pledges totaled $26 billion. The key objectives of the adjustment program were to restore market confidence, bring about an orderly adjustment in the current account, limit the decline in output growth, and contain the inflationary impact of exchange rate depreciation. The initial response to the program was positive, market confidence improved, and the rupiah strengthened.

Contagion from other emerging markets soon reemerged and the exchange rate fell precipitously during December 1997–January 1998, notwithstanding massive interventions that lowered gross official reserves to less than four months of imports. The downfall of the rupiah against the U.S. dollar from Rp2,400 in the pre-crisis period to Rp14,000–15,000 led to a collapse in corporate balance sheets and resulting sharp economic contraction. The increase in the cost of living and poverty led to widespread social and political unrest. Key factors contributing to the macroeconomic deterioration included stop-and-go monetary policy, swinging between support for the exchange rate and strong liquidity expansion in the face of financial sector difficulties and runs on deposits. Implementation of important structural measures was uneven and market sentiment worsened ahead of the presidential election in mid-1998.

A strengthened program was announced in early January 1998, but markets remained skeptical. In addition to a commitment to tight monetary policy and an extensive package of structural reforms, the program stressed a comprehensive bank restructuring plan, which did not move quickly enough to address the problems of corporate debt, however. Implementation of structural reforms continued to lag, and the macroeconomic program quickly ran off track, with base money growing rapidly, fueled by the liquidity support for failing financial institutions. Program implementation was further sidetracked by futile discussions about the introduction of a currency board and preparations for the March presidential election. The economic downturn deepened and the economy hovered on the verge of a vicious circle of currency depreciation and hyperinflation.

Following the re-election of President Suharto and formation of a new government, the first review was completed on May 4, 1998 on the basis of another substantial modification of the program. After a promising start, including successful talks with private creditors regarding the restructuring of corporate sector obligations and the rollover of short-term bank debt, the program was cast off track by severe civil unrest, which led to the resignation of President Suharto on May 21, 1998. The rupiah nose-dived and hit an all-time low of Rp16,650 against the U.S. dollar in mid-June 1998 (a cumulative depreciation of 85 percent since June 1997). Although some progress was made on restructuring of interbank debt, restoration of a trade facility, and creation of a framework for the voluntary restructuring of corporate debt involving a government exchange guarantee scheme (INDRA scheme), the economy experienced a severe slump (real GDP fell by a staggering 14 percent in 1998).

In view of the deep-seated nature of Indonesia's structural and balance of payments problems, the IMF's Executive Board in late August 1998 approved the authorities' request to replace the Stand-By Arrangement with an Extended Arrangement with the same access ($6.3 billion, or 312 percent of quota, for the remaining 26 months) and phasing as envisaged under the Stand-By Arrangement. The program succeeded in improving market sentiment, the domestic currency appreciated to about Rp7,500 against the U.S. dollar, and, as a result, inflation declined sharply. Unlike in other cases of capital account crises, however, a V-shaped recovery in economic activity did not take place and the economy declined by a further 1 percent in 1999. Although macroeconomic policies remained broadly on track in 1999, continued political and social unrest weighed on economic policies. Implementation of much needed structural policies remained poor and the slow progress in bank and corporate restructuring was particularly damaging to the economy.

The EFF was cancelled in early 2000 and, at the same time, a new EFF for the period through December 2002 was approved, following the election of President Wahid and formation of his government. The arrangement provided access equivalent to some $5 billion and focused on macroeconomic stabilization, bank and corporate restructuring, rebuilding of public institutions, and improvement in natural resource management. Progress under this arrangement has been mixed, especially in the structural area. Although the economy bottomed out in 1999 and grew modestly—by 2.5 percent—in 2000, the recovery remained fragile. The continued social unrest hampered economic policies and, to date, Indonesia has been unable to benefit from a sustained rebound in economic activity.

Korea (1997–98)

Korea's external position became vulnerable during the 1990s as domestic banks borrowed offshore to finance domestic firms. Although contagion from

Thailand and Indonesia, and a lack of promptness in responding to market pressures, brought Korea to the brink of default, the authorities soon started to act decisively by implementing their program and bringing private lenders to the negotiating table. In the end, the ensuing crisis was relatively mild.

Korea initially appeared little affected by the crisis in the region, with the exchange rate remaining essentially stable through October 1997. With a high level of short-term debt in relation to international reserves, however, the economy was vulnerable to a shift in market sentiment. Although macroeconomic fundamentals were favorable, concerns about the soundness of financial institutions and *chaebol* (industrial conglomerates) had intensified in early 1997. As Korean banks began to face difficulties rolling over their short-term foreign liabilities, in mid-1997 the Bank of Korea found itself lending its dwindling foreign exchange reserves to the banks' offshore branches and the government announced a guarantee of foreign borrowing by Korean banks. External financing conditions deteriorated further in late October 1997 and the won fell sharply. Monetary policy was tightened briefly, but was soon relaxed in light of concerns about the impact of higher interest rates on the highly leveraged corporate sector. By early December 1997, the won had depreciated by over 20 percent against the U.S. dollar and usable foreign exchange reserves had declined to $6 billion (from $22.5 billion at the end of October 1997).

On December 4, 1997, the IMF's Executive Board approved a three-year Stand-By Arrangement with Korea, equivalent to $21 billion (1,939 percent of quota), with additional financing totaling $37 billion. To establish conditions for an early return of market confidence, the underlying program aimed to bring about an orderly reduction in the current account deficit, build up foreign exchange reserves, and contain inflation through a tightening of monetary policy and some fiscal measures. In addition, the program included a range of structural reforms in the financial and corporate sectors to address the root causes of the crisis. Upon approval of the program, Korea was able to draw $5.5 billion from the IMF.

The positive impact of the announcement of the program was short-lived and the won dropped sharply. Confidence was undermined by doubts about the commitment to the program as the leading candidates for the mid-December presidential election hesitated to publicly endorse it. Moreover, with new information becoming available about the state of financial institutions, the level of usable reserves, and short-term obligations falling due, markets became concerned about a widening financing gap.

With the won in free-fall and a few days of reserves left, a temporary agreement was reached with private bank creditors on December 24, 1997 to maintain their exposure to Korea. In addition, Korea requested a rephasing of purchases under the Stand-By Arrangement to permit an advancement of drawings. At the same time, the program accelerated financial sector restructuring to facilitate capital inflows into the domestic stock and bond market. Interest rates had been raised significantly, and conditions for the provision of foreign currency liquidity support to banks had been tightened.

In January 1998, early signs of stabilization emerged. Rollover rates increased significantly after the agreement with the banks on a voluntary rescheduling of short-term debt (equivalent to some $22 billion), usable international reserves stabilized, and the won appreciated moderately against the U.S. dollar. The current account had moved into surplus, but owing to the large depreciation of the exchange rate, inflation started to rise. In February, against the background of contracting domestic demand, program targets were adjusted to accommodate fiscal stimulus: the fiscal target for 1998 was lowered from a surplus of 0.2 percent of GDP in the original program to a deficit of 0.8 percent of GDP. Monetary policy was expected to remain tight as long as the exchange market situation continued to be fragile. The program's comprehensive structural reform agenda was expanded further to include commitments in financial sector restructuring, capital account and trade liberalization, the social safety net, labor market flexibility, and corporate restructuring and governance.

The program remained on track and market confidence in the new government's commitment strengthened. By July 1998, Korea had made substantial progress in overcoming its external crisis. A global sovereign bond issue was launched successfully, the central bank registered significant capital inflows into the domestic stock and bond markets, and usable reserves exceeded $30 billion. The sharp decline in economic activity, however, was weighing heavily on corporations, necessitating an acceleration of structural reforms. Interest rates had been lowered somewhat, but monetary policy continued to focus on maintaining exchange market stability. In view of the weaker outlook for growth, the program incorporated an additional fiscal stimulus.

Macroeconomic policies were further eased in the second half of 1998 to mitigate the severity of the recession: interest rates declined to pre-crisis levels, and a supplementary budget was prepared to support economic activity and strengthen the social safety net. Although output declined by 6 percent in 1998, exports recovered, and the current account surplus exceeded 12 percent of GDP.

In 1999, the macroeconomic situation was fully stabilized and Korea experienced a V-shaped recovery (although there remained serious structural issues in the financial corporate sectors that remained to be tackled). With GDP growing by more than 6 percent amid price stability, the won appreciated by 13 percent, while the current account stayed in a healthy surplus of 6 percent of GDP. Although Korea stopped drawing from the IMF at mid-1999, it continued with scheduled quarterly reviews. Of the total committed amount at the onset of the crisis, only about one-half was actually disbursed, almost all of it from international financial institutions.

Mexico (1994–95)

The Mexican financial crisis of 1994–95—the first "crisis of the 21st century"—plays a central role in any analysis of crises driven by capital account reversals as it bears many similarities to subsequent events in Asia and Brazil.

The Mexican crisis erupted after several years of impressive macroeconomic performance and an economic boom made possible by large capital inflows. These inflows, which amounted to about $95 billion during 1990–94, were facilitated by a return of confidence following the "lost decade" of the 1980s. Similar to the Asian episode, Mexican capital inflows were short-term and unhedged in the context of a fixed exchange rate regime which had led to an appreciating real exchange rate and a growing external current account deficit. Mexico's vulnerabilities became a full-blown crisis when the confluence of changes in external conditions and a succession of domestic political shocks led to a loss of market confidence in the authorities' ability to defend the exchange rate. On the external front, U.S. monetary policy was gradually tightened over the course of 1994. Internally, Mexico suffered from a series of adverse political shocks that included a revolt in the southern state of Ciapas and political assassination.

Capital outflows and exchange rate pressures first surfaced in March–April 1994. The Mexican authorities responded by doubling interest rates from 9 to 18 percent and using $11 billion worth of reserves to defend the peso. However, the extent of intervention was kept secret. Moreover, the government decided to change the composition of its debt by issuing dollar-linked securities (tesobonos) to replace maturing peso-denominated securities (cetes) in an effort to reduce its direct funding costs. Although interest rates were some 6 percentage points lower than cetes rates, tesobonos offered an exchange rate guarantee. These actions were successful in calming market conditions in the period to August.

Market turbulence resumed in October–November after yet another assassination, prompting a decline in the stock market and a resumption of outflows. Monetary policy was tightened, but this did not prove sufficient to stem the loss of reserves (about $4 billion in the last two weeks of November). The peso came under renewed pressure in mid-December and it was finally allowed to float on December 22 after reserves had dipped to a low of $6 billion as compared to $25 billion in early November. The immediate problem following the float of the peso was how to refinance $29 billion of tesobonos and $18 billion in short-term bank credit lines, with the amortization schedule particularly heavy during the first quarter.

Prior to the approval of the program, an $18.5 billion official line of credit was committed on January 2, 1995. Markets viewed the size of the package as insufficient, however, while the Mexican government was perceived as procrastinating. With the crisis deepening, a larger package of $40 billion in loan guarantees was proposed on January 12. Finally, on January 31, with Mexico on the brink of default, the U.S. administration proposed a package of more than $50 billion from the U.S. Treasury, the IMF, the Bank for International Settlements, and private institutions.

The IMF-supported program provided for financing of SDR5.3 billion (300 percent of quota), to be disbursed over an 18-month period. In light of the unrelenting crisis, the financing was increased to SDR12.1 billion (688 percent of quota) on February 1, 1995. The program aimed to bring about a gradual real depreciation of the peso (by 14 percent over the life of the program) which was expected to cut the current account deficit in half (to 4 percent of GDP) by triggering a modest (7 percent) decline in imports and a much larger (25 percent) increase in exports of manufactures.

With the program failing to stem capital outflows, the crisis continued unabated. Between January and March, the exchange rate depreciated sharply, interest rates rose substantially, and the banking system came under severe pressure. Financial markets doubted the realism of the program and the adequacy of its financing. The program had to be revised in March 1995 through a tightening of monetary conditions, a further consolidation of public finances (by the equivalent of 1.7 percent of GDP), and by a comprehensive set of policies to deal with the banking crisis. The revised program was ultimately successful in stemming capital outflows, stabilizing the peso, and amortizing the entire stock of tesobonos.

The financial crisis led to a sharper-than-expected contraction in real GDP of about 7 percent in 1995, while end-of-period consumer price inflation amounted to 52 percent. The tightening of financial policies and a sizable real depreciation of the peso led to a large turnaround in the balance of payments: the current account shifted to approximate balance, fueled by a 32 percent increase in exports (in dollar terms) and a 21 percent decline in imports. The 1995 fiscal targets were met with significant margins, with the overall budget achieving a surplus of about 1 percent of GDP. Implementation of policies agreed in the context of the program led to a consolidation of financial market stability in 1996, quick recovery, and restoration of low inflation.

The 1995 downturn combined with high domestic interest rates led to a banking crisis. The government strategy of dealing with the crisis emphasized burden-sharing between bank shareholders and the government, and the spreading of the fiscal costs of bank restructuring over time. Immediate steps taken in January–June 1995 included (1) a government commitment to protect all depositors; (2) provision of peso liquidity by the Bank of Mexico to the banking system; (3) a temporary bank recapitalization through the PROCARTE program; (4) a program of dollar loans to help banks meet their external short-term obligations through FOBAPROA, the deposit protection agency administered by the Bank of Mexico; and (5) a strengthening of banking supervision and relaxation of limits on foreign participation in Mexican banks. While these measures contained the crisis and prevented the collapse of several banks, the banking system remained fragile in 1995–96.

The extent of the Mexican crisis caught the financial markets by surprise and prompted a lot of soul searching as to the reasons behind the failure to detect the early warning signs. Three reasons were identified. First, weak financial systems were unable to intermediate efficiently large capital inflows into productive investments, creating firm-level vulnerabilities. Second, the Mexican government procrastinated for several months in 1994, in effect undermining confidence in its policies. Third, the authorities' lack of transparency, especially with regard to international reserves in the early days of the crisis, fueled negative market sentiment.

The Philippines (1997)

When the 1997 crisis struck, the Philippines had a long-running IMF program already in place.[113] The authorities acted decisively, the program was quickly amended, and, in the end, the country weathered the crisis better than expected.

[113]The Philippines has had a long history of IMF programs. The Extended Fund Facility, with total access of SDR0.8 billion, had been in place from June 1994. At the first sign of the Thai crisis, the arrangement was extended for an additional nine months in July 1997 and the total amount approved was augmented. A new two-year Stand-By Arrangement, with total access of SDR1 billion, was approved in April 1999.

The Philippines' better-than-expected performance can be explained as a combination of a comparatively smaller asset bubble and a faster and more decisive reaction by the authorities. First, in their macroeconomic performance in the 1970s and 1980s, the Philippines lagged behind their neighbors and only after reforms in the early 1990s did the economy begin to attract substantial foreign capital. Consequently, signs of overheating and asset bubbles began to show much later than in other countries and the resulting financial imbalances were correspondingly smaller. Second, at the time of the crisis, an IMF arrangement was already in place and, when the crisis struck, the authorities acted without delay. Moreover, the consensus for sound economic policies survived the May–July 1998 transition from one presidential administration to another.

At the onset of the crisis, the Philippines presented a somewhat different pattern of strengths and vulnerabilities than the "tigers" most heavily affected by the crisis. Current account deficits averaged 4–5 percent during pre-crisis years and private sector credit grew 50 percent in 1996. By regional standards, however, the pre-crisis growth rates of real GNP were more modest than in other countries and external exposure by domestic private corporations, including short-term debt, was relatively small. Moreover, levels of corporate leverage were significantly lower, major banks were well capitalized, and the reforms of the past 10 years or so had created a reasonably open, market-oriented economy. In summary, the structural vulnerabilities were much smaller and their roots—unlike in other countries—were known and some of them had already been addressed in previous IMF programs.

The initial impact of the Asian crisis—in terms of the initial drop in share prices, currency depreciation, and loss in international reserves—was comparable to that of the Philippines' neighbors. On the other hand, the ensuing recession was relatively mild and most of the macroeconomic and financial indicators rebounded faster than in the Philippines' neighbors. This may have reflected, in large part, the lesser degree of vulnerability of the Philippine economy. In particular, the rebound was associated with more favorable export performance than in neighboring countries: unlike in other Asian crisis countries, where monthly U.S. dollar export growth rates were negative for most of 1998, the Philippines recorded an uninterrupted period of double-digit growth rates. The high level of exports throughout the crisis likely reflected the stability of firms' balance sheets vis-à-vis exchange rate fluctuations. Of course, as a result of the massive depreciation of the peso, imports fell between 1997 and 1998 by some 8 percent of GNP, forcing a trade balance adjustment of 13 percent of GNP.

As in other countries, capital outflows and sharp falls in the stock market led to mounting pressures on the peso. The authorities initially tightened monetary policy by raising interbank interest rates from about 15 percent to reach peaks of 40–60 percent (for a few days in late August 1997) and intervened in the foreign exchange market to maintain the de facto peg of the peso. However, the system lost its viability with the flotation of the Thai baht and the peso was accordingly floated in July 1997. The new exchange rate arrangement was accompanied by strengthened fiscal, monetary, and structural policies in the context of the existing IMF program. The thrust of the program was on improved fiscal performance and the related long-standing revenue measure: the Comprehensive Tax Reform Package.

After initial monetary and fiscal tightening, as the peso stabilized,[114] the stance became neutral and eventually shifted toward supporting the emerging recovery. Interest rates were brought down during the second half of 1998 and monetary policy was eased significantly in early 1999, after firm turnarounds in the balance of payments and inflation were established. Fiscal policy followed a similar path: from a pre-crisis surplus target of 1 percent of GNP for 1998, the program was revised to an eventual deficit target of 3 percent of GNP.

Financial markets remained volatile until the last quarter of 1998, as a result of both external developments (short-term outflows amounted to $3 billion, a reversal of some 7 percent of GNP, and the net position on medium-term loans worsened by another $2.5 billion) and domestic uncertainties (including political uncertainties associated with a new administration that took office in early 1998). Since September 1998, however, financial markets strengthened continually, with share prices up by more than 100 percent above their trough, the peso appreciating by some 20 percent in real effective terms, and official reserves rising well above their pre-crisis level. By mid-1999, the economic slowdown appeared to be over, with industrial production showing significant growth. After recording zero growth in 1998, GNP grew by more than 3½ percent in 1999.

Thailand (1997–98)

Contagion started to spread from Thailand in 1997, where a period of fast growth led to large current account deficits. In addition, chaotic deregulation in the early 1990s created an unsupervised and vulnerable financial sector and contributed to the emergence of asset bubbles, especially in the real estate sector.

Pressures on the baht started in late 1996 and built up in early 1997 against the background of an unsustainable current account deficit, significant real appreciation of the domestic currency, rising short-term foreign debt, and growing problems in the financial sector. Reserve money growth accelerated sharply as the Bank of Thailand provided liquidity support for ailing financial institutions. The policy response to the pressures in the foreign exchange market focused on intervention, the introduction of capital account controls, and minor fiscal tightening.

The baht was floated on July 2, 1997, following mounting speculative attacks and amid concerns about the reserve position. The accompanying policy response was inadequate and failed to bolster market confidence. The baht depreciated by 20 percent against the U.S. dollar during July, partly because short-term interest rates were allowed to decline sharply after a temporary increase.

On August 20, 1997, the IMF's Executive Board approved a three-year Stand-By Arrangement with Thailand, equivalent to $4 billion (505 percent of quota), with additional financing totaling $13 billion. The underlying adjustment program was aimed at restoring confidence, bringing about an orderly reduction in the current account deficit, while maintaining positive growth rates, reconstituting foreign exchange reserves, and limiting the rise in inflation to the one-off effects of the depreciation. Key elements of the program included measures to restructure the financial sector (including closure of insolvent financial institutions); fiscal adjustment equivalent to some 3 percent of GDP; and control of domestic credit, with indicative ranges for interest rates. Upon approval of the program, Thailand drew more than $5 billion from the IMF and other sources.

In subsequent months, the baht continued to depreciate as the country was unable to roll over its short-term debt. While macroeconomic policies were in line with the program and nominal interest rates were raised, market confidence was adversely affected by delays in the implementation of financial sector reforms, political uncertainty, and initial difficulties in communicating key aspects of the program to the public. It also became clear that the slowdown in economic activity was more pronounced than anticipated. Against this background, a new government took office in November 1997 and soon thereafter the program was strengthened and additional fiscal measures were introduced to achieve the original fiscal target. Reserve money and net domestic assets of the Bank of Thailand were to be kept below the original program limits, the indicative range for interest rates was raised, and a specific timetable for financial sector restructuring was announced.

[114]The decline in both nominal and real exchange rates was the smallest of all Asian-crisis countries.

The crisis in Thailand started to abate in early 1998, in tandem with other countries in the region. After falling to an all-time low against the U.S. dollar in early January 1998, the baht began to strengthen in early February as market confidence revived. Contracting domestic demand helped to keep inflation in check and contributed to a larger-than-expected adjustment in the current account and growth deceleration. In view of stabilizing exchange market conditions and the changed economic outlook, the program was revised significantly in March 1998. Monetary policy focused on the exchange rate, while fiscal policy shifted to a more accommodating stance. In addition, the program included measures to strengthen the social safety net, and broadened the scope of structural reforms to strengthen the core banking system and promote corporate restructuring.

By mid-1998, the domestic currency appreciated some 35 percent vis-à-vis the U.S. dollar from its low in January and foreign exchange reserves increased. Nevertheless, the economy sank into a deep recession. To stimulate demand, the fiscal deficit target for 1997–98 was increased from 2 percent to 3 percent of GDP. In addition, the social safety net was strengthened and the program for financial sector and corporate restructuring was further specified. However, the financial sector began to show signs of strain, economic activity slowed down again, and exports failed to pick up. The large adjustment in the current account reflected mostly a compression of imports. Restructuring of financial institutions was complicated by corporate sector problems.

At end-1998, the policy framework was refocused on supporting the nascent recovery without sacrificing stabilization gains. Foreign exchange market conditions remained relatively stable—in spite of the Russian crisis—providing room for a further lowering of interest rates, while the fiscal position remained expansionary. The program for financial and corporate sector restructuring was broadened significantly, and the structural reform agenda in other areas (privatization, foreign ownership, and social safety net) was strengthened. The implementation of structural measures remained inconsistent, however.

In 1999, the Thai economy started to grow again (by about 4 percent), mostly fueled by buoyant exports, but the recovery was weak and less pronounced than in neighboring countries. The current account balance remained highly positive, despite a fiscal deficit of 3 percent. The rate of growth stayed comparatively low in 2000, partly owing to sluggish domestic demand. Thai financial markets underperformed compared to their peers as foreign investors started to pull out of the country because of unresolved issues related to financial and corporate sector restructuring.

Thailand was hard hit by the 1997–98 crisis—only Indonesia experienced a larger decline in real GDP—and the subsequent recovery was milder than in other countries. More important, investor confidence remained low, pending the resolution of structural vulnerabilities.

Turkey (1994)

The Turkish 1994 crisis foreshadowed several of the subsequent capital account crises with a massive swing in capital outflows of some 8 percent of GNP. The IMF-supported program was successful in the sense that it quickly restored confidence, even though the national authorities procrastinated on longer-term structural measures.

Following the liberalization of the economy during the 1980s, Turkey enjoyed high, albeit very variable, real GNP growth rates (Table A5.1). At the same time, macroeconomic imbalances became increasingly pronounced as a result of expansionary public sector policies, especially after 1988. These imbalances resulted in persistently high inflation—in the range of 60–70 percent per year—and a weakening external position.

Capital inflows and outflows prior to 1993 had been modest (typically less than 1 percent of GNP) and total external debt at end-1992 stood at 35 percent of GNP (about three-quarters of which represented public debt).

Real GNP continued to grow rapidly in 1993, as strong increases in both consumption and investment were fueled by a loosening of monetary policy and by an increase in the fiscal deficit. The overall public sector deficit rose to 13 percent of GNP (up from 12 percent in 1992), while the central government deficit grew from 5.4 percent to 6.3 percent of GNP. This widening deficit primarily reflected higher interest payments, with the primary deficit actually improving from 7 percent of GNP to 5.6 percent of GNP in 1993.[115]

Against the backdrop of growing resource demands by the public sector, the current account deteriorated from a deficit of about 1 percent of GNP in 1992 to more than 5 percent of GNP in 1993. The associated relaxation of monetary policy reflected the authorities' attempt to reduce the interest cost of public debt, with the ex post real interest rate on treasury bills falling from 20 percent a year in the first quarter of 1993 to about 9 percent for the rest of the year.

[115]The figures given here differ from those reported at the time because of subsequent changes to the coverage of public sector accounts and a comprehensive revision to the national accounts data (including the level of GNP).

Table A5.1. Macroeconomic Indicators in Capital Account Crisis Programs

	t – 3	t – 2	t – 1	t	t + 1	t + 2	t + 3
1. Argentina (1995)	1992	1993	1994	1995	1996	1997	1998
Real GDP (growth, percent per year)	10.3	6.3	5.8	–2.8	5.5	8.1	3.8
Consumer Price Index (growth, percent per year)	24.9	10.6	4.2	3.4	0.2	0.5	0.9
Real exchange rate (growth, percent per year)	13.4	11.7	–0.4	–5.0	–0.3	5.6	3.1
Private Savings (as percent of GDP)	13.4	15.8	17.5	17.9	17.2	15.7	15.6
Public Savings (as percent of GDP)	0.5	1.4	0.4	–1.6	–1.5	–0.4	–0.5
Investment (as percent of GDP)	16.7	19.1	19.9	17.9	18.1	19.4	19.9
Current Account (as percent of GDP)	–2.8	–3.4	–4.3	–1.9	–2.4	–4.1	–4.8
Capital and financial account (as percent of GDP)	3.1	3.3	4.1	1.6	3.0	4.5	4.7
Net private capital flows (as percent of GDP)	4.5	–8.0	2.1	0.3	0.4	3.1	3.2
General government balance (as percent of GDP)	0.4	–0.2	–1.8	–2.3	–3.2	–2.1	–2.1
External debt (as percent of GDP)	27.4	30.5	33.3	38.1	40.3	42.6	47.3
2. Brazil (1998)	1995	1996	1997	1998	1999	2000	2001
Real GDP (growth, percent per year)	4.2	2.7	3.3	0.2	0.8	4.2	. . .
Consumer Price Index (growth, percent per year)	66.0	15.8	6.9	3.2	4.9	7.0	. . .
Real exchange rate (growth, percent per year)	9.4	5.9	4.2	–2.3	–33.6	9.1	. . .
Private Savings (as percent of GDP)	22.9	21.4	21.0	21.8	24.1	19.5	. . .
Public Savings (as percent of GDP)	–3.2	–3.4	–3.4	–4.9	–8.3	–3.1	. . .
Investment (as percent of GDP)	22.3	20.9	21.5	21.2	20.4	20.5	. . .
Current Account (as percent of GDP)	–2.6	–3.0	–3.8	–4.3	–4.7	–4.2	. . .
Capital and financial account (as percent of GDP)	2.3	3.2	4.2	4.9	4.6	4.1	. . .
Net private capital flows (as percent of GDP)	4.3	4.5	3.1	2.4	2.2	4.8	. . .
General government balance (as percent of GDP)	–7.0	–5.9	–6.1	–7.9	–10.0	–4.6	. . .
External debt (as percent of GDP)	22.6	23.2	24.8	30.7	45.6	39.7	. . .
3. Indonesia (1997)	1994	1995	1996	1997	1998	1999	2000
Real GDP (growth, percent per year)	7.5	8.2	8.0	4.5	–13.1	0.8	4.8
Consumer Price Index (growth, percent per year)	8.5	9.4	7.9	6.2	58.0	20.7	3.8
Real exchange rate (growth, percent per year)	–0.7	–3.4	5.1	–5.6	–51.6	45.2	–2.0
Private Savings (as percent of GDP)	21.6	22.0	21.9	19.4	10.8	11.0	14.7
Public Savings (as percent of GDP)	7.6	7.0	6.8	7.3	6.4	6.4	7.4
Investment (as percent of GDP)	31.1	31.9	32.1	31.8	16.8	12.2	17.9
Current Account (as percent of GDP)	–1.7	–3.3	–3.2	–1.7	4.2	4.1	4.2
Capital and financial account (as percent of GDP)	4.4	3.3	5.1	1.7	–4.2	–4.1	–4.2
Net private capital flows (as percent of GDP)	3.9	6.2	6.3	7.1	–3.0	–3.6	–0.9
General government balance (as percent of GDP)	0.0	0.8	1.2	–1.1	–2.3	–1.5	–3.1
External debt (as percent of GDP)	57.0	56.3	53.4	63.3	148.4	112.1	96.5
4. Korea (1997)	1994	1995	1996	1997	1998	1999	2000
Real GDP (growth, percent per year)	8.3	8.9	6.8	5.0	–6.7	10.9	8.8
Consumer Price Index (growth, percent per year)	6.3	4.5	4.9	4.4	7.5	0.8	2.2
Real exchange rate (growth, percent per year)	0.8	1.2	3.5	–6.0	–25.6	13.5	8.1
Private Savings (as percent of GDP)	25.4	25.8	23.4	22.4	23.0	22.3	20.9
Public Savings (as percent of GDP)	10.2	9.7	10.2	10.1	11.0	10.4	10.2
Investment (as percent of GDP)	36.5	37.2	37.9	34.2	21.2	26.7	28.7
Current Account (as percent of GDP)	–1.0	–1.7	–4.4	–1.7	12.7	6.0	2.4
Capital and financial account (as percent of GDP)	1.4	2.0	4.2	2.7	–10.7	–5.2	–2.7
Net private capital flows (as percent of GDP)	2.7	0.7	4.1	–4.6	–2.7	3.3	1.8
General government balance (as percent of GDP)	1.0	1.3	1.0	–0.9	–3.8	–2.7	2.5
External debt (as percent of GDP)	18.0	17.5	22.2	28.1	43.5	. . .	. . .

Table A5.1 *(continued)*

	t − 3	t − 2	t − 1	t	t + 1	t + 2	t + 3
5. Mexico (1995)	1992	1993	1994	1995	1996	1997	1998
Real GDP (growth, percent per year)	3.6	2.0	4.4	−6.2	5.2	6.8	4.9
Consumer Price Index (growth, percent per year)	15.5	9.8	7.0	35.0	34.4	20.6	15.9
Real exchange rate (growth, percent per year)	8.2	7.6	−3.6	−33.1	13.0	17.8	1.9
Private Savings (as percent of GDP)	10.0	10.1	10.3	14.5	18.5	21.5	18.3
Public Savings (as percent of GDP)	6.6	5.1	4.4	4.8	3.9	2.5	2.2
Investment (as percent of GDP)	23.3	21.0	21.7	19.8	23.1	25.9	24.3
Current Account (as percent of GDP)	−6.7	−5.8	−7.0	−0.6	−0.7	−1.9	−3.8
Capital and financial account (as percent of GDP)	6.7	6.5	8.1	1.7	0.4	1.4	3.5
Net private capital flows (as percent of GDP)	6.8	8.6	4.6	1.4	4.0	3.9	4.4
General government balance (percent of GDP)	1.5	0.7	−0.2	−0.2	0.3	−1.0	−1.3
External debt (as percent of GDP)	31.3	32.7	33.8	59.0	49.6	38.2	38.4
6. Philippines (1998)	1995	1996	1997	1998	1999	2000	2001
Real GDP (growth, percent per year)	4.7	5.8	5.2	−0.6	3.3	3.9	...
Consumer Price Index (growth, percent per year)	8.0	9.0	5.9	9.7	6.6	4.3	...
Real exchange rate (growth, percent per year)	2.7	9.3	−0.5	−18.4	8.6	−6.8	...
Private Savings (as percent of GDP)	14.4	15.5	15.4	20.9	27.0	29.0	...
Public Savings (as percent of GDP)	3.4	3.8	4.1	1.7	1.1	−0.7	...
Investment (as percent of GDP)	22.5	24.0	24.8	20.2	18.6	17.6	...
Current Account (as percent of GDP)	−2.7	−4.8	−5.3	2.4	10.0	12.4	...
Capital and financial account (percent of GDP)	2.1	8.4	11.7	−5.6	−6.7	−7.7	...
Net private capital flows (as percent of GDP)	5.0	13.3	6.9	−4.0	−1.2	−7.7	...
General government balance (as percent of GDP)	−1.4	−0.4	−0.8	−2.7	−4.3	−4.7	...
External debt (as percent of GDP)	54.9	55.0	61.6	81.7	75.7	75.7	...
7. Thailand (1997)	1994	1995	1996	1997	1998	1999	2000
Real GDP (growth, percent per year)	9.0	9.3	5.9	−1.4	−10.8	4.2	4.3
Consumer Price Index (growth, percent per year)	5.1	5.8	5.9	5.6	8.1	0.3	1.5
Real exchange rate (growth, percent per year)	0.1	−1.8	6.8	−7.0	−15.5	5.1	−3.1
Private Savings (as percent of GDP)	22.5	21.0	20.6	20.3	26.1	24.1	23.7
Public Savings (as percent of GDP)	12.1	12.8	13.0	10.9	7.0	6.0	6.2
Investment (as percent of GDP)	40.2	41.8	41.6	33.3	20.3	19.9	22.4
Current Account (as percent of GDP)	−5.4	−7.8	−7.9	−2.1	12.8	10.2	7.6
Capital and financial account (as percent of GDP)	5.5	8.6	8.8	7.8	−13.6	−14.5	−8.2
Net private capital flows (as percent of GDP)	8.2	11.8	9.2	−5.3	−16.3	−13.5	−10.7
General government balance (as percent of GDP)	1.9	3.0	2.5	−0.9	−2.6	−2.9	−2.3
External debt (as percent of GDP)	51.6	59.9	59.6	72.3	93.9	78.4	65.8
8. Turkey (1994)	1991	1992	1993	1994	1995	1996	1997
Real GDP (growth, percent per year)	0.8	5.0	7.7	−4.7	8.1	6.9	7.5
Consumer Price Index (growth, percent per year)	66.0	70.1	66.1	106.3	93.7	82.3	85.7
Real exchange rate (growth, percent per year)	2.6	−3.7	8.9	−24.8	6.9	2.3	6.4
Private Savings (as percent of GDP)	19.6	22.1	24.2	23.8	21.8	21.6	20.4
Public Savings (as percent of GDP)	0.7	−0.8	−2.7	−1.1	−0.1	−1.8	0.8
Investment (as percent of GDP)	22.4	23.2	26.3	21.3	24.9	24.5	25.1
Current Account (as percent of GDP)	0.2	−0.6	−3.5	2.8	−0.5	−1.4	−1.4
Capital and financial account (as percent of GDP)	−0.7	1.8	5.0	−3.6	−0.3	2.4	2.7
Net private capital flows (as percent of GDP)	−2.8	3.0	3.7	−2.4	2.7	5.5	4.8
General government balance (as percent of GDP)	−6.9	−6.7	−9.1	−6.0	−5.8	−10.3	−9.4
External debt (as percent of GDP)	33.0	34.8	36.9	50.2	42.2	45.1	46.8

Table A5.1 *(concluded)*

	t − 3	t − 2	t − 1	t	t + 1	t + 2	t + 3
9. Russia (1998)	1995	1996	1997	1998	1999	2000	2001
Real GDP (growth, percent per year)	–4.2	–3.4	0.9	–4.9	3.2	7.5	. . .
Consumer Price Index (growth, percent per year)	197.4	47.6	14.7	27.7	85.7	20.8	. . .
Real exchange rate (growth, percent per year)	9.7	22.1	5.6	–11.4	–29.3	12.1	. . .
Private Savings (as percent of GDP)	33.1	33.7	28.9	18.5	28.3	34.8	. . .
Public Savings (as percent of GDP)	–6.3	–8.2	–5.9	–3.4	–0.9	1.6	. . .
Investment (as percent of GDP)	25.4	24.6	23.1	15.7	15.1	18.0	. . .
Current Account (as percent of GDP)	1.4	0.9	–0.1	–0.6	12.4	18.4	. . .
Capital and financial account (as percent of GDP)	0.9	1.1	1.4	3.8	–8.3	–13.4	. . .
Net private capital flows (as percent of GDP)	7.3	0.4	–5.3	–4.0	–5.8	–6.9	. . .
Central government balance (as percent of GDP)	–5.8	–6.5	–6.7	–4.9	–1.4	2.6	. . .
General government balance (as percent of GDP)	–6.1	–8.9	–7.5	–7.0	–0.2	4.5	. . .
Primary balance (as percent of GDP)	–2.5	–3.0	–2.8	–3.0	3.4	7.0	. . .
External debt (as percent of GDP)	37.9	32.5	30.9	54.8	79.9	61.5	. . .
10. Malaysia (1997)	1994	1995	1996	1997	1998	1999	2000
Real GDP (growth, percent per year)	9.2	9.8	10.0	7.3	–7.4	5.8	8.5
Consumer Price Index (growth, percent per year)	3.7	3.4	3.5	2.7	5.3	2.8	1.5
Real exchange rate (growth, percent per year)	–2.6	0.6	4.3	–2.4	–20.5	2.9	2.6
Private Savings (as percent of GDP)	16.8	17.5	19.9	18.8	24.7	24.2	24.3
Public Savings (as percent of GDP)	17.2	16.4	16.1	18.1	14.9	14.1	13.7
Investment (as percent of GDP)	41.6	43.6	41.5	43.0	26.6	22.3	27.0
Current Account (as percent of GDP)	–7.6	–9.7	–4.4	–5.9	13.1	15.9	9.7
Capital and financial account (as percent of GDP)	5.9	10.6	6.9	8.2	–9.7	–14.3	–6.7
Net private capital flows (as percent of GDP)	–0.3	–0.4	0.8	0.2	–0.3	–0.3	2.2
General government balance (as percent of GDP)	3.3	2.2	2.3	4.1	–0.4	–3.7	0.4
External debt (as percent of GDP)	19.9	18.0	15.6	16.8	25.1	. . .	. . .

At end-1993, foreign exchange reserves stood at some $8 billion or about 2½ months worth of imports, while total external debt stood at $67 billion (37 percent of GNP). Three-quarters of this was medium- and long-term debt, and most of the medium- and long-term debt was in the form of public sector debt. The exchange crisis broke in January 1994, and through the period January–March 1993 (when the central bank stopped intervening), the Turkish lira depreciated some 60 percent and the central bank lost $3 billion of its foreign exchange reserves. The capital account, which had registered a net inflow of $8.7 billion in 1993, recorded a net outflow of $4.2 billion in 1994. Much of this occurred through the banking system, which initially had been borrowing heavily from abroad to take advantage of high domestic interest rates; short-term flows to domestic banks swung from an inflow of $4 billion in 1993 to an outflow of $7 billion in 1994: a swing of more than 7 percent of GNP.

The Treasury's continued reluctance to sell securities at market rates paralyzed the primary and secondary bond markets and led to heavy borrowing from the central bank. In turn, this placed mounting strains on the interbank market, with interest rates reaching well into the four-digit levels. In the end, the banking system proved vulnerable to the exchange rate depreciation (even the generous net foreign exchange position limits were routinely flouted), the slowdown in economic activity, and the extremely high interbank interest rates. As a result, three small banks and a number of brokerage houses collapsed in April 1994. In May, the authorities narrowly avoided large-scale bank runs by extending the government's guarantee to cover 100 percent of all domestic and foreign currency deposits.

The program, approved in July 1994, centered on frontloaded fiscal adjustment—amounting to some 9 percent of GNP—while the low level of reserves and turbulence in the financial markets precluded an exchange rate anchor. The Treasury eschewed further monetary financing, and successfully reentered the bond market in June 1994. The macroeconomic adjustment was to be followed by far-reaching structural reforms, particularly in the banking, social security, and agricultural sectors, as well as privatization, so as to lower the level of public debt and the strain on public finances. The program foresaw a swing in the current account of about 4 percent of GNP, all of which could be accounted for by an improvement in the public sector savings-investment balance.

The program was successful in that the external situation was stabilized. The current account swung into a surplus of 3 percent of GNP in 1995 (at the expense of a GNP decline of some 5 percent against a program expectation of a 1½ percent decline), and the short-term capital outflows were reversed. In the short term, public finances also improved, with the overall deficit falling from 13 percent of GNP in 1993 to 10 percent of GNP in 1994, and 6.4 percent of GNP in 1995. Many of the structural reforms, however, were not undertaken (particularly privatization and the social security reform) which would, in later years, again place unsustainable demands on public sector finances.[116]

Taken as a whole, the Turkish 1994 crisis and program—which predated the Mexican crisis by several months—combined elements of traditional balance of payments crises with features of the later capital account crises. On the one hand, there were clear macroeconomic imbalances prior to the currency crisis. On the other hand, the massive swings in capital flows—amounting to some 8 percent of GNP—were a presage of crises to come.

[116]By 1998, the overall public sector deficit had grown to 16 percent of GNP and, by 1999, the deficit reached almost 24 percent of GNP.

Table A5.2. Balance of Payment Developments in Selected Asian Countries
(Quarterly flows, as a percent of quarterly GDP)[1]

	Indonesia				Korea			
	1997Q4	1998Q1	1998Q2	1998Q3	1997Q4	1998Q1	1998Q2	1998Q3
Current Account	–0.4	4.2	2.8	7.1	3.3	13.4	13.8	12.2
Financial Account	2.5	–5.1	–3.6	–5.7	0.1	–13.4	–11.3	–10.4
Excluding IMF and Reserve Assets	–15.6	–26.2	0.9	–9.8	–17.2	–6.7	0.4	–4.7
A. Direct Investment	–0.6	–2.1	1.5	–0.7	–0.2	0.0	0.7	0.8
B. Portfolio Investment	–9.9	–15.0	7.8	0.5	0.4	5.1	1.0	–4.7
Assets	0.0	0.0	0.0	0.0	1.8	1.4	–1.6	–0.2
Liabilities	–9.9	–15.0	7.8	0.5	–1.4	3.7	2.5	–4.5
Equity securities	–10.0	–15.0	–3.6	0.6	–1.2	3.4	0.0	–0.2
C. Other Investment	0.5	–9.1	–4.2	2.6	–8.2	–6.4	1.4	0.6
Assets	0.0	0.0	0.0	0.0	–6.1	–1.3	2.0	3.8
Liabilities	0.5	–9.1	–4.2	2.6	–2.1	–5.1	–0.6	–3.3
Trade credits	0.0	0.1	0.0	0.0	–2.0	–7.0	–1.6	–0.3
Loans	0.5	–9.2	–4.2	2.6	–0.6	2.7	0.9	–2.7
Monetary authorities	5.6	0.0	4.2	12.2	9.1	5.1	2.3	1.2
of which: IMF	5.6	0.0	4.2	12.2	9.1	5.1	2.3	1.2
General government	0.2	3.7	5.2	5.8	4.0	3.8	0.0	0.1
Banks	–1.2	–3.5	–4.5	–0.9	–9.0	–4.2	–0.7	–2.7
of which: Short-term	0.0	0.0	0.0	0.0	–9.7	–3.7	–9.1	–2.3
Other sectors	–4.1	–9.3	–9.2	–14.5	–4.7	–1.9	–0.7	–1.3
of which: Short-term	0.0	0.0	0.0	0.0	–5.3	–2.4	–5.8	–1.1
Currency and deposits	...	...	...	...	–0.7	–0.1	0.1	0.2
Banks	...	...	...	...	–0.5	0.0	0.1	0.1
Other liabilities	...	...	...	...	1.2	–0.7	0.0	–0.5
Banks	...	...	...	...	0.1	0.0	0.0	–0.2
Other sectors	...	...	...	...	1.0	–0.7	0.0	–0.3
Net Errors and Omissions	–2.1	0.8	0.8	–1.4	–3.3	0.1	–2.9	–1.7
Reserve Assets (–: increase)[2]	12.5	21.1	–8.6	–8.1	8.2	–11.7	–14.1	–6.9

Source: IMF, *Balance of Payments Statistics Yearbook*.
[1]In percent of equal quarters of annual GDP.
[2]Change in reserve assets equals –(current account + (financial account – reserve assets – IMF) + IMF + net errors and omissions + capital account (not shown)).

Philippines				Thailand				
1997Q4	1998Q1	1998Q2	1998Q3	1997Q2	1997Q3	1997Q4	1998Q1	1998Q2
−3.5	−0.2	1.1	2.9	−8.3	−1.8	7.7	15.0	10.0
4.2	1.5	4.6	−7.8	11.0	3.2	−6.1	−10.4	−7.1
−5.3	5.1	10.5	−8.2	−4.6	−6.3	−13.4	−9.5	−10.8
0.4	2.3	2.9	1.5	1.2	3.2	2.8	7.2	9.0
−3.2	−2.4	1.5	−4.3	4.1	6.3	1.1	1.4	−0.2
0.1	−0.7	−0.4	−0.9	−0.1	−0.1	0.0	0.2	0.0
−3.3	−1.7	1.9	−3.4	4.2	6.4	1.1	1.2	−0.2
−0.4	2.3	0.1	−1.6	2.4	5.5	1.3	1.6	−0.5
−2.9	5.1	7.9	−5.4	−9.9	−11.5	−15.1	−17.2	−19.1
0.5	5.9	0.6	−1.3	−0.1	−2.3	−3.1	2.3	−9.4
−3.4	−0.8	7.3	−4.1	−9.8	−9.2	−12.0	−19.5	−9.7
...	...	...	...	−0.4	−0.2	−1.5	−1.1	−0.2
3.1	−1.4	3.3	0.4	−3.1	3.4	−0.4	−8.0	−6.1
−0.3	0.0	1.7	0.0	0.0	12.6	7.6	7.1	1.7
−0.3	−0.1	1.9	0.0	0.0	4.3	2.2	1.0	0.5
−1.2	0.5	−1.7	−0.2	0.2	0.1	2.2	1.2	0.5
−0.9	−0.6	0.1	0.3	−1.2	−7.1	−5.0	−10.1	−6.0
−1.3	−0.7	−0.2	0.0	...	...	...	...	...
5.6	−1.4	3.2	0.4	−2.1	−2.2	−5.2	−6.3	−2.3
0.6	−3.6	−1.5	−0.9	−3.4	−3.0	−3.9	−6.5	−2.8
−5.7	1.6	4.0	−5.4	−5.6	−13.2	−9.6	−11.0	−2.8
−5.7	1.6	4.0	−5.4	0.0	0.2	0.0	0.0	−0.1
−0.9	−1.0	0.0	0.9	−0.7	0.8	−0.6	0.7	−0.5
−0.9	−1.0	0.0	0.9	0.1	−1.2	−1.1	0.1	−0.1
0.0	0.0	0.0	0.0	−0.7	0.7	0.5	0.6	−0.3
−0.7	−1.3	−5.7	4.8	−2.7	−1.3	−1.6	−4.6	−2.9
9.9	−3.6	−7.7	0.4	15.6	5.2	5.2	−1.8	3.2

Table A5.3. Balance of Payment Developments in Selected Latin American Countries
(Quarterly flows, as a percent of quarterly GDP)[1]

	Argentina				Brazil			
	1995Q4	1995Q1	1995Q2	1995Q3	1998Q3	1998Q4	1999Q1	1999Q2
Current Account	–4.4	–4.1	0.3	–1.6	–4.6	–5.8	–4.1	–5.3
Financial Account	5.5	4.7	–1.5	3.5	4.2	5.5	3.8	6.1
Excluding IMF and Reserve Assets	7.8	–4.3	–0.1	3.6	–8.4	2.7	–4.1	8.2
A. Direct Investment	2.1	0.8	1.2	1.8	4.6	4.9	5.8	4.6
B. Portfolio Investment	4.3	–2.8	0.9	1.9	–3.8	2.0	–5.9	4.5
Assets	–0.6	–1.9	–1.3	–0.4	–0.7	0.4	–0.3	0.6
Liabilities	4.9	–0.9	2.2	2.3	–3.1	1.6	–5.6	3.8
Equity securities	1.0	0.7	0.4	0.1	–4.4	–0.7	0.2	1.3
C. Other Investment	1.1	–2.4	0.1	0.3	–9.3	–1.8	–4.0	2.9
Assets	–0.8	–5.7	–5.0	–0.1	–3.5	0.0	–0.2	–1.4
Liabilities	1.9	3.2	5.1	0.5	–5.8	–1.7	–3.9	4.3
Trade credits	0.1	–0.1	–0.1	0.0	–0.6	–1.3	–0.8	–0.3
Loans	2.4	3.5	4.5	–0.2	–3.6	2.2	–2.5	5.1
Monetary authorities	–0.2	–0.2	2.5	0.3	0.0	4.4	–0.1	6.4
of which: IMF	–0.2	–0.1	2.3	0.4	0.0	2.4	0.0	3.7
General government	1.3	0.8	1.6	–0.3	...	...	0.1	0.0
Banks	0.5	2.5	0.1	–0.4	–3.6	–2.2	–1.1	–1.8
of which: Short-term	0.5	2.5	0.1	–0.4	–2.8	–1.7	0.3	–1.7
Other sectors	0.8	0.3	0.4	0.2	0.0	–0.1	–1.4	0.5
of which: Short-term	0.0	0.0	0.0	0.0	0.1	0.0	–0.3	0.7
Currency and deposits	–0.3	–0.8	0.3	0.2	–0.1	0.0	–0.6	–0.6
Other liabilities	–0.3	0.7	0.3	0.5	–1.5	–2.6	0.0	0.0
Banks	–0.3	0.7	0.4	0.5	0.0	–1.1	0.0	0.0
Other sectors	0.0	0.0	0.0	0.1	–1.5	–1.5	0.0	0.0
Net errors and ommissions	–1.1	–0.6	1.2	–1.9	0.3	0.3	0.2	–0.9
Reserve assets (–: increase)[2]	–2.0	9.2	–3.7	–0.5	12.7	0.4	7.9	–5.7

Source: IMF, *Balance of Payments Statistics Yearbook.*
[1]Equal quarters of annual GDP.
[2]Change in reserve assets equals –(current account + (financial account – reserve assets – IMF) + IMF + net errors and omissions + capital account (not shown)).

Mexico				Turkey				
1994Q3	1994Q4	1995Q1	1995Q2	1993Q4	1994Q1	1994Q2	1994Q3	1994Q4
–7.5	–7.1	–1.9	0.5	–3.5	–3.5	4.3	6.2	1.0
3.8	6.0	4.6	–1.5	4.9	11.7	–10.0	–13.8	–1.3
4.2	–3.4	–4.9	3.5	4.0	2.6	–7.5	–7.3	–0.6
2.7	1.6	2.8	4.1	0.4	0.2	0.4	0.4	0.8
3.1	–5.1	–10.5	–5.6	3.9	4.3	–0.2	–0.9	0.3
–0.4	0.1	–0.2	–0.2	–0.5	0.6	–0.3	–0.4	0.2
3.5	–5.2	–10.3	–5.4	4.4	3.7	0.1	–0.5	0.0
0.7	–0.4	0.2	0.1	0.7	2.1	0.7	0.0	0.3
–1.8	–0.1	13.3	4.6	–0.3	–1.9	–7.7	–6.1	–1.3
–0.2	–1.4	0.2	–0.6	–6.1	6.3	1.6	–1.5	1.0
–1.6	1.3	13.1	5.2	5.7	–8.2	–9.3	–4.5	–2.3
0.0	0.0	0.0	0.0	1.5	–1.3	–1.9	–0.9	1.7
–0.6	1.1	15.8	5.9	3.0	–8.2	–7.1	–5.5	–5.2
–0.3	–0.2	13.5	–0.4	0.0	0.0	–0.2	0.7	0.3
–0.3	–0.2	10.4	–0.4	0.0	0.0	0.0	0.7	0.3
–0.3	0.0	3.4	6.9	–1.0	–1.8	–1.9	–2.6	–1.3
–0.1	1.8	–2.0	–1.2	3.3	–7.1	–6.3	–3.9	–3.8
0.5	1.2	1.0	–0.2	3.3	–7.3	–6.2	–2.8	–3.8
0.1	–0.5	0.8	0.5	0.7	0.7	1.3	0.3	–0.4
0.1	–0.8	–0.2	0.4	–0.3	–0.1	0.1	–0.1	–0.2
–1.1	0.2	–2.7	–0.7	1.2	1.2	–0.3	1.8	1.2
				0.0	0.0	0.1	0.1	0.0
3.7	1.2	–2.7	1.0	–1.4	–8.2	5.7	7.6	0.3
–0.1	9.5	–1.0	–4.5	0.9	9.1	–2.4	–7.3	–1.1

References

Agénor, Pierre-Richard, C. John McDermott, and E. Murat Uçer, 1997, "Fiscal Imbalances, Capital Inflows, and the Real Exchange Rate: The Case of Turkey," *European Economic Review*, Vol. 41 (April), pp. 819–25.

Aghion, Philippe, Philippe Bacchetta, and Abhijit Banerjee, 2000, "A Simple Model of Monetary Policy and Currency Crises," *European Economic Review*, Vol. 44 (May), pp. 728–38.

Alesina, Alberto, and Allan Drazen, 1991, "Why Are Stabilizations Delayed?" *American Economic Review*, Vol. 81 (December), pp. 1170–88.

Basurto, Gabriela, and Atish R. Ghosh, 2000, "The Interest Rate-Exchange Rate Nexus in the Asian Crisis Countries," *Staff Papers*, Special Issue—IMF Annual Research Conference, International Monetary Fund, Vol. 47, pp. 99–120.

Berg, Andrew, 1999, "The Asia Crisis: Causes, Policy Responses, and Outcomes," IMF Working Paper 99/138 (Washington: International Monetary Fund).

———, and Catherine Pattillo, 1999, "Are Currency Crises Predictable?: A Test," *Staff Papers*, International Monetary Fund, Vol. 46 (June), pp. 107–38.

Blanchard, Olivier J., and Danny Quah, 1989, "The Dynamic Effects of Aggregate Demand and Supply Disturbances," *American Economic Review*, Vol. 79 (September), pp. 655–73.

Boorman, Jack, Timothy Lane, Marianne Schulze-Ghattas, Ales Bulir, Atish R. Ghosh, Javier Hamann, Alex Mourmouras, and Steven Phillips, 2000, "Managing Financial Crisis: The Experience in East Asia," *Carnegie-Rochester Conference Series on Public Policy*, No. 53 (Amsterdam: North-Holland).

Burnside, Craig, Martin S. Eichenbaum, and Sergio Rebelo, 1999, "Prospective Deficits and the Asian Currency Crisis," Policy Research Working Paper No. 2174 (Washington: World Bank).

Calvo, Guillermo A., 1996, "Varieties of Capital-Market Crises" (unpublished; College Park: University of Maryland). Available via the Internet: http://www.bsos.umd.edu/econ/ciecrp.htm

———, 1999, "Fixed versus Flexible Exchange Rates: Preliminaries of a Turn-of-Millennium Rematch" (unpublished; College Park: University of Maryland). Available via the Internet: http://www.bsos.umd.edu/econ/ciecrp.htm

———, and Enrique G. Mendoza, 1996, "Mexico's Balance-of-Payments Crisis: A Chronicle of a Death Foretold," *Journal of International Economics*, Vol. 41 (November), pp. 235–64.

Chalk, Nigel A., and Richard Hemming, 2000, "Assessing Fiscal Sustainability in Theory and Practice," IMF Working Paper 00/81 (Washington: International Monetary Fund).

Chand, Sheetal K., 1992, "Fiscal Impulses and Their Fiscal Impact," IMF Working Paper 92/38 (Washington: International Monetary Fund).

Chang, Roberto, and Andres Velasco, 1998, "Financial Fragility and the Exchange Rate Regime," NBER Working Paper No. 6469 (Cambridge, Massachusetts: National Bureau of Economic Research).

Chu, Ke-Young, and Sanjeev Gupta, 1998, eds., *Social Safety Nets: Issues and Recent Experiences* (Washington: International Monetary Fund).

Claessens, Stijn, Simeon Djankov, and Giovanni Ferri, 1998, "Corporate Distress in East Asia: Assessing the Impact of Exchange Rate and Interest Rate Shocks" (unpublished; Washington: World Bank).

Claessens, Stijn, Simeon Djankov, and Tatiana Nenova, 2000, "Corporate Risk Around the World," Policy Research Working Paper No. 2271 (Washington: World Bank).

Cline, William R., 2000, "The Role of the Private Sector in Resolving Financial Crises" (unpublished; Washington: Institute for International Finance).

Corsetti, Giancarlo, Paulo Pesenti, and Nouriel Roubini, 1999, "What Caused the Asian Currency and Financial Crisis? Part II: The Policy Debate," *Japan and the World Economy*, Vol. 11, No. 3, pp. 305–73.

Dell'Ariccia, Giovanni, Isabel Gödde, and Jeromin Zettelmeyer, 2000, "Moral Hazard and International Crisis Lending: A Test," paper presented at the first IMF Research Conference, Washington, November.

Dollar, David, and Mary Hallward-Driemeier, 2000, "Crisis, Adjustment, and Reform in Thailand's Industrial Firms," *World Bank Research Observer* (International), Vol. 15 (February), No. 1, pp. 1–22.

Domaç, Ilker, and Giovanni Ferri, 1998, "The Real Impact of Financial Shocks: Evidence from Korea," Policy Research Working Paper No. 2010 (Washington: World Bank).

Dornbusch, Rudiger, and Alejandro Werner, 1994, "Mexico: Stabilization, Reform, and No Growth," *Brookings Papers on Economic Activity: 1*, Brookings Institution, pp. 253–315.

Drazen, Allan, and Vittorio Grilli, 1993, "Benefits of Crises for Economic Reforms," *American Economic Review*, Vol. 83 (June), pp. 598–607.

Edwards, Sebastian, 2000, "Contagion," *The World Economy*, Vol. 23 (July), pp. 873–900.

Eichengreen, Barry, 1999, "Is Greater Private Sector Burden Sharing Impossible?" *Finance & Development,* Vol. 36 (September), pp. 16–19.

Fane, George, and Ross H. McLeod, 1999, "Lessons for Monetary and Banking Policies from the 1997–98 Economic Crises in Indonesia and Thailand," *Journal of Asian Economics*, Vol. 10 (Fall), No. 3, pp. 395–413.

Feldstein, Martin, 1998, "Refocusing the IMF," *Foreign Affairs*, Vol. 77 (March–April), pp. 20–33.

———, 1999, "A Self-Help Guide for Emerging Markets," *Foreign Affairs*, Vol. 78 (March–April), pp. 93–109.

Flood, Robert P., and Nancy P. Marion, 1998, "Perspectives on Currency Crisis Literature," IMF Working Paper 98/130 (Washington: International Monetary Fund).

Frankel, Jeffrey A., 1999, "The Balance Between Adjustment and Financing," paper presented at the International Monetary Fund seminar, "Key Issues in Reform of the International Monetary System," Washington, May.

Furman, Jason, and Joseph E. Stiglitz, 1998, "Economic Crises: Evidence and Insights from East Asia," *Brookings Papers on Economic Activity: 2*, Brookings Institution, pp. 1–35.

Ghosh, Swati R., and Atish R. Ghosh, 2000, "East Asia in the Aftermath: Was There a Crunch?" in *European Monetary Union, Emerging Markets and Econometric Issues in International Finance*, ed. by Cornelius, Gottschling, and Kreuter (Frankfurt, Campus Verlag).

———, 2001, "Structural Factors in Currency Crises" (unpublished; Washington: International Monetary Fund).

Giavazzi, Francesco, and Marco Pagano, 1990, "Can Severe Fiscal Contractions Be Expansionary? Tales of Two Small European Countries," NBER Working Paper No. 3372 (Cambridge, Massachusetts: National Bureau of Economic Research).

Goldfajn, Ilan, and Taimur Baig, 1998, "Monetary Policy in the Aftermath of Currency Crises: The Case of Asia," IMF Working Paper 98/170 (Washington: International Monetary Fund).

Goldfajn, Ilan, and Poonam Gupta, 1999, "Does Monetary Policy Stabilize the Exchange Rate Following a Currency Crisis?" IMF Working Paper 99/42 (Washington: International Monetary Fund).

Goldstein, Morris, 2001, "IMF Structural Policy Conditionality: How Much Is Too Much?" IIE Working Paper No. 01–4 (Washington: Institute for International Economics).

Gould, David M., and Steven B. Kamin, 2000, "The Impact of Monetary Policy on Exchange Rates During Financial Crises," U.S. International Finance Discussion Papers No. 669 (Washington: U.S. Board of Governors of the Federal Reserve System, International Finance Division).

Guitián, Manuel, 1981, *Fund Conditionality: Evolution of Principles and Practices*, IMF Pamphlet Series, No. 38 (Washington: International Monetary Fund).

Hutchison, Michael M., 2001, "A Cure Worse Than the Disease? Currency Crises and the Output Costs of IMF-Supported Stabilization Programs," NBER Working Paper No. 8305 (Cambridge, Massachusetts: National Bureau of Economic Research).

Institute of International Finance, 1999, *Report of the Working Group on Financial Crises in Emerging Markets* (Washington).

International Monetary Fund, 1999, Policy Development and Review Department, "Involving the Private Sector in Forestalling and Resolving Financial Crises" (Washington). Available via the Internet: http://www.imf.org/external/pubs/ft/series/01/index.htm

———, 2000a, Policy Development and Review Department, "Review of Fund Facilities—Preliminary Considerations" (Washington). Available via the Internet: http://www.imf.org/external/np/pdr/fac/2000/index.htm

———, 2000b, Public Information Notice 00/37, "Debt and Reserve-Related Indicators of External Vulnerability." Available via the Internet: http://www.imf.org/external/np/sec/pn/2000/pn0037.htm

———, 2001a, Policy Development and Review Department, "Conditionality in Fund-Supported Programs—Overview" (Washington). Available via the Internet: http://www.imf.org/external/np/pdr/cond/2001/eng/overview/index.htm

———, 2001b, Policy Development and Review Department, "Conditionality in Fund-Supported Programs—Policy Issues" (Washington). Available via the Internet: http://www.imf.org/external/np/pdr/cond/2001/eng/policy/index.htm

———, 2001c, Policy Development and Review Department, "Structural Conditionality in Fund-Supported Programs" (Washington). Available via the Internet: http://www.imf.org/external/np/pdr/cond/2001/eng/struct/index.htm

Kaminsky, Graciela, and Carmen M. Reinhart, 1999, "The Twin Crises: The Causes of Banking and Balance of Payments Problems," *American Economic Review*, Vol. 89 (June), pp. 473–500.

Kaplan, Ethan, and Dani Rodrik, 2001, "Did the Malaysian Capital Controls Work?" NBER Working Paper No. 8142 (Cambridge, Massachusetts: National Bureau of Economic Research).

Kenen, Peter B., 2000, "Financial-Sector Reform in Emerging-Market Countries: Getting the Incentives Right," paper prepared for the Per Jakobsson Foundation panel discussion, "Strengthening the Resilience of Global Financial Markets," Lucerne, Switzerland, June.

Kopits, George, 2000, "How Can Fiscal Policy Avert Currency Crises?" IMF Working Paper 00/185 (Washington: International Monetary Fund).

Kraay, Aart, 2000, "Do High Interest Rates Defend Currencies During Speculative Attacks?" Policy Research Working Paper No. 2267 (Washington: World Bank).

Krueger, Anne, and Aaron Tornell, 1999, "The Role of Bank Restructuring in Recovering from Crises: Mexico 1995–98," NBER Working Paper No. 7042 (Cambridge, Massachusetts: National Bureau of Economic Research), pp. 28–34.

Krugman, Paul, 1979, "A Model of Balance-of-Payments Crises," *Journal of Money, Credit and Banking*, Vol. 11 (August), pp. 311–25.

———, 1998, "What Happened to Asia?" (unpublished; Cambridge, Massachusetts: Massachusetts Institute of Technology).

Krugman, 2001, "Crises: The Next Generation?" (unpublished; Princeton: Princeton University).

Lane, Timothy D., Atish R. Ghosh, Javier Hamann, Steven Phillips, Marianne Schulze-Ghattas, and Tsidi Tsikata, 1999, *IMF-Supported Programs in Indonesia, Korea, and Thailand: A Preliminary Assessment*, IMF Occasional Paper No. 178 (Washington: International Monetary Fund).

Lane, Timothy D., and Steven Phillips, 2000, "Does IMF Financing Result in Moral Hazard?" IMF Working Paper 00/168 (Washington: International Monetary Fund).

Lindgren, Carl-Johan, Thomas J.T. Balino, Charles Enoch, Anne-Marie Gulde, Marc Quintyn, and Leslie Teo, 1999, *Financial Sector Crisis and Restructuring: Lessons from Asia*, IMF Occasional Paper No. 188 (Washington: International Monetary Fund).

McBrady, Matthew R., and Mark S. Seasholes, 2000, "Bailing-In" (unpublished; Berkeley: University of California at Berkley).

Milesi-Ferretti, Gian Maria, and Assaf Razin, 1996, "Current Account Stability," Princeton Studies in International Finance No. 81 (Princeton, New Jersey: International Finance Section, Department of Economics, Princeton University).

Mulder, Christian, Roberto Perelli, and Manuel Rocha, 2001, "The Role of Corporate, Legal, and Macro Balance Sheet Indicators in Crisis Detection and Prevention" (unpublished; Washington: International Monetary Fund).

Mussa, Michael, and Miguel A. Savastano, 1999, "The IMF Approach to Economic Stabilization," IMF Working Paper 99/104 (Washington: International Monetary Fund).

Musso, Alberto, and Steven Phillips, 2001, "Comparing Projections and Outcomes of IMF-Supported Programs," IMF Working Paper 01/ 45 (Washington: International Monetary Fund).

Nunnenkamp, Peter, 1999, "The Moral Hazard of IMF Lending: Making a Fuss About a Minor Problem?" Kiel Discussion Papers, March (Kiel: Institut für Weltwirtschaft).

Olivier, Jeanne, and Jeromin Zettelmeyer, 2001, "International Bailouts, Moral Hazard, and Conditionality," paper prepared for the 33rd Economic Policy Panel meeting, Stockholm, April.

Oxford Analytica, 2001, "Russia: Internal Debt (E)," *Oxford Analytica Brief* (November 9, 2001, Part 1).

Özatay, F., 2000, "The 1994 Currency Crisis in Turkey," *Journal of Policy Reform*, Vol. 3, pp. 327–52.

Radelet, Steven, and Jeffrey D. Sachs, 1998, "The East Asian Financial Crisis: Diagnosis, Remedies, Prospects," *Brookings Papers on Economic Activity: 1*, Brookings Institution, pp. 1–90.

Rodrik, Dani, 1999, "The New Global Economy and Developing Countries: Making Openness Work," Policy Essay No. 24 (Washington: Overseas Development Council; Baltimore, Maryland: Johns Hopkins University Press).

Sachs, Jeffrey D., Aaron Tornell, and Andrés Velasco, 1996, "The Collapse of the Mexican Peso: What Have We Learned?" *Economic Policy*, No. 22 (April), pp. 15–63.

———, 1996, "Financial Crises in Emerging Markets: The Lessons from 1995," NBER Working Paper No. 5576 (Cambridge, Massachusetts: National Bureau of Economic Research).

Sargent, Thomas J., and Neil Wallace, 1985, "Some Unpleasant Monetarist Arithmetic," *Quarterly Review*, U.S. Federal Reserve Bank of Minneapolis, Vol. 9 (Winter), pp. 15–31.

Summers, Lawrence H., 2000, "International Financial Crises: Causes, Prevention, and Cures," *American Economic Review*, Papers and Proceedings (U.S.), Vol. 90 (May), pp. 1–16.

Tanner, Evan, 2000, "Exchange Market Pressure and Monetary Policy: Asia and Latin America in the 1990s," *Staff Papers*, International Monetary Fund, Vol. 47, No. 3, pp. 311–33.

Üçer, E., Murat, C., Caroline van Rijckeghem, and R. Yolalan, 1998, "Leading Indicators of Currency Crises: A Brief Literature Survey and an Application to Turkey," *Yapi Credit Economic Review*, Vol. 9 (December), No. 2.

West, Kenneth D., 1990, "The Sources of Fluctuations in Aggregate Inventories and GNP," *Quarterly Journal of Economics*, Vol. 105 (Winter), pp. 939–71.

Willett, Thomas D., 2000, "Understanding the IMF Debate," School of Politics and Economics Working Paper (Claremont, California: Claremont Graduate University).

Zhang, Xiaoming Alan, 1999, "Testing for 'Moral Hazard' in Emerging Markets Lending," IIF Research Paper No. 99–1 (Washington: Institute of International Finance).

Recent Occasional Papers of the International Monetary Fund

210. IMF-Supported Programs in Capital Account Crises, by Atish Ghosh, Timothy Lane, Marianne Schulze-Ghattas, Aleš Bulíř, Javier Hamann, and Alex Mourmouras. 2002.

209. Methodology for Current Account and Exchange Rate Assessments, by Peter Isard, Hamid Faruqee, G. Russell Kincaid, and Martin Fetherston. 2001.

208. Yemen in the 1990s: From Unification to Economic Reform, by Klaus Enders, Sherwyn Williams, Nada Choueiri, Yuri Sobolev, and Jan Walliser. 2001.

207. Malaysia: From Crisis to Recovery, by Kanitta Meesook, Il Houng Lee, Olin Liu, Yougesh Khatri, Natalia Tamirisa, Michael Moore, and Mark H. Krysl. 2001.

206. The Dominican Republic: Stabilization, Structural Reform, and Economic Growth, by Alessandro Giustiniani, Werner C. Keller, and Randa E. Sab. 2001.

205. Stabilization and Savings Funds for Nonrenewable Resources, by Jeffrey Davis, Rolando Ossowski, James Daniel, and Steven Barnett. 2001.

204. Monetary Union in West Africa (ECOWAS): Is It Desirable and How Could It Be Achieved? by Paul Masson and Catherine Pattillo. 2001.

203. Modern Banking and OTC Derivatives Markets: The Transformation of Global Finance and Its Implications for Systemic Risk, by Garry J. Schinasi, R. Sean Craig, Burkhard Drees, and Charles Kramer. 2000.

202. Adopting Inflation Targeting: Practical Issues for Emerging Market Countries, by Andrea Schaechter, Mark R. Stone, and Mark Zelmer. 2000.

201. Developments and Challenges in the Caribbean Region, by Samuel Itam, Simon Cueva, Erik Lundback, Janet Stotsky, and Stephen Tokarick. 2000.

200. Pension Reform in the Baltics: Issues and Prospects, by Jerald Schiff, Niko Hobdari, Axel Schimmelpfennig, and Roman Zytek. 2000.

199. Ghana: Economic Development in a Democratic Environment, by Sérgio Pereira Leite, Anthony Pellechio, Luisa Zanforlin, Girma Begashaw, Stefania Fabrizio, and Joachim Harnack. 2000.

198. Setting Up Treasuries in the Baltics, Russia, and Other Countries of the Former Soviet Union: An Assessment of IMF Technical Assistance, by Barry H. Potter and Jack Diamond. 2000.

197. Deposit Insurance: Actual and Good Practices, by Gillian G.H. Garcia. 2000.

196. Trade and Trade Policies in Eastern and Southern Africa, by a staff team led by Arvind Subramanian, with Enrique Gelbard, Richard Harmsen, Katrin Elborgh-Woytek, and Piroska Nagy. 2000.

195. The Eastern Caribbean Currency Union—Institutions, Performance, and Policy Issues, by Frits van Beek, José Roberto Rosales, Mayra Zermeño, Ruby Randall, and Jorge Shepherd. 2000.

194. Fiscal and Macroeconomic Impact of Privatization, by Jeffrey Davis, Rolando Ossowski, Thomas Richardson, and Steven Barnett. 2000.

193. Exchange Rate Regimes in an Increasingly Integrated World Economy, by Michael Mussa, Paul Masson, Alexander Swoboda, Esteban Jadresic, Paolo Mauro, and Andy Berg. 2000.

192. Macroprudential Indicators of Financial System Soundness, by a staff team led by Owen Evans, Alfredo M. Leone, Mahinder Gill, and Paul Hilbers. 2000.

191. Social Issues in IMF-Supported Programs, by Sanjeev Gupta, Louis Dicks-Mireaux, Ritha Khemani, Calvin McDonald, and Marijn Verhoeven. 2000.

190. Capital Controls: Country Experiences with Their Use and Liberalization, by Akira Ariyoshi, Karl Habermeier, Bernard Laurens, Inci Ötker-Robe, Jorge Iván Canales Kriljenko, and Andrei Kirilenko. 2000.

189. Current Account and External Sustainability in the Baltics, Russia, and Other Countries of the Former Soviet Union, by Donal McGettigan. 2000.

188. Financial Sector Crisis and Restructuring: Lessons from Asia, by Carl-Johan Lindgren, Tomás J.T. Baliño, Charles Enoch, Anne-Marie Gulde, Marc Quintyn, and Leslie Teo. 1999.

187. Philippines: Toward Sustainable and Rapid Growth, Recent Developments and the Agenda Ahead, by Markus Rodlauer, Prakash Loungani, Vivek Arora, Charalambos Christofides, Enrique G. De la Piedra, Piyabha Kongsamut, Kristina Kostial, Victoria Summers, and Athanasios Vamvakidis. 2000.

186. Anticipating Balance of Payments Crises: The Role of Early Warning Systems, by Andrew Berg, Eduardo Borensztein, Gian Maria Milesi-Ferretti, and Catherine Pattillo. 1999.

185. Oman Beyond the Oil Horizon: Policies Toward Sustainable Growth, edited by Ahsan Mansur and Volker Treichel. 1999.

184. Growth Experience in Transition Countries, 1990–98, by Oleh Havrylyshyn, Thomas Wolf, Julian Berengaut, Marta Castello-Branco, Ron van Rooden, and Valerie Mercer-Blackman. 1999.

183. Economic Reforms in Kazakhstan, Kyrgyz Republic, Tajikistan, Turkmenistan, and Uzbekistan, by Emine Gürgen, Harry Snoek, Jon Craig, Jimmy McHugh, Ivailo Izvorski, and Ron van Rooden. 1999.

182. Tax Reform in the Baltics, Russia, and Other Countries of the Former Soviet Union, by a staff team led by Liam Ebrill and Oleh Havrylyshyn. 1999.

181. The Netherlands: Transforming a Market Economy, by C. Maxwell Watson, Bas B. Bakker, Jan Kees Martijn, and Ioannis Halikias. 1999.

180. Revenue Implications of Trade Liberalization, by Liam Ebrill, Janet Stotsky, and Reint Gropp. 1999.

179. Disinflation in Transition: 1993–97, by Carlo Cottarelli and Peter Doyle. 1999.

178. IMF-Supported Programs in Indonesia, Korea, and Thailand: A Preliminary Assessment, by Timothy Lane, Atish Ghosh, Javier Hamann, Steven Phillips, Marianne Schulze-Ghattas, and Tsidi Tsikata. 1999.

177. Perspectives on Regional Unemployment in Europe, by Paolo Mauro, Eswar Prasad, and Antonio Spilimbergo. 1999.

176. Back to the Future: Postwar Reconstruction and Stabilization in Lebanon, edited by Sena Eken and Thomas Helbling. 1999.

175. Macroeconomic Developments in the Baltics, Russia, and Other Countries of the Former Soviet Union, 1992–97, by Luis M. Valdivieso. 1998.

174. Impact of EMU on Selected Non–European Union Countries, by R. Feldman, K. Nashashibi, R. Nord, P. Allum, D. Desruelle, K. Enders, R. Kahn, and H. Temprano-Arroyo. 1998.

173. The Baltic Countries: From Economic Stabilization to EU Accession, by Julian Berengaut, Augusto Lopez-Claros, Françoise Le Gall, Dennis Jones, Richard Stern, Ann-Margret Westin, Effie Psalida, Pietro Garibaldi. 1998.

172. Capital Account Liberalization: Theoretical and Practical Aspects, by a staff team led by Barry Eichengreen and Michael Mussa, with Giovanni Dell'Ariccia, Enrica Detragiache, Gian Maria Milesi-Ferretti, and Andrew Tweedie. 1998.

171. Monetary Policy in Dollarized Economies, by Tomás Baliño, Adam Bennett, and Eduardo Borensztein. 1998.

170. The West African Economic and Monetary Union: Recent Developments and Policy Issues, by a staff team led by Ernesto Hernández-Catá and comprising Christian A. François, Paul Masson, Pascal Bouvier, Patrick Peroz, Dominique Desruelle, and Athanasios Vamvakidis. 1998.

169. Financial Sector Development in Sub-Saharan African Countries, by Hassanali Mehran, Piero Ugolini, Jean Phillipe Briffaux, George Iden, Tonny Lybek, Stephen Swaray, and Peter Hayward. 1998.

168. Exit Strategies: Policy Options for Countries Seeking Greater Exchange Rate Flexibility, by a staff team led by Barry Eichengreen and Paul Masson with Hugh Bredenkamp, Barry Johnston, Javier Hamann, Esteban Jadresic, and Inci Ötker. 1998.

167. Exchange Rate Assessment: Extensions of the Macroeconomic Balance Approach, edited by Peter Isard and Hamid Faruqee. 1998

166. Hedge Funds and Financial Market Dynamics, by a staff team led by Barry Eichengreen and Donald Mathieson with Bankim Chadha, Anne Jansen, Laura Kodres, and Sunil Sharma. 1998.

165. Algeria: Stabilization and Transition to the Market, by Karim Nashashibi, Patricia Alonso-Gamo, Stefania Bazzoni, Alain Féler, Nicole Laframboise, and Sebastian Paris Horvitz. 1998.

164. MULTIMOD Mark III: The Core Dynamic and Steady-State Model, by Douglas Laxton, Peter Isard, Hamid Faruqee, Eswar Prasad, and Bart Turtelboom. 1998.

Note: For information on the title and availability of Occasional Papers not listed, please consult the IMF Publications Catalog or contact IMF Publication Services.